Practising Feminist Criticism

For Dan, another future

'for my son in the autumn
  of the unjust war'

from Paul Goodman 'Hokku for Mathew'

Practising Feminist Criticism
An Introduction

Maggie Humm
Co-ordinator of Women's Studies
University of East London

PRENTICE HALL
HARVESTER WHEATSHEAF

London New York Toronto Sydney Tokyo Singapore
Madrid Mexico City Munich

First published 1995 by
Prentice Hall/Harvester Wheatsheaf
Campus 400, Maylands Avenue
Hemel Hempstead
Hertfordshire, HP2 7EZ
A division of
Simon & Schuster International Group

Typeset in 10/12pt Palatino
by Hands Fotoset, Leicester

Printed and bound in Great Britain by
Biddles Ltd, Guildford and King's Lynn

Library of Congress Cataloging in Publication Data

Available from the publisher

British Library Cataloguing in Publication Data

A catalogue record for this book is available from
the British Library

ISBN 0-13-355371-X

1 2 3 4 5   99 98 97 96 95

Contents

Acknowledgements

Practising Feminist Criticism has already been 'practised' at UEL and grew from the stimulating thoughts of students and colleagues. An important influence has been the ideas of feminist critics Cheris Kramarae, Dale Spender my co-editors of *The International Encyclopedia of Women's Studies*, feminist teachers in Israel, Bulgaria and Pakistan on my British Council tours and friends and members of the British WSN (Women's Studies Network). Mel Landells, a co-editor of *The International Handbook of Women's Studies (WISH)*, kindly supplied invaluable glossary entries. My family and Rachael gave me needed encouragement and new suggestions and the book could not have appeared without Shiona Burris's *excellent* work. My major debt is to Jackie Jones, now at Edinburgh University Press, who commissioned the book and whose professional and feminist expertise has inspired many Harvester authors, not only myself.

The author and publishers wish to make the following acknowledgements. Every effort has been made to trace copyright holders, but if any has been inadvertently overlooked the publishers will be pleased to make the necessary arrangement at the first opportunity.

Smedley, Agnes, extracts from *Daughter of Earth*, copyright © The Estate of Agnes Smedley 1950; Lowell, Robert, lines from *Notebook*, copyright © Faber and Faber Ltd 1974; LeGuin, Ursula, extracts from *The Left Hand of Darkness*, copyright © Ursula K. LeGuin 1969; Atwood, Margaret, extracts from *Surfacing*, André Deutsch, copyright © Margaret Atwood 1972; Steedman, Carolyn, extracts from *Landscape for a Good Woman*, Virago Press, copyright © Carolyn Steedman 1986; Sinclair, May, extracts from *Mary*

Olivier: A Life, Virago Press, copyright © Mrs H. L. Sinclair 1946; Lessing, Doris, extracts from *The Golden Notebook*, Michael Joseph, copyright © Doris Lessing 1962; Murdoch, Iris, extracts from *The Unicorn*, Chatto and Windus, copyright © Iris Murdoch 1963; Wolf, Christa, extracts from *The Quest for Christa T.*, Virago Press, copyright © Christa Wolf 1968; Kingston, Maxine Hong 1975, extracts from *The Woman Warrior*, Alfred A. Knopf Inc, copyright © Maxine Hong Kingston 1975, 1976; Robins, Elizabeth, extracts from *The Convert*, Women's Press, copyright © The Backsettown Trustees 1980; Weldon, Fay, extracts from *Female Friends*, William Heinemann, copyright © Fay Weldon, 1974; Plath, Sylvia extracts from *The Bell Jar*, Faber and Faber Ltd, copyright © Sylvia Plath 1963; Hurston, Zora Neale, extracts from *Their Eyes Were Watching God*, Virago Press, copyright © John C. Hurston and Joel Hurston 1965; Kuzwayo, Ellen, extracts from *Call Me Woman*, The Women's Press, copyright © Ellen Kuzwayo 1965; Colette, extracts from *Claudine at School*, copyright © Martin Secker and Warburg Ltd 1956; Lorde, Audre, extracts from *Zami*, Sheba Feminist Publishers, copyright © Audre Lorde 1982; Conrad, Joseph, extracts from *Heart of Darkness*, copyright © St Martin's Press Inc 1989; Rhys, Jean, extracts from *Wide Sargasso Sea*, Hodder and Stoughton, copyright © Jean Rhys.

Introduction: Feminist criticism

Feminist criticism includes both literary theories and reading practices; it grew out of the dissatisfaction many feminists felt with the gender blindness of much literary criticism. While the ideas and techniques I am labelling 'feminist criticism' are not always as radical as feminists would like to believe, *Practising Feminist Criticism* offers a starting point: an introduction to a variety of feminisms dating from the late 1960s. Weaving feminism into the academy involved feminists in a kind of critical cross-dressing, having to wear the clothes of other disciplines, particularly those of psychoanalysis. Hence the book's rather large number of disciplinary informed approaches. In addition the book brings *together* theory and practice – always an uneasy, if not unhappy, marriage. Too often critics either describe the density of theory or discuss the ways in which texts address readers in isolation from the theory which informed their criticism in the first place. *Practising Feminist Criticism* is both theory *and* practice, working on the assumption that feminist criticism will always take into account feminist issues but should translate these into ways of reading of practical use to students.

This still leaves open the big question: what is feminist criticism? To state the obvious, although 'feminist' is an adjective like the 'New' of New Criticism, the function of *feminist* criticism is to correlate a particular politics with literary practice. So that whereas New Criticism is now somewhat confusingly called 'traditional', it is hoped that feminist criticism will have a brighter future. If I emphasize the 'feminist', it is because it seems to me that the theoretical best helps us understand the critical.

FEMINISM

Feminism is not simply an additive explanatory model alongside other political theories. To centralize women's experiences of sexuality, work and the family inevitably challenges traditional frameworks of knowledge. Feminism incorporates diverse ideas which share three major perceptions: that gender is a social construction which oppresses women more than men; that patriarchy shapes this construction; and that women's experiential knowledge is a basis for a future non-sexist society. These assumptions inform feminism's double agenda: the task of critique (attacking gender stereotypes) and the task of construction. Without this second task (sometimes called feminist praxis) feminism has no goal.

Although feminism is an expansive, international phenomenon, it does have particular features. First, certain themes – reproduction, representation, the sexual division of labour – recur. Second, feminism as a political activity can be discerned in most countries of the world and as a current of thought is intensely interdisciplinary. Third, and most striking, feminism has created a new vocabulary, new concepts such as 'sexism' and 'sexual harassment', to address absences in existing knowledge as well as the social discriminations these concepts describe. Fourth is a sharing of women's subjective and objective experiences in the creation of knowledge. The starting point is often consciousness raising, where the personal can become political.

These themes give feminism a particular interest in *cultural* constructions of gender, including those in literature. The cultural practices of literature are pervasive in schools, higher education and in the media. Literature produces representations of gender difference which contribute to the social perception that men and women are of unequal value. Women often become feminists by becoming conscious of, and *criticizing*, the power of symbolic misrepresentations of women.

CRITICISM

The term 'criticism' applies to any kind of textual evaluation, including close readings and book reports; it is the most common activity in literary study. Criticism trains students, and encourages readers, to engage self-consciously with literary texts, as well as with language in general, alerting readers to hidden features and new frames of reference. Criticism offers various ways of interpreting texts, trying to see how texts work, what kinds of work texts do and why texts work in particular ways. While all texts can be critically reworked, no text is simply *there*, offering a transparent collection of ideas. Literary texts are often full of contradictions and competing levels, and readers, too, read texts in different and competing ways. For these reasons *feminist* criticism has a difficult task: it has to clarify contradictions while not losing sight of the fact that contradictions often contribute to misrepresentations of women.

FEMINIST CRITICISM

Feminist criticism rarely resembles the 'propagandist', 'lesbian plot', 'narrow', 'ideological' labels stored in the filofaxes of politically correct Conservatives. Rather, feminist critics take advantage of the coupled term by making critiques about gender representations while remaining within a shared vocabulary of knowledge. Feminism is not prescriptive or essentialist, but inhabits critical practice in stimulating shapes. There is no single feminism but many different interpretative methods, including those in this book: Black feminisms, poststructuralism, the psychoanalytic and so forth. Feminist criticism has no party line but brings together many ways of looking which in turn draw on different disciplines and debates. What brings feminist critics together is a common belief that gender is constructed through language and that writing style must thus articulate, consciously or unconsciously, gender constructions. By giving a systematic account of the interaction between gender and literary form, feminist critics hope to open up literary topics to include issues of power and sexual divisions. Feminist criticism aims to redress the imbalances of literary history by examining gender stereotypes and giving full weight to hitherto ignored women's writing.

1960s TO THE PRESENT

In the late 1960s the notion of *origin*, of the significance of male
or female authorship, was a key feature of feminist criticism.
Second wave feminism is often characterized as the break with
the fathers because critics such as Kate Millett, Germaine Greer
and Mary Ellmann made revisionary readings of what Ellmann
calls 'phallic' writing (Millett, 1970; Greer, 1971; Ellmann, 1968).
Critics focused on sexist vocabulary and gender stereotypes in
the work of male authors and highlighted the ways in which
these writers commonly ascribe particular features, such as
'hysteria' and 'passivity', only to women. In the 1970s feminist
criticism grew into a new phase, often called gynocriticism or the
study of women writers and women identified themes. Critics,
including Ellen Moers and Elaine Showalter, described women's
literary expressions and 'sub-cultures' and defined and celebrated women's literary history as a progressive tradition (Moers,
1976; Showalter, 1977). Building on these acts of retrieval, Sandra
Gilbert and Susan Gubar focused on the psychoanalytic themes
of the double and the domestic in nineteenth- and twentieth-
century women's writing to argue the existence of a female
aesthetic (Gilbert and Gubar, 1979). In one decade feminist
criticism proved, first, that 'literature' was not simply a collection
of great texts but was deeply structured by sexist ideologies; and,
secondly, that women's writing offered new ways of understanding these ideologies as well as revisionary images. The decade
also witnessed an innovative and self-conscious marriage of
creative writing and criticism in the work of Alice Walker and
Adrienne Rich, among others (Walker, 1984; Rich, 1980a).

Yet for the 1980s and 1990s feminist criticism needed to answer
other more substantial questions about literary meaning making
which the formulation of a women's tradition did not solve. The
writings of poststructuralists, Derrida and French feminists were
refiguring the powerful and sexually expressive relation between
men and women's psyches and language. These critics argued
that the universalism of binaries such as man/woman, culture/
nature, in which 'woman' was the inferior term, led to women's
language (*écriture féminine*) lying mute in patriarchy (Derrida,
1976; Irigaray, 1974). These theories called into question the
identification of female author and female text; yet also evaded

differences between white and Black feminists, heterosexual and lesbian.

From the mid-1980s on, differences of colour and sexual preference became a key focus in feminist criticism as Black feminists began to create a Black aesthetic (Smith, 1983). Several themes emerge in this work: the significance of spirituality, oral culture, female friendship and mothering. Similarly, lesbian and queer theorists were recovering lost lesbian writers and critiquing the heterosexism of the literary academy (Bulkin, 1981). These critics exposed the racism and homophobia shaping literary structures. By focusing on autobiography, and on themes of place and displacement, critics such as Gloria Anzaldúa and Gayatri Spivak brought feminist criticism into the post-colonial, postmodern world (Anzaldúa, 1987; Spivak, 1987). None of these approaches can simply be thought of as *new*, as offering entirely new paradigms and new ways of reading. Many of these critics have been attacked and particular issues, such as 'essentialism', are frequently revisited and rethought. Feminist criticism, like any other, suffers the trauma of historical change; yet more than any other criticism, it invites readers to look up at the world outside the covers of books. The companion volume to this book – *A Reader's Guide to Contemporary Feminist Literary Criticism* – describes these debates and critical revisions.

STRUCTURE OF THE BOOK

The chapters that follow constitute an overview, and include as many approaches as possible, of the *practices* of feminist literary criticism. Each chapter begins by describing a different approach, focusing on the main themes and critics, and then goes on to apply that approach to individual texts. A single section can be read in isolation if a reader is interested purely, for example, in how to analyze Sylvia Plath's *The Bell Jar*. But collectively I hope that the book offers a more total picture of feminist strategies as well as of some of the disagreements between interpretations. The sheer *range* of feminist work is not always believed. For that reason I offer two different practices of each approach. These are not arbitrarily chosen but are there to show how all approaches can be alternatively applied and to encourage readers perhaps to argue with my interpretations and construct other ways of reading. I also hope that readers will enjoy working with critical theories and be stimulated into reading the primary critical texts I introduce.

The choice of practical examples is limited, of course, both by the length of the book as well as my own enthusiasms. While there is a specific focus on women writers I include many writers who are now 'members' of Britain's National Curriculum school 'canon', as well as established figures in higher education literary studies. These include Thomas Hardy, Joseph Conrad, Virginia Woolf, Margaret Atwood, Sylvia Plath, Jean Rhys and Fay Weldon. I have also tried to balance white/Black/lesbian writers and the 'classics' as well as to balance genres (autobiography, historical fiction, feminist, utopian, romance, poetry, modernism, postmodernism).

I make no apology for my women-centred perspective. It appears that feminist thinking has fractured into a poststructuralist rejection of the essentialism involved in such a perspective (Riley, 1984); attacks on the ethnocentricism implied by its exclusions (Spelman, 1988; Spivak, 1987); psychoanalytic attacks on a unified subjectivity (Mitchell and Rose, 1982); and anxieties about the heterosexism of a singular perspective (Fuss, 1991). Yet a desire to focus on women's books is felt very strongly, not least by students entering women's studies, and I share those feelings.

Practising Feminist Criticism also tries to offer a flexible critical structure to match the new and changing world of higher education. Modular and area subjects like women's studies are growing, and literature modules are often taken by students who may be knowledgeable about feminist theory but have not had time to acquire literary critical tools. Conversely, other students who are attracted to courses with women in the title, for example my own 'Women's life histories', are already familiar with literary criticism but seek a new topic focus. While this curriculum model is much more common in American universities, where I enjoyed teaching literature to students from several disciplines, including math and health studies, the model has only recently become a major feature of British academic life. So *Practising Feminist Criticism* is essentially *practical*, guiding readers to make involved, detailed and gender aware readings based on the assumption that understanding feminist theory means being able to practise it.

No text exists that is without a few 'problematic' features and *Practising Feminist Criticism* is no exception. I realize that I am in danger of over-simplifying or misrepresenting chronologically distant criticism by use of the term 'traditional' when I could simply say 'pre-1968'. In addition I am guilty (like many others) of critical clichés. Trying to make literary criticism an active and stimulating event unfortunately seems to encourage a vocabulary more appropriate to a war zone – 'challenging', 'battling', 'subversive' – as well as the ubiquitous 'problematic' which opens this paragraph. Yet to refuse current terminology *completely* I think patronizes readers; it assumes that they can only cope with a 'restricted' everyday language rather than the 'elaborate' critical codes which they will need in order to perform well as students. I therefore attach a glossary of all the main terms to help the reader. Getting to know a critical dialect does not mean asking it to share your life for ever.

Finally, to contain any single feminist critic inside a room of her own assumes a false homogeneity *within* a critical approach as well as strong differences between them. Critics can be Black, lesbian, Third World *and* deconstructionists all at the same moment. Rather than pluralist it would be better to describe *Practising Feminist Criticism* as comparative. But I hope I have avoided any grand claims. For example, this book does not suggest that 'to theorise one's *own* practice – is to enfranchise oneself in the constituency of cultural politics', because I am not sure where to find this constituency or even what one looks like (Selden and Widdowson, 1993, p. 8). *Practising Feminist Criticism* has a very simple aim: to answer the question of what gender means when we read.

INTRODUCTORY READING

The following are some useful introductory books in the field of feminist criticism.

Anzaldúa, G. (ed.), (1990) *Making Face, Making Soul: Haciendo Caras: Creative and Critical Perspectives by Women of Color*, Aunt Lute Foundation Books: San Francisco.

Bell, P. R., Parker, B. J. and Guy-Sheftall, B. (eds), (1979) *Sturdy Black Bridges: Visions of Black Women in Literature*, Anchor Press: Garden City, NY.

Belsey, C. and Moore, J. (1989) *The Feminist Reader: Essays in Gender and the Politics of Literary Criticism*, Macmillan: London.

Benstock, S. (ed.), (1987) *Feminist Issues in Literary Scholarship*, Indiana University Press: Bloomington.

Braxton, J. M. and McLaughlin, A. N. (eds), (1990) *Wild Women in the Whirlwind: Afra–American Culture and the Contemporary Literary Renaissance*, Serpents Tail: London.

Donovan, J. (ed.), (1989) *Feminist Literary Criticism: Explorations in Theory*, 2nd edition, University Press of Kentucky: Lexington.

Eagleton, M. (ed.), (1991) *Feminist Literary Criticism*, Longman: London.

Gallop, J. (1992) *Around 1981: Academic Feminist Literary Theory*, Routledge: London.

Gates, H. L. Jr. (ed.), (1990) *Reading Black: Reading Feminist: A Critical Anthology*, Meridian: New York.

Gilbert, S. and Gubar, S. (1979) *The Madwoman in the Attic: The Woman Writer and the Nineteenth Century Literary Imagination*, Yale University Press: New Haven, CT.

Humm, M. (1986) *Feminist Criticism: Women as Contemporary Critics*, Harvester: Brighton.

Humm, M. (1994) *A Reader's Guide to Contemporary Feminist Literary Criticism*, Harvester Wheatsheaf: Hemel Hempstead.

Jay, K. and Glasgow, J. (eds), (1990) *Lesbian Texts and Contexts: Radical Revisions*, New York University Press: New York.

Meese, E. A. (1990) *(EX)tensions: Re-Figuring Feminist Criticism*, University of Illinois, Urbana.

Moi, T. (1985) *Sexual/Textual Politics: Feminist Literary Theory*, Methuen: London.

Rich, A. (1979) *On Lies, Secrets, and Silence: Selected Prose 1966–1978*, W. W. Norton: New York.

Sellers, S. (1991) *Language and Sexual Difference: Feminist Writing in France*, Macmillan: London.

Showalter, E. (ed.), (1985) *The New Feminist Criticism: Essays on Women, Literature and Theory*, Pantheon: New York.

Stimpson, C. R. (1988) *Where the Meanings Are: Feminism and Cultural Spaces*, Routledge: London.

Wall, C. A. (ed.), (1989) *Changing Our Own Words: Essays on*

Criticism, Theory and Writing by Black Women, Rutgers University Press: New Brunswick.

Walker, A. (1984) *In Search of Our Mothers' Gardens*, The Women's Press: London.

Warhol, R. R. and Herndl, D. P. (1991) *Feminisms: An Anthology of Literary Theory and Criticism*, Rutgers University Press: New Brunswick.

1 Second wave feminism

SECTION 1: AGNES SMEDLEY, *DAUGHTER OF EARTH*

The late 1960s, the moment of second wave feminism, witnessed vigorous challenges to postwar democracy. A questioning of authority, demands for political engagement and an attention to marginalized groups were the common currency of feminist, student, civil rights and New Left movements. Political strikes in Europe and student campaigns combined with feminist consciousness raising groups to call for a culture of *relevance*. Second wave feminism talked about self-realization for women not as an individualistic politics but as a collective and crucial challenge to the years of the feminine mystique. These were also the years of Black power writing, the French New Novel and feminist fiction. Literature played an important role in consciousness raising of all kinds at a moment when situationist art, New Journalism and women's writing were all drawn into the political concerns of radical movements. The shared reading of key novels such as Doris Lessing's *The Golden Notebook* helped many women locate individual experience within a wider framework of meaning. Contemporary women's novels, in particular, were a crucial source of new meanings of gender identity. This period of a revitalized yet embryonic political feminism also saw the emergence of new forms of cultural and critical thought, as existentialism, structuralism and second wave feminism began to subvert the conservative academy. Issues of historical agency and representations of sexual politics were new items on the menu of traditional criticism.

Simone de Beauvoir's *The Second Sex* (1949) followed by Kate Millett's *Sexual Politics* threw into question the cultural and ethical values of many literary representations. Scrutinizing texts by male modernists such as D. H. Lawrence, both de Beauvoir and Millett drew attention to the way in which the greater social power men have over women is translated into textual conventions (de Beauvoir, 1949; Millett, 1970). What second wave critics did was to question the idealism of literary works and show how literature, like any other social institution, embodies the cultural ideology of the society in which it is formed. Along with institutional critiques came a radical challenge to literary history as critics drew attention to hitherto unrecognized women writers and began to publish lost or undervalued women's texts.

The growing number of 'new' works and 'new' writers demanded new critical strategies, even new aesthetic criteria, as well as the creation of a new literary tradition. Many second wave feminists at first focused on the novel. If literature was to give women a sense of individual and collective significance then the novel was a likely source of positive images. For many women, as I have suggested, reading women's novels such as Marge Piercy's *Small Changes* and Marilyn French's *The Women's Room* was a formative part of political thinking. If contemporary writing was beginning to provide positive images of women, then it would be important to find similar images in earlier fiction. In addition, the novel has conventionally been regarded as a women's genre since novel writing offered the only 'professional' career to many nineteenth-century women.

Several critics turned their energies to creating a female literary tradition. Elaine Showalter and Ellen Moers made the novel a special focus of their work taking it to be a major source of values and experiences relevant to contemporary women's thinking (Showalter, 1977; Moers, 1976). The fact that women *had* created a vast literary landscape excited critics into investigating a greater range of styles and conventions. Moers's *Literary Women* is a good example of the strengths and the problems in second wave feminist criticism. Moers focused on literary influences and connections across writing from Europe, America and Britain, linking each author's life with particular images or themes in her work. Moers claims that there are specific female modes (the Gothic), specific female motifs (birthing, landscape) and specific female symbols (birds, flowers). *Literary Women* opened up a new way of thinking about the literary conflicts of women writers and how writers set about resolving these, for example by sharing experiences in a sorority of letter writing. Yet Moers unquestioningly assumes that female consciousness *can* find direct expression in writing. Far more problematic was her creation of a literary history in which Black women and lesbians, Black or white, took no part.

What second wave criticism *did* achieve was to place literature in historical and social frameworks and point to the gendered, and sometimes sexist, features of those frames. The conventions of literary representations, second wave critics claimed, were as misogynist as the social conventions on which literature draws. In this sense second wave feminists set out a whole new agenda for literary criticism by suggesting affinities between social and literary discourses.

Second wave critics began with the premise that women's experience mattered, and that it mattered to literature. By focusing on powerful textual affirmations of experience, critics argued, literature offered challenges to patriarchy by creating new role models and new patterns of living. Although this raised the issue that isolating texts from their own literary forerunners might leave out a great deal, it is certainly the case that common experiences such as menstruation and reproduction could significantly shape literary representations. Critics characteristically concerned themselves with women characters in terms of realism or stereotype, and with the relation between author and text. For these reasons one special focus was the autobiographical novel since an author/character's growing into consciousness and 're-vision' of her life might offer important insights for contemporary readers. Novels which were written in a confessional mode or *unobtrusive* third person, such as Kate Chopin's *The Awakening* and Agnes Smedley's *Daughter of Earth*, took on a new significance as potential feminist models. The commercial success of reprints attested to women readers' desire for positive pleasures. The forefronting of authorial presence by critics and readers, together with an emphasis on social and political action, suggested the need not only to reshape literary history but also critical foci. Critics now felt sufficiently liberated from New Criticism to highlight a character's emotional states, her rejection of authority and discarding of tired social roles.

Autobiographical novels most usually describe a journey to selfhood (in critical terms called a *Bildungsroman*). In some senses fictional representations of positive female development risk conservatism, if only because they suggest that individual women *can* triumph over social obstacles. However, such journeys are often hugely appealing to women readers because readers and characters can share experiences in common – sexual abuse, reproductive difficulties, social discriminations. Agnes Smedley's *Daughter of Earth* genderizes genre in this way. The novel shares many characteristics of the autobiographical novels favoured by feminists: the depiction of a heroine strong in will and in physique; a quasi-confessional form full of conversations engaging intimately with a reader; an emphasis on social/psychological constraints; and a belief in individual self-development.

Marie Rogers tells of her struggle against rural poverty in nineteenth-century Missouri and of her journey through education and across America into political activism. Agnes Smedley was born in 1892 into an illiterate rural Missourian family, journeyed similarly across America from Arizona, San Diego to New York, studying part time at university while writing for socialist journals. Smedley's involvement with Indian resistance movements brought her imprisonment. On release she worked as a journalist and activist in Berlin, China and the Soviet Union. The apparent match between Marie Rogers' life and Smedley's career affirms second wave feminism's belief that women's writing should draw on personal and historical perspectives.

A key focus of second wave critical attention would therefore be on the ways in which the novel's scenes and vocabulary provide a mirror of life. In *Daughter of Earth* descriptions of rural life – of cooking, cleaning and work routines – are intensely detailed and evoke the historical conditions of America's rural poor at the turn of the century. Characters are exactly placed and believable. Vocabulary and dramatized and narrated conversations seem to carry historical accuracy. Smedley interconnects social and economic forces and individual morality and development. In this way her novel answers the call of second wave feminism for literary reflections of historical, social and economic issues.

Even more important to second wave feminists would be Smedley's descriptions of men and her account of the sexual politics of daily life. *Daughter of Earth* illustrates Kate Millett's premise that patriarchy shapes masculinity and all forms of social power relations. Male characters have patriarchal beliefs. Marie's father is a shiftless, violent man who finally leaves his wife when she refuses to tell him 'howrye goin' to vote' (p. 53). Other male characters also share patriarchal attitudes towards women. Even Anand, the Indian revolutionary whom Marie loves, hypocritically resents her physical relationships with other men. The frank and accurate depiction of sexuality is an important focus of second wave readings. In *Daughter of Earth* there are detailed and realistic accounts of the everyday existence of married life which function to dispel any feminine mystique Marie might have about romance. For these and other reasons Marie, like Olive Schreiner, decides that prostitution is as honourable as marriage. Having chosen one partner by correspondence, separating from her first husband Knut Larsen after an abortion and coming to reject Anand's 'primitive' beliefs, Marie is finally free from patriarchal emotional constructs.

Second wave feminists would approve the depiction of strong and collective women's friendships which Smedley paints as an opposing picture to male oppressions. Rural women are active workers and deft story tellers. Aunt Helen works as a prostitute to support Marie's whole family and is 'as sensitive as a photographic plate' (p. 43). Helen is evidently an emotional being and yet in control of her life. There are other depictions of supportive women. Marie is encouraged to study and take the country teacher's examination by a woman from a Normal School, who eases Marie's educational future. *Daughter of Earth* is full of detailed sketches of women's work, including the laundry routines of Marie's mother and Marie's own domestic labour; but it presents these not so much as *drudgery* but as examples of collective *friendships*. Taken together, Smedley's themes echo second wave feminists' love of women centred texts.

By way of example here is the end of Part 5 and the beginning of Part 6 of the novel – two significant and contrasting passages.

> On a still moonlight night before they left, Knut rode by my side over the bridge, down through the outskirts of the town, and along the

white hard road leading through the desert. Something maddened my horse, and it took the bit in its teeth and tore through the cold night air. When I felt the peculiar fierce movements of its body beneath me I remembered that down deep somewhere I had always feared horses – feared them even as I rode them, and that now blind fear was seizing me. Desperately I turned my head and called to Knut; the horse perhaps sensed my fear, for it dashed ahead more fiercely still. Knut's face was desperate as he answered my call; he spurred his horse savagely to reach my bridle bit. Neck to neck we rode, the wind sweeping his hair back from a high white forehead. He was bending far out over his horse's neck, then his hand caught my bridle and with a terrific jerk he brought my horse under control. With the animal rearing and whirling, white, lathering, mad, I leaped to the earth. My legs trembled from exhaustion and I sank into the shadow of a clump of sage-brush. Knut's voice came from a distance where he was soothing the animals and fastening them to the brush. In a few moments his steps came rapidly toward me. I bent down and I reached up to grasp his arm . . . A tremor swept through his muscles! He dropped on his knees by my side, his arms were around me and I felt the quivering heart-beats through his soft white shirt. He was whispering as if the lonely desert might hear him . . . elemental things, ecstatic things. A great peace swept through my body and mind in the all-embracing gentleness of his touch . . . and his lips were as caressingly tender as the moonlight falling on a quiet sheet of water.

Part 6

What was love? I considered it: a confused, colourful mingling of the fairy tales I had read as a child and novels I had read later on; a very lovely but forbidden thing. Still it was not connected with that other forbidden expression, – sex. Sex had no place in love. Sex meant violence, marriage or prostitution and marriage meant children, weeping nagging women and complaining men; it meant unhappiness, and all the things that I feared and dreaded and intended to avoid.

Since I had known Knut such thoughts had often passed through my mind. I was ashamed of the desire for love, tenderness and companionship that existed beneath my rough and defiant manner. I was nearly nineteen, undeveloped in emotions and not fully developed in body. I had thought little but acted much. My fear of sex expression had grown with the years. Yet I resented virginity, and the so-called 'purity' of woman, and reacted violently to any suggestion about it. It had always shamed me that men judged women by such a standard.

In my hatred of marriage, I thought that I would rather be a prostitute than a married woman. I could then protect, feed, and respect myself, and maintain some right over my own body. Prostitutes did not have children, I contemplated; men did not dare beat them; they did not have to obey. The 'respectability' of married women seemed to rest in their acceptance of servitude and inferiority. Men don't like free, intelligent women. I considered that before marriage men have relations with women, and nobody thought it wrong – they were but 'sowing their wild oats'. Nobody spoke of 'fallen men' or men who had 'gone wrong' or been 'ruined'. Then why did they speak so of women? I found the reason! Women had to depend upon men for a living; a woman who made her own living, and would always do so, could be as independent as men. That was why people did not condemn men.

(From *Daughter of Earth*, Virago, London, 1977, pp. 121–4)

At first glance the opening appears to mirror the potent feminine fantasies of cheap romances. As in the classic formula, there is a fetishistic focus on the female sex drive crudely represented in a conventional trope of the escaping horse and its subsequent capture by the male hero Knut. Phrases such as 'I felt the peculiar fierce movements of its body' . . . 'down deep somewhere' . . . 'my legs trembled from exhaustion and I sank' seem a typical display of romance conventions, both in their vocabulary and appeal to female passivity. Knut seems to have the persona of a formulaic romance hero. He is more knowledgeable and better educated than the correspondingly younger, less experienced Marie. Yet where male sexuality is presented in traditional romance as compelling, often brutal, violent and certainly dark, here Knut is 'soothing', 'quivering', 'whispering', 'gentle' with his 'soft white shirt'. Marie's desire is *not* transmitted into a conventional rape fantasy. Marie's liberated sexuality is triggered not *only* by the male but, more significantly, by a recovery of feminine fluidity. Knut's body is identified as feminine and objectified 'a desperate face'. The passage reverses the male gaze to deny Knut subjectivity while aligning the reader with Marie's embodied point of view.

What the passage *does* share with romance, however, is a powerful textual 'interpellation' of a female reader. Interpellation is the process by which writing attracts a reader into participating in the text by deployment of characterization, symbols, plot structure and so forth. Romances typically interpellate a female reader by describing strong male heroes and happy endings. Textually, romances achieve reader identification with hetero-sexuality through descriptions of the male gaze and suppressed violence.

The dominant characteristic of this passage, however, is a juxtaposition between a feminized hero and Marie's interrogative voice asking the reader a series of crucial questions about the *social* context of romance and likely *social* outcomes: 'children, weeping nagging women and complaining men'. Second wave feminists would focus on how Marie's individualism is achieved *through* interrogation of the confining roles and stereotypes of romance. Marie moves in the direction of freedom *from* hetero-sexual outcomes ('children') as she takes responsibility for her multifaceted response to sexual awakening. Marie's focus is on the gap between social institutions such as marriage and mother-hood and individual feelings. Marie understands very well that female sexuality is socially constructed as 'prostitute', 'wife', 'mother', while she still openly confesses her psychic pleasures. The passage's juxtaposition of private psychic needs with the public languages of sexuality might seem a confused clashing of rhetorical registers. Yet the fractured point of view – the move from the inner preconscious to public interrogative – might well mirror a female reader's own feelings about her own fractured roles. Second wave feminists would approve a text where closure, as here, is not into romance but into independent thinking.

For a second wave critic, the breaks in narrative, Smedley's move from the psychic to the abstract, do not mark a *loss* of narrative control but rather make the point that the personal is always political. The form of the passage matches its theme: in a mixture of romance genre with individual interrogatives. Describing the writing of mid nineteenth-century women, Nina Baym points to a similar feature. Baym argues that women writers often placed journeys to self-fulfilment in forms such as romance in order to accomplish moderate and feasible resistances to patriarchy (Baym, 1978).

There is one major feminist theme which my analysis has not addressed – the question of a female/feminist aesthetic. Attempts to characterize a female aesthetic are more the concern of later feminist critics (see French feminism). Second wave feminist critics focus instead on literary representations of women's social oppressions and social triumphs. *Daughter of Earth* embodies both in its form (a journey to intellectual awakening) *and* in its rhetoric (multigeneric registers) some of the liberating impulses of second wave feminism.

SECTION 2: ROBERT LOWELL, *NOTEBOOK*

The publication of Kate Millett's *Sexual Politics* in 1970 inaugurated the debate about gender and representation within second wave feminism. Although the 1960s was a time of challenge and demystification, the intellectual framework of the American academy was conservative and shaped by postwar New Criticism. This 'orthodox' influential critical school argued that the author had only an impersonal presence in any text and that one of the first principles of literary criticism was to ignore an author's biography. Instead critics should focus purely on literary features such as genres and symbolism. Syntactical organization could safely be studied in isolation from biographical antecedents. New Critics further argued that the experiences and feelings of readers were not relevant to the kind of objective literary critique which readers should make (Brooks, 1947). With the arrival of *Sexual Politics*, what was thought to be a gender-free technical process was exposed as the ideological projection of a masculine point of view.

The second wave feminist critics Kate Millett and Germaine Greer argued that literary history was only a collection of 'great' texts largely written by 'great' men (the canon) because literature, like other cultural practices, was dominated by men (Millett, 1970; Greer, 1971). Inevitably, literary history would represent women unequally rather than reflect the reality of women's experience and lives. The power structures of literary institutions, these critics argued, reflect power structures in society at large. The critical analysis of literature should involve, in second wave feminist minds, the laying bare of the ideologies which underpinned these power structures. A major element in a second wave reading is concern with women's experience. In this way feminists hoped to contest negative images of women with a more adequate account of women's roles in literature and culture. Second wave criticism involved rereading, resisting and 're-vision', whether the focus was on single authors, literary history or particular genres. Literary texts, in other words, were thought to reflect, as well as to create, imbalances between men and women.

Second wave feminists asked new and crucial critical questions. Why is woman so frequently represented as the Other to man in books written by men? Why are so *many* women characters stereotypes? How does the world view of an author contribute to the shaping of his literary work?

As well as asking new questions about literature, second wave feminists tested the previously accepted limits of literary criticism. Drawing on the perceptions of sociology, history and cultural studies, a distinguishing feature of second wave feminism is its *hybridity*. Critics fruitfully straddled the disciplines, creating multigeneric mixtures of political ideas, literary techniques and aesthetics. The years since have only intensified these exciting new perceptions. The borders between disciplines had to be fluid to unravel the encoding of social beliefs. Literature, these critics argued, was emblematic of patriarchal fears and beliefs, and in turn acted as a major instrument of socialization. In attempting to define the nature of patriarchal beliefs critics found Simone de Beauvoir's *The Second Sex* an important inheritance. In the literary section of her book describing the work of Lawrence, Claudel and Breton, among others, de Beauvoir argued that each author constructed characters in mythical terms: as Muse, as Flesh or as Nature (de Beauvoir, 1949). For example, D. H. Lawrence, de Beauvoir claims, portrays Gudrun in *Women in Love* as a masochist, and men in Lawrence's novels make instrumental uses of women.

A crucial theme in second wave criticism became the idea that literature presents gender discriminations and inequalities as the product of the individual psyche rather than the playing out of a socially allotted role. Critics further claimed that literature represented social values directly, for example, Germaine Greer suggests that Shakespeare's plays transparently reflect Elizabethan views about romance and marriage (Greer, 1971).

But it was the publication of Kate Millett's *Sexual Politics*, above all, which marked the enduring innovation of second wave feminism. The very title, *Sexual Politics*, sums up Millett's theory of patriarchy. She argues that patriarchal power is ubiquitous. There is a deeply entrenched politics of sexuality, beginning with the reproduction of patriarchy through psychosocial conditioning in the family, which operates in all economic and cultural structures. Millett's argument is that ideological indoctrination (for example through literature) as much as economic inequality is the cause of women's oppression. The book is a pioneering synthesis of literary, social and historical images of masculinity. Millett's fundamental conviction is that sexual power shapes all personal, cultural and social relationships (including literary criticism). Twenty-five years on, *Sexual Politics* remains one of the clearest accounts of women's cultural oppressions.

The specific focus of Millett's attack was male writers, including D. H. Lawrence, Henry Miller and Norman Mailer, whose work is directly quoted in a section called 'Instances of sexual politics'. By directly quoting many misogynist passages, Millett could argue that a patriarchal sexual politics self-evidently pervaded this writing and that, in turn, this misogyny reflected the sexist attitudes of each author. In order to highlight the enduring sexism of male authors, Millett tackled the issue of how literary *forms*, as well as content, might reinforce social values. Millett argued that features of patriarchy, such as sexual violence, were visible in literary texts not only in character stereotypes but also in symbolic patterns of dominance and subordination. This led Millett to make three major charges in *Sexual Politics*: that male authors create stereotypical female characters; that such misrepresentations work through association (equating women and passivity); and third, that the narrative structures of fiction in some way resemble the other cultural structures of patriarchy.

As Millett points out, the coercive sexual power men have over women (whether direct or indirect) was not, at least in 1970, discussed openly; but it did exist through literary and media reproductions. The *representation* of sexuality was therefore a fundamental feature of men's power because women's *complicity* with such representations accounted for a great deal of women's social subordination. Hence second wave critics went on to argue that narrator viewpoint and autobiographical revelations *did* represent an author's ethics.

Since Millett's critique requires the interweaving of character and author, of text and biography, she in the main discusses modernist and contemporary writing, where the narrator focus is clear. Millett's main critical technique is paraphrase, translating texts into 'documentary' accounts of male sexual violence, and highlighting vocabulary. In her account of D. H. Lawrence, Millett notes how Lawrence frequently describes independent, intellectual women like Hermione Roddice and Gudrun Brangwen in *Women in Love* as 'repulsive' and 'macabre'. In turn Lawrence praises married women like Ursula Brangwen as enjoying 'submission absolute'. Millett shows how Lawrence routinely abuses women's own sexual choices (Millett, 1970).

Millett's fresh evaluation of the sexual politics of literature was continued by many other second wave critics. Their contribution was summarized by Elaine Showalter in 'Toward a feminist poetics' (1985) as the 'woman as reader' approach, because second wave feminists so often addressed only women. Second wave critics claimed that this was necessary as so much of literature was addressed to men. In short, second wave feminists agree that patriarchy works through psychological and cultural controls, of which literature is a major example. While later critics attacked Millett and others for creating binary oppositions between men and women and for their sometimes separatist and essentialist views, Millett's profound scepticism transformed feminist thinking. Any polemical critique will necessarily be prescriptive.

The American Robert Lowell is an autobiographical poet whose poems have often been characterized as quests for self-rediscovery. For this reason Lowell's poems could be read from a second wave perspective as reflections of the author's beliefs. Lowell characteristically mixes life events, meditations and commentary, although leaving the literal facts of his life history unclear. Lowell writes as if autobiography, within poetry, allows for a true historical sense and he often comments self-reflexively on processes of composition. Lowell's early poems are soaked in the passionate consciousness of the history and literature of New England. By the last decade of his life Lowell's introspective autobiographical poems reveal his uneasy relationship with this Puritan inheritance.

> . . . Yet tonight means something, something we
> must let go willingly, and smash:
> *all flesh is grass, and like the flower of the grass–*
> no! lips, breasts, eyes, hands, lips, hair–
> the overworked central heating bangs the frame,
> as the milkhorse in childhood would clang the morning milk-can.

> The Charles River (4)
> Seen by no visible eye, our night unbroken–
> our motel bedroom is putty-gray and cold,
> the shivering winds thrust through its concrete cube.
> A car or two, then none; since midnight none.
> Highways on three levels parallel the river,
> roads patrol the river in her losing struggle,
> a force of nature trying to breathe beneath
> a jacket of lava. We lie parallel,
> parallel to the river, parallel
> to six roads–unhappy and awake,
> awake and naked, like a line of Greeks,
> facing a second line of Greeks–like them,
> willing to enter the battle, and not come out . . .
> morning's breathing traffic . . . its unbroken snore.

> Searching
> I look back to you, and cherish what I wanted:
> your flashing superiority to failure,
> hair of yellow oak leaves, the arrogant
> tanned brunt in the snow-starch of a loosened shirt–
> your bullying half erotic rollicking . . .
> The white bluffs rise above the old rock piers,
> wrecked past insuring by two hurricanes.
> As a boy I climbed those scattered blocks and left
> the sultry Sunday seaside crowd behind,
> seeking landsend, with my bending fishing rod
> a small thread slighter than the dark arc of your eyebrow . . .
> Back at school, alone and wanting you,
> I scratched my four initials, R.T.S.L.
> like a dirty word across my bare, blond desk.

> > (From *Robert Lowell's Poems*, ed. J. Raban, Faber and Faber,
> > London, 1982, pp. 127, 126 and 119)

Notebook 1967–68 was published in 1969 and revised and enlarged in *Notebook* published in 1970. In these extracts we can see the poet linking great moments from history with those from his private life. Lowell describes himself, his morality and his historical place. The poems, as second wave critics would note, constantly intersperse personal feelings with public events. Although the forms of the poems are not similar, experiential themes are constant. Lowell's purchase of poetic form is continually counterbalanced by often hysterical and violent images. Second wave critics would draw attention to Lowell's contemporary life history, in which he was experiencing many difficult relationships: with his wife, lovers and daughter Harriet. The poems describe a poet reflecting on his masculinity and balancing sexually private with public moments.

Lowell uses the intimate voice of inner monologue to negotiate sexual experiences. The focus is always on *his* thoughts about *his* reality rather than the representation of actual events. Lowell relies heavily on a vocabulary of rivers and borders, 'a line of Greeks', to separate himself from relationships in a structural ideogram of mental frontiers. Second wave critics would argue that since other figures are represented but allowed no subjectivity (no speech or quotation) the subject of each poem is masculine difference. Everything is turned inwards. The blank verse is removed from vivid immediacy. Lowell tells us about himself at 50, with a body where 'overworked central heating bangs the frame'.

Art and life commingle in Lowell's use of quotation: *'all flesh is grass, and like the flower of the grass'* and direct address: 'I look back to you'. By means of intertextuality, Lowell attempts to make life *into* art. The numerous intertextual and historical echoes, more importantly, make the past more significant than the banality of present sexual relations and 'motel bedroom'. The past has become a surrogate for the present because the poet is intensely fearful of the immediate future: death where he will 'not come out'. This diminishes a potential elegiac tone and its imagery of battle. As second wave critics would point out, Lowell's poems represent processes of repression. 'Searching' is an Oedipal scenario of alienated longing. Lowell's view of sexuality is repressive. Current erotic longings are diffused by distancing his desires into the objectified setting of adolescence. Lowell's rejection of a contemporary androgynous figure is the burden of his memory of adolescence. The emblematic figure with 'hair of yellow oak leaves' can be brutally effaced by scratching 'my four initials, R.T.S.L. like a dirty word across my bare, blond desk'. What would particularly disturb a second wave feminist is not only Lowell's objectification of the figure but the sexual violence which objectification entails. The ellagic acid (from oak trees) is transformed from blond oak desk to yellow oak hair. Lowell avoids thinking through and representing the full extent of his feelings. Lowell represents the past not as vividly *true* but only as a surrogate for his immediate emotions.

In 'The Charles River', Lowell and his lover become two parallel Greek armies engaged in a mental civil war. Like the river they lie beside, their passion is policed and patrolled in a 'losing struggle'. The couple are paradoxically 'Greek' and 'putty-gray and cold'. The verbal ambiguities make the dissimilar, similar. Further ambiguities proliferate: each individual is 'seen by no visible eye', yet 'awake' while the traffic has an 'unbroken snore'. According to Kate Millett the *institution* of heterosexuality is a root cause of patriarchal oppression. Lowell presents us here with that unpleasant and stark reality.

In *No Man's Land* Sandra Gilbert and Susan Gubar pose the issue of Lowell's misogyny and repressions among those of other twentieth-century men of letters faced with the feminization of American culture. The savagery of Lowell's writing, as Gilbert and Gubar argue, is part of that same psychoanalytic masculine model of loss and anger 'feelings that the mother-muse had abandoned them' (Gilbert and Gubar, 1988, p. 160). Second wave feminists would agree that Lowell's poems are a good example of the ways in which a patriarchal sexual politics shapes poetic form. 'Reflectionists', or second wave feminists, would go on to argue that misogynist views, like Lowell's, are universal. It is this belief in the universal features of patriarchy, together with the critical practice of conflating author and text, which many later feminists contested. Yet Millett and her contemporaries were not offering complex readings of particular authors but rather highlighting the power relations shaping all cultural institutions. The fact that literary institutions are key structures of cultural construction is not in doubt.

2 Myth criticism

SECTION 3: URSULA LeGUIN, *THE LEFT HAND OF DARKNESS*

Science fiction, more than any other kind of literature, describes worlds beyond existing politics and history. Myths, whether Biblical or classical, often shape the concepts, plots and structures of science fiction novels. Similarly, at the centre of feminism is the belief that we should try to move beyond contemporary political formations in order to transform and humanize society.

Feminist myth criticism therefore seems to offer a useful way of reading utopian texts when these, like feminism, work against the grain of contemporary culture. Of course, no literary text, as I have argued in the introduction, can be fully explained by *one* form of criticism, nor can our understanding of texts and authors be reduced to a single reading; but myth criticism, in particular, offers more universal ways of reading in a historically fluctuating time. The strategies and forms of utopian fiction can be made more comprehensible if we look at some of their mythical patterns. In one sense science fiction writing may seem to *defy* patterning because it so often includes metaphoric landscapes, new species and behaviours. But in another sense, science fiction often figuratively transforms existing social mythical patterns and so imagines future worlds.

At first glance traditional myths seem remarkably anti-woman. The Greek stories we remember are full of angry male gods (Zeus, Apollo), and 'heroines' are frequently duplicitous (Eve, Helen) or women known only for their support of men (Penelope). Judeo-Christian myths similarly often characterize women as evil, as temptresses or as passive holy figures. Feminist critics argue that Graeco-Roman myths are often masculine constructs whose narratives only reflect the anxieties of male psyches. The main project of feminist myth critics is to move away from these constructs, perhaps to find that myths are originally feminine or at least to discover the outlines of some earlier, more specifically female, mythologies. One good example is Virginia Woolf's interest in Egyptian myths. Woolf used Isis iconography in her work to reject a contemporary and patriarchal obsession with Greek myths and heroes.

Concepts of spirituality are amply interpretable. Mythology can help to reformulate traditional historical accounts of women's lives with female centred stories. Feminists have argued that myth criticism helps us redress the huge and distorting impact of many traditional religions on women's roles, by pointing to recurrent powerful images which are associated with the feminine, such as the motif of the rainbow serpent in Aboriginal Australian culture. Other myths which have been retrieved by feminist critics centre on menstruation and women's 'power' over cyclical time, the moon and tides.

Myths also have a typology which is future orientated, based on the assumption that there is some meaning and point to history, however bizarre or extreme. Myths call attention to the fiction making ability of humans and to the significance of ethics and moral tales. Myths are always, and simultaneously, private *and* public: they often feature dreams and forbidden personal feelings while having a high public status as the source of a society's legends, the classics or scripture. Myths centre on eternal, even primal, human 'truths' which claim to be valid in any society or historical context. Most importantly, myths are also, and primarily, about power and gender.

It is not surprising that myth criticism and science fiction writing played such a major role in feminist thinking in the 1970s. Second wave feminism took shape in a utopian mode. One early text of feminist criticism, Shulamith Firestone's *The Dialectic of Sex*, called for new ways of organizing reproduction, contraception and childbearing. Firestone described the whole area of future reproductive technology and the kinds of changes in power and language it would bring (Firestone, 1970). Firestone's vision was both radical and utopian. This utopian impulse took shape in what came to be called cultural feminism; it has utilized myth critiques more than any other form of feminist thinking. Mary Daly's *Gyn/Ecology* and Monique Wittig's *Les Guérillères* both created a new women's language in order to describe new forms of women's communities and political action (Daly, 1978; Wittig, 1971). This concern with utopias and women's identity was inextricably linked to questions about literary authority.

Attention to the genres of romance, fantasy and utopias was a major part of feminist literary criticism in the 1970s in the work of Janice Radway, Tania Modleski and Joanna Russ, herself a leading science fiction author. Feminist critics put forward a novel, but crucial, argument that these genres should not be relegated to popular culture and dismissed from academic attention; they had important political and mythical dimensions. Feminist critics, informed by consciousness raising practices, wanted to draw attention to new kinds of writing and speculative plots. Joanna Russ's key essay 'What can a heroine do? or why women can't write' summed up this feminist thinking by attacking the canon for its omissions and distortions. Utopian texts often speak to women's dissatisfaction with myths of male superiority and with the institutions of marriage, the family and heterosexuality (Russ, 1972). If the traditional literary canon, Russ argued, only offered women negative or demeaning representations, then myths and utopian writing (of which Russ's own *The Female Man* is a prime example) offered new possibilities. One danger, of course, is to fall into the trap of celebrating an 'eternal feminine'. Ursula LeGuin's *The Left Hand of Darkness* avoids this slip into an easy essentialism.

Although myth is often thought of as a contrast with the everyday, feminist myth critics suggest that myth and the everyday can be aspects of a similar reality if both narratives share similar patterns. And even if traditional myths frequently portray women as avaricious or dangerous, critics point out, myths also describe women's curiosity and search for knowledge (Pandora) and women's literary skills (Scheherazade). Many contemporary women poets, like Adrienne Rich, often incorporate stories of mythical heroines as a way of writing positively about socially unacceptable female attributes such as eroticism or anger (Rich, 1976). Since the aim of feminist myth critics is to attack traditional gender archetypes and revalue other mythical representations, a particular focus of feminist critics is on alternative narrative images and conventions. Science fiction above all is a genre dedicated to rethinking conventional representations of consciousness and social roles. Challenging gender stereotypes inevitably raises questions about realism.

Ursula LeGuin's *The Left Hand of Darkness* describes a future world – Gethen – where it is always winter, inhabited by androgynous people who change to a feminine gender at cyclical moments (Kemmer) in order to reproduce. Out of Kemmer the inhabitants are largely sexless, and the physiological characteristics of sexuality only appear if stimulated by another's foreplay. Individuals can become male or female with either partner choosing to reproduce. The 'mother' is female only until the conclusion of breast feeding and 'she' then reverts to an androgynous state. Gethen is a society in which the male principle of force is opposed to a female principle of anarchy. But it is the female principle which concludes the novel. There is no myth of progress since the current year is always Year One.

The novel begins with the visit of a heterosexual male envoy, Ai, representing the League of All Worlds, a kind of interplanetary United Nations. Through Ai's eyes we learn about Gethen's strange mode of exgenetic reproduction, its bisexuality and its organic culture of 'hysterical foretellers' and barbaric cities. The opposition hysterical/barbaric is one often associated with female/male. The novel has been criticized by some feminist writers, of whom Joanna Russ is one, for its use of a male protagonist and masculine pronouns (or the generic masculine); Russ feels that LeGuin is unable to incorporate a feminist, or even a collective, model of social transformation. Yet Ai's self-deceiving noblesse oblige and inability to disengage fully from gender stereotypes are flagged as dilemmas for us all, which LeGuin wants to address.

Myth is the active setting for all these concerns. The organization of Gethen is undertaken by the Ekumen Council, a name resonant of Christian terminology. LeGuin also introduces a form of Taoist belief in which characters claim to unlearn, not just to learn. The novel follows a classic myth pattern of a picaresque romance ending with a long, dangerous journey undertaken by Ai and his bisexual companion Estraven on which Ai gains wisdom and self-knowledge.

LeGuin's bleak winter landscape contrasts with the bountiful surpluses of many nineteenth-century utopias and this, together with contrasts of urban and rural dwellers, acts to focus readers' attention on the iconic structure of character opposites or archetypes. LeGuin's vocabulary of 'spiderwebs' and 'weaving', together with her almost constant use of visual analogies, helps to create a metaphoric rather than realist or documentary narrative.

A significant feature in the novel is LeGuin's subversion of patriarchal constructs. 'Family' descent in Gethen is from the *mother*, the 'parent in the flesh'. LeGuin gives her protagonist Ai a rather different goal for his quest from the traditional gold or land. Ai is searching for a spiritual, psychological and mystical holism. The plot of *The Left Hand of Darkness* resembles a traditional myth in its ending: Ai's journey with Estraven across an icy and forbidding landscape to safety. Both men suffer many trials and survive many perils on their journey in the traditional way, but unlike a typical epic hero, Ai is far less knowledgeable, less purposefully active, than the more effeminate, bisexual Estraven. It is Estraven's *feminine* fluid thinking and his ability to use a form of Gestalt psychology (a psychology of holism) which enables both men to survive the ice. Finally, Estraven deliberately causes his own death at the hands of border guards so that Ai can be captured alive and live.

LeGuin's most explicit challenge to traditional myth archetypes of strong and boastful heroes occurs in the episode of Ai's stay with the Foretellers, whose forest town is a peaceful, rural alternative to the dark and hierarchically ordered cities of Gethen.

> Time was unorganised except for the communal work, field labor, gardening, woodcutting, maintenance, for which transients such as myself were called on by whatever group most needed a hand. Aside from the work, a day might pass without a word spoken; those I talked with most often were young Goss, and Faxe the Weaver, whose extraordinary character, as limpid and unfathomable as a well of very clear water, was a quintessence of the character of the place. In the evenings there might be a gathering in the hearth-room of one or another of the low, tree-surrounded houses; there was conversation, and beer, and there might be music, the vigorous music of

Karhide, melodically simple but rhythmically complex, always played extempore. One night two Indwellers danced, men so old that their hair had whitened, and their limbs were skinny, and the downward folds at the outer eye-corners half hid their dark eyes. Their dancing was slow, precise, controlled; it fascinated eye and mind. They began dancing during Third Hour after dinner. Musicians joined in and dropped out at will, all but the drummer who never stopped his subtle changing beat. The two old dancers were still dancing at Sixth Hour, midnight, after five Terran hours. This was the first time I had seen the phenomenon of *dothe* – the voluntary, controlled use of what we call 'hysterical strength' – and thereafter I was readier to believe tales concerning the Old Men of the Handdara.

(From *The Left Hand of Darkness*, Panther, London, 1973, pp. 46–7)

In this novel of a journey and individual transformation, LeGuin draws on the structure of myth while re-envisioning its content. This passage emphasizes Ai's concrete perceptions and his frame of meaning since he is an historian of an unrecorded world. Feminist myth critics typically focus on writers' strategies of de-familiarization, the techniques science fiction writers commonly use to subvert the messages of traditional myth. In this passage LeGuin mimics the character portraits of traditional epics with an unheroic figure, 'as limpid and unfathomable as a well of very clear water'. LeGuin's emphasis on Ai's *concrete* perceptions, on his careful empiricism, avoids a traditional myth narrative which would emphasize personal attributes of power, large physique and individual strength rather than powers of observation.

Ai the narrator keeps a careful record of his observations of the 'low, tree-surrounded houses', and of the exact numbers of dancers – 'two Indwellers'. His observations record intervals of foreteller life like a good ethnographer, and it is from these that Ai begins to get an understanding of the futuristic Handdara thought processes, not from any expectations set up by mythical patterns or from imprecise, imagistic feelings. The authenticity of Ai's account is reinforced by LeGuin's deliberate eschewing of the conventional vocabulary of myth.

Another defamiliarization technique which LeGuin employs is a refusal of sacred or liturgical syntax. There are no choral or lyrical elements. There are no exaggerated metaphors or superhuman qualities (except those which Ai has carefully observed). Antiphonal clauses, or alternating responses, which can take the form of actual dialogue between two characters or internalized dialogue in the form of one character's inner thoughts, are a common feature of spiritual or liturgical writing. Here LeGuin defamiliarizes this common feature of myths by creating a marked contrast between the two *levels* of Ai's thoughts. On the one hand Ai is presented as a careful empiricist, a portrait painter extraordinaire who even notices the precise detail of Indweller eyes ('the downward folds at the outer eye-corners half hid their dark eyes'). Ai appears to use description as a transparent medium as if he is simply and faithfully recording reality. Pitted against this level is Ai's consistent use of the conditional: 'in the evenings there may be', 'there might be music'. In this second level of Ai's thoughts, he assembles information not by observation but purely by inference, supplying possible events which are not timed or necessarily sequential. Since these 'events' or 'actions' are in effect supplied by the viewer we cannot be certain of the truth or value of Ai's thoughts. Ai's inferencing is a kind of contextual signal to the reader to check the logic of Ai's deductions against other evidence we may have already acquired earlier in the novel. LeGuin's extensive use of defamiliarization allows the 'marvellous' mythical framework to create a rich and dense world while at the same time, unlike traditional myth telling, she invites her readers to interrogate that world.

In this way LeGuin's own style matches, or encapsulates, Foreteller existence where 'time was unorganised except for the communal work'. A key concern of feminist myth critics is to celebrate the *communal* features of women's stories rather than any traditional hierarchic formula where stories are transmitted from seer to son. In the passage the elderly are not venerated but active strong individuals. Ai observes that the elders' 'controlled use' of *dothe* is not derived simply from their age or high social status among the Indwellers but is a visible and active demonstrable strength. *The Left Hand of Darkness* does not glorify the typical attributes of mythical heroes, such as military prowess. The old men are not presented here as immortals but as incredibly strong survivors. It is not insignificant that this strength is a form of feminine 'hysteria'. Hysterics, along with witches and midwives, according to Hélène Cixous and

Catherine Clément in *The Newly Born Woman*, are feminist anticipations of the culture to come (Cixous and Clément, 1986). Such individuals, they argue, exist in the gaps between the symbolic system of patriarchy (in Gethen terms the barbaric city) and the imaginary or the unknown. Hysterics have all the power, or *dothe*, of any repressed group, but exist in a space, Clément claims, where time has no meaning (or is 'unorganised').

Finally, feminist myth critics would share LeGuin's discomfort with a cosmic, mythical perspective and conquering hero. *The Left Hand of Darkness* deliberately challenges the 'A1' quality of Ai, who has no traditional unifying wisdom. A schematic allegory of myth emerges in Ai's journey with Estraven across the ice. The journey is a conventional metaphor of spiritual progress. But Ai is forced to admit his *unheroic* qualities, to turn to Estraven, to the feminine, to survive. Ai is a fluid character whose certainties are constantly under threat in the Gethen world which he never fully understands. Indeed, the point of the novel is precisely to challenge the notion of an intact, confident vision and contrast this with forms of thinking and consciousness raising which are communal, even telekinetic. In denying access to identification with the mythical hero, LeGuin defamiliarizes a major convention of traditional myth. Ai chooses the ecological wisdom of the Foretellers over the military barbarians of the city. LeGuin deliberately swerves from the military bathos beloved of traditional epics. Ideas are more significant here than golden fleeces. But nor does LeGuin privilege the gardens and woods of the Foretellers as a mythical model of a bountiful, perfect world, since Ai's report is at best a hypothesis full of syntactical inferences. As Joanna Russ argues, the defamiliarization of traditional myths and the creation of new myths in speculative fictions are an unchartered territory of new literary and social archetypes (Russ, 1972).

SECTION 4: MARGARET ATWOOD, *SURFACING*

Myth is a relative term which can apply to imaginary worlds which are not real, as well as to metaphoric versions of actual events which were not documented in written form. Myths are also created by writers, and existing myths drawn upon by writers, to make imaginative interpretations of the psychological states of characters. Literature, especially the novel, offers a writer the space and complexity necessary to represent *probable* truths as well as 'truthful' reality. Writers can use myths to explain what is really happening in a novel or what motivations trigger events partly because mythical knowledge is often shared by readers. Listening to stories, myths or fantasies is a common part of many childhoods. Fictional representations of myths draw on this frame of reference. In addition, myths offer a kind of rhetorical vision, which can give aspects of women's culture, for example, a public status. Myths can depict in imaginary and symbolic form some of the social processes affecting women. As Sandra M. Gilbert and Susan Gubar suggest, myths can even be more *accurate* than documentary because myths can reduce historical change and social issues to quintessential emblems (Gilbert and Gubar, 1979). For this reason many women writers turn to myths as familiar frames which can be reshaped and remade to give a truer picture of women's experience.

Myths generally are powerful imagistic accounts fed by fragments of real history. Classic myth stories centre on a quest for identity or a search for a parent figure, where the sweep of the narrative orders pieces of the world into an allegory of individual development. Through imagery and vocabulary myths metamorphize individual doubts into major quest events. Myths are always gendered, and are usually about male rites of passage and initiation ceremonies. They reveal Oedipal anxieties about father–son relations or male fears of terrifying mother figures at the heart of Western culture. Yet in a paradoxical way this means that myths mark the *fragility* of patriarchy, which constantly needs to repeat mythical paradigms in order to hold together cultural order.

So although traditional myths create images of women as terrifying Medusas or passive Snow Whites, as women *outside* culture and society, that nature/culture binary also suggests that the animal nature associated with women *is* sexual. A more expansive description of nature, and its Demeter-like qualities, could represent a metaphorical untamed experience for women to escape gender oppressions. In this way feminist retellings of myth, and particularly those myths to do with the environment, could enable women readers to come to terms with a new sexual and gendered identity.

Fiction, in particular, often gives myths a more resonant, less static shape. By their very nature myths are often sacred, affirmative stories describing epic journeys outside social controls. Such journeys, like those of Jason and the Argonauts, are often undertaken to *escape* social/national restrictions. So that while myths have some historical trigger, they often describe journeys *away* from powerful tyrants, away from social discourses into a natural world of beauty and freedom.

Myths are particularly important sources of alternative history for groups denied a place in mainstream culture. There is a rich Afrocentric history of story telling and oral culture which excites contemporary Black women writers such as Alice Walker and Audre Lorde. Mythical language and themes nourish Black women struggling to define a womanist culture in a racist, masculine literary tradition. Myths can help 'minority' groups to express communal reality through analogy or masks. Audre Lorde creates matrilineal diasporas which explicitly mythologize relationships between mothers and daughters by drawing on African myths (see Section 20). The Chicana feminist Gloria Anzaldúa draws on Mexican serpent and nature myths to reclaim a mythical identity untouched by a sexist and racist 'host' society (Anzaldúa, 1987). In some ways the psychological paradigms which often structure myths, like the id of The Beast loving Beauty, provide groups with a psychic release from social processes. Toni Morrison is another Black feminist writer whose work is flooded with supernatural and ancestor motifs. *Jazz* is a quest novel for a lost mother who is lost *in* the natural world, literally a cave, Kristeva's Platonic emblem for the semiotic (Morrison, 1992). The mother takes on the mantle of a primary archetype embodying values of survival and endurance. In Alice Walker's *The Color Purple*, Celie learns a great deal from the natural world and her love of nature, particularly purple flowers, gives Celie the strength to withstand sexual violence (Walker, 1983).

So how do feminist myth critics describe the distinctive and alternative myths created by writers? What techniques are important? Describing the new literary vocabularies spawned by myth is one task. Susan Griffin invents a unique, associative style in *Woman and Nature* (Griffin, 1978). Sometimes critics utilize Jungian archetypes and other psychoanalytic categories to describe organic, paradigmatic images. Myth symbols might reveal a writer's psychological state and in turn help a reader to understand her own psychological images and dreams. Critics often focus on religious rituals, such as Native American myths, in fictions where these are important vehicles for social messages. One good example of an alternative reading of Virginia Woolf's *To The Lighthouse* would be to describe the novel, not as I do in Section 8 in terms of French feminism, but as a novel about an androgynous fertility figure, Mrs Ramsay. Myth criticism aims not so much to present *detailed* explanations of literary features but to link literary features with mystical experiences which have their own explanatory models. As Carol Christ suggests, women's mystical experiences are often ineffable – inexpressible in full – but can be poetic or illuminatory (Christ, 1980). Critics usually *overlay* meanings *from* myths on to texts, forming filters of critical explanation. This is how Carol Christ describes those fictionalized quests of awakening in which women characters gain a new sense of themselves and the world, particularly through a mystical awareness of nature. Similarly, Mary Daly, in *Gyn/Ecology* describes the worlds of nature and prehistory which Christianity has stripped of their Goddess religions. The book ends with an outline of a new woman-centred language and ethics, a collective consciousness in tune with the environment (Daly, 1978).

It seems to me that a consideration of Margaret Atwood's *Surfacing* might draw in many of these issues. Margaret Atwood pays enormous attention throughout her work to myths, religious philosophies (including sufism in *The Handmaid's Tale*) and existentialism. These concerns lead Atwood to experiment with a range of genres including the Gothic, poetry, utopian or dystopian fiction as well as the mythical quest narrative of *Surfacing*. These genres are not static in her work since she interplays a variety of rhetorical styles and devices drawn from women's magazines as much as high culture. Like all fiction, Atwood's novels can be read on many levels; *Surfacing* could be called a ghost story, a detective novel, and a novel of development.

As her second novel, *Surfacing* is also closer in time and

therefore influence to Atwood's literary mentorship with North-rop Frye, Canada's leading critic. Frye created a new critical school for the burgeoning, newly independent country during the 1960s, one which drew on mythical archetypes appropriate to Canada's landscape and new national identity. It was Frye's writing and teaching which encouraged Atwood to make her own investigations into North American myths and landscape which Atwood, unlike Frye, sees in specifically gendered ways.

Surfacing is about a young woman's search for a missing (presumed dead) father as well as her internal search for memories of her dead mother. In this sense *Surfacing* has a classical mythic structure. The novel foregrounds questions about paternity/maternity, language and identity. By rewriting the myth of a questing hero, Atwood attempts to revise the social stereotypes of female identity by giving significance to maternal relations, which are usually devalued in classical myth. *Surfacing* is almost contemporary with Adrienne Rich's *Of Woman Born* and both books share a climate of thinking in contemporary feminism about motherhood. The subtitle of Rich's now classic text, *Motherhood as Experience and Institution*, highlights Rich's innov-ative argument. Rich splits the representation of mothering into 'experience', which can be an energizing part of all women's lives, whether or not they choose to be biological mothers, and 'institution' which is the social construction and devaluing of mothering (Rich, 1976). Rich celebrates the 'experience' of mothering by taking this back to prehistory and endowing 'experience' with mythic symbols and figures. She argues that a number of fertility myths can be read as historical archetypes of female power. Atwood's heroine similarly goes back to her own 'prehistory' to try to understand the importance of a maternal presence/absence in her life by returning to the island where she lived as a child. In some ways the novel resembles an inverted version of the great myth of *Paradise Lost*, with an alternative account of a myth of origins. The heroine of *Surfacing* similarly returns to the rigours of nature in order to reach the 'heaven' of self-knowledge. While not violating a patriarchal decree, as Satan does, she has certainly chosen an artistic career in opposition to her scientific father, and both narratives could be described as supremely visionary.

It is the *gendered* quality of Atwood's myth making which is the key. Myth provides Atwood with a wonderful mechanism for incorporating themes of women's double consciousness and maternal relations, as well as women's exclusions from the social. The images of Atwood's myths become a grammar, a kind of alternative feminist language. The 'grammar' helps the novel's readers to understand the meanings of Atwood's symbolic plot literally like the heroine in the passage I will examine in a moment – we surface. By forging a mythical and alternative fictional account of a return to origins, or Oedipal crisis, Atwood offers the reader the emotional satisfaction of a half-remembered familiar structure. *Surfacing* leads straight to the key issue of feminist myth criticism. How can women celebrate nature myths without invoking stereotypes of essentialism, of earth women?

The narrator in *Surfacing* leaves her city home, together with three friends, David, an amateur film maker, Anna, David's wife, and Joe, the narrator's lover, on a vacation trip to search for clues to her father's disappearance. Returning to her distant childhood island home, the narrator pieces together memories of her father and her mother, dead some years earlier, together with recovered childhood objects and 'pictographs' left by her father. In a spectacularly mythical conclusion the narrator finds the body of her father who drowned in the lake as he photographed underwater Native American cave paintings. She herself begins to acquire the body language and understanding of Shamanism. The coming together of these concerns gives the narrator a kind of cognitive mastery over her past as well as coinciding with a new fertility as she conceives Joe's child.

Atwood links the social marginalization of the narrator, a failed commercial artist, with the marginalization of Native American myths and spirituality. This issue Atwood shapes as a contrast between masculine totems and female myth imagery. Men's misuse and women's use of nature in *Surfacing* is specifically gendered. American hunters string up a dead heron as a 'totem' of their hunting success. To the narrator, an illustrator of folk tales, birds become totemic emblems of her dead mother. Not surprisingly sketches, which the narrator draws to illustrate the story of a king 'who learned to speak with animals and the fountain of life', got 'no further than a thing that looked like a football player' (Atwood, 1973, p. 84).

To celebrate as uniquely female powers such activities as the mother's conversations with birds risks falling into the trap of existing feminine stereotypes. But Atwood associates women with fertility and men with environmental abuse specifically as a metaphor of the violation of women by men. In *Surfacing* men leave a detritus of used beer cans which spoils the fruit and vegetable bounty of nature. Throughout her work, Atwood returns again and again to myth rituals and Shamanism. Shamans are spiritual people who cross from human shape into animals, plants and the sky in order to return with natural powers. The ascription of Shamanism to women is problematic. In many cultures Shamans are men, and women are thought to be incompatible with spirituality. In other cultures women are regarded as the primary human representatives of spirituality.

Yet in many ways Shamanism expresses a number of feminist myth themes: one is a concern to spiritually affirm 'feminine' features such as intuition; another is an interest in imagery often associated with the feminine, such as water and matriarchal imagery. Atwood roots women's sensitivity and ethics in spirituality, or Shamanism. Like feminist myth critics, she identifies women with ecology and holism in opposition to male hunters and meat eaters. The narrator in *Surfacing* learns to possess myth and identify her parents with Native American totems in her visions because she has a concern for ecological survival. Atwood's women often gain a self-identity by returning to their ancestors and the wilderness.

> When nothing is left intact and the fire is only smouldering I leave, carrying one of the wounded blankets with me, I will need it until the fur grows. The house shuts with a click behind me.
>
> I untie my feet from the shoes and walk down to the shore; the earth is damp, cold, pockmarked with raindrops. I pile the blanket on the rock and step into the water and lie down. When every part of me is wet I take off my clothes, peeling them away from my flesh like wallpaper. They sway beside me, inflated, the sleeves bladders of air.
>
> My back is on the sand, my head rests against the rock, innocent as plankton; my hair spreads out, moving and fluid in the water. The earth rotates, holding my body down to it as it holds the moon; the sun pounds in the sky, red flames and rays pulsing from it, searing away the wrong form that encases me, dry rain soaking through me,

warming the blood egg I carry. I dip my head beneath the water, washing my eyes.

Inshore a loon; it lowers its head, then lifts it again and calls. It sees me but it ignores me; accepts me as part of the land.

When I am clean I come up out of the lake, leaving my false body floated on the surface, a cloth decoy; it jiggles in the waves I make, nudges gently against the dock.

They offered clothing as a token, formerly; that was partial but the gods are demanding, absolute, they want all.

The sun is three-quarters, I have become hungry. The food in the cabin is forbidden, I'm not allowed to go back into that cage, wooden rectangle. Also tin cans and jars are forbidden; they are glass and metal. I head for the garden and prowl through it, then squat, wrapped in my blanket. I eat the green peas out of their shells and the raw yellow beans, I scrape the carrots from the earth with my fingers, I will wash them in the lake first. There is one late strawberry, I find it among the matted weeds and suckers. Red foods, heart colour, they are the best kind, they are sacred; then yellow, then blue; green foods are mixed from blue and yellow. I pull up one of the beets and scratch the dirt from it and gnaw at it but the rind is tough, I'm not strong enough yet.

At sunset I devour the washed carrots, taking them from the grass where I've concealed them, and part of a cabbage. The outhouse is forbidden so I leave my dung, droppings, on the ground and kick earth over. All animals with dens do that.

I hollow a lair near the woodpile, dry leaves underneath and dead branches leaned over, with fresh needle branches woven to cover. Inside it I curl with the blanket over my head. There are mosquitoes, they bite through; it's best not to slap them, the blood smell brings others. I sleep in relays like a cat, my stomach hurts. Around me the space rustles; owl sound, across the lake or inside me, distance contracts. A light wind, the small waves talking against the shore, multilingual water.

(From *Surfacing*, André Deutsch, London, 1973, pp. 177–8)

The passage follows a classic myth narrative – one where the protagonist, in order to be 'reborn' or gain knowledge has to descend into hell or into the wilderness. The moment is very near the end of the novel just when the protagonist has left her companions and, alone on the island, literally returns to nature as she unravels her past and gains a new identity. The passage directly describes a number of themes from Shamanism, including spiritual images and initiation rites. The first is the heroine's withdrawal from her social (or tribal) world: 'nothing is left intact' and 'the house shuts with a click behind me'. This is symbolized by the discarding of clothing; 'I leave, carrying one of the wounded blankets with me', where the blanket is anthropomorphized, or endowed with her qualities. The protagonist explicitly associates clothing with the social scripts she will leave behind. Earlier in the novel she leaves a sweatshirt as an offering to the gods on a ledge feathered by reindeer moss close to the site of her father's pictographs. Learning that such tokens can only be 'partial' emblems it is at this point that she slashes her clothing creating the 'wounded' blanket. The description of renunciation 'I take off my clothes, peeling them away from my flesh like wallpaper. They sway beside me, inflated, the sleeves bladders of air' resembles life-saving routines where children learn to inflate their clothing so that their bodies can 'surface'.

Feminist myth critics would also draw attention to food rituals, which are a frequent and important mythical motif. The protagonist eats only preordained food and creates her own mystical rituals since 'the food in the cabin is forbidden'. Not surprisingly, her food has to have *primary* colours 'Red foods, heart colour, they are the best kind, they are sacred; then yellow, then blue, green foods are mixed from blue and yellow'. Like Huichol Shamans the protagonist eats 'hearts' in order to fly. This internal monologue does not use the natural stress of ordinary speech but has the didactic quality of religious rituals. The language organizes the protagonist's experience via material action processes rather than mental processes. The sentences are short clauses with an agent, 'I' swiftly acting on an object – 'pull up', 'leave', 'I know', so that the sensations of each phenomenon are less important than their *primary* features. The protagonist is presented as an effective and active agent rather than a *receiving*, sensing being. This form of transivity, or relation between person and object, is very common in religious rituals.

An additional focus of myth criticism would be on the symbolic associations of animals and birds. Throughout her work, Atwood makes plain that by investigating specific animal analogies or metaphors (one favourite is the dinosaur) women can recover a source of archaic knowledge and come to know themselves. In this passage the protagonist crosses over the boundary between animal and human. She has a 'den', she 'gnaws' and 'scratches' and will grow 'fur'. There is an affinity between her and the natural world symbolized by the loon 'who accepts me as part of the land'. Shamanism also encourages humans to adopt the potencies of animal shape, even outwardly transforming their physical human shapes into other forms.

All literary symbols combine an image with a concept which may be public or private – a rose signifies beauty. In myth criticism it is public or universal symbols which are of interest – journeys and water and light. Water is an organizing motif in *Surfacing*. Responses to water structure the plot (in the events of the narrator's brother's drowning and her father's death). In this passage we find 'water' has many variations – 'damp', 'rain', 'floating' – to express abstract ideas. Water is a metaphor of change (as when the protagonist makes a final dive into the lake and into her Shaman powers). In Shamanism and other religions, immersion in water is the mark of a transition into religious knowledge or sanctified life. Like Irigaray, Atwood describes fluid as multiple and feminine, 'multilingual water'.

Another kind of symbolism which attracts myth critics is known as the transcendental, where concrete objects or natural features are used as symbols to represent an ideal world. Light is a key transcendental symbol in all religions. In this passage it is light from heaven which transforms the protagonist into a spiritual being: 'the sun pounds in the sky, red flames and rays pulsing from it, searing away the wrong form that encases me'. The protagonist gains the power of light 'washing her eyes' free of social constructions. In Shamanism, perception is often called 'dermoptic perception' or skin vision; it enables Shamans to detect colours without seeing. Coloured light gives a kind of psychic protection.

The symbols of Shamanism – water, light, and totems – in the passage are signs of female power. The protagonist does not respect the totems from her father which she describes as complicated and tangled, but respects maternal totems, her mother's pictographs – the heroine's own childhood drawings which were saved. The interpretation of pictographs often depends on a seer or spiritual leader. In addition the meaning of pictographs is often fluid, open ended, unlike the meanings transmitted phonetically in literate cultures, which are fixed and given.

Atwood paints here, feminist myth critics would claim, a powerful mythical picture of the natural world with its Shaman heroine. The protagonist follows Shaman rituals to cross the borders of human and animal into a new multilingual cosmology. The placing of the feminine *within* a spiritual sign system helps Atwood to escape from conservative associations of women and nature. Part of her success is due to a use of parallelism which builds a repeated thematic association between the female narrator and nature. Parallelism is a common literary device for holding together different meanings. Here there is the evocative mystical voice with its vocabulary of 'pulsing', 'staring', 'sacred' set into a very simple prose voice. In this way Atwood is able to associate two models of consciousness: the mythical with conscious personal actions. Syntactic parallelism is, of course, a marked feature of Christian writing – as in the Psalms.

The protagonist's monologues in *Surfacing* certainly erase any meaningful difference between objective realism and myth. Spiritual rituals – the discarding of clothing, special diet, the symbolic importance of water and light – give the protagonist, feminist myth critics would claim, a new epistemology, or way of organizing knowledge. Myths are structural devices, ways of organizing female reality. *Surfacing* uses its mythic frame, self-consciously, to explore issues of feminist ethics. Myth is not presented simply as a nostalgic recreation of a familiar world but as a viable narrative of self-identity.

3 Marxist/socialist criticism

SECTION 5: THOMAS HARDY, *TESS OF THE D'URBERVILLES*

Where deconstructionists are interested in the ways in which texts often *prevent* or play with fixed and definite social values, Marxist/socialist feminists are concerned with the *impact* of social and political values and forces. Our ideas and values, Marxist/socialists believe, do not spring only from our individual psyches but also from our consciousness of class and patriarchal exploitation.

While most critics ask questions about a text's context, Marxist/socialist feminism pays special attention to the ideology(ies) evident in, or implied by, textual features. In general, a person's ideology is the set of beliefs and ideas s/he carries around with them. Feminist ideologies include ideas about the sexist social divisions of any particular society. Sexist ideologies about women's domestic place are attacked by feminists because these ideas depict a static and conservative image of women's social condition. By analyzing ways in which these ideologies evolve historically and perpetuate women's inferiority, feminist critics draw attention to issues of cultural change. Marxist/socialist feminist critics focus on the representations of ideology *within* literature. Following the French Marxist Louis Althusser's view that ideology is an *imaginary* way in which people *represent* their own social relationships, feminist critics believe that texts reveal imaginary reproductions of the relations of unequal sexual power (Althusser, 1971).

According to Althusser, ideology works through systems,

representations and rituals of daily life and culture. In *Lenin and Philosophy and Other Essays* he argued that literature, together with the other arts and sports, is a 'cultural state apparatus', and that with other ideological state apparatuses (ISAs), including the church, education and the family, literature 'colludes' in reproducing ideology (Althusser, 1971). Ideologies may not be represented by *actual* historical events or characters, but literary texts always project a sense of political and historical reality. Marxist/socialist feminist critics believe that to understand the *gendered* features of historical representations and meanings is to know more about societies past and present and how social change might occur.

How do we know that literary representations are ideological, and what does this suggest for critical practice? Marxist/socialist feminists rarely describe textual features in terms of a writer's *personal* political beliefs (if known). This approach is more characteristic of second wave feminists, who have often been attacked for being too 'reductive' because they argued that stereotypical features in a text represent an author's feelings (see Kate Millett's attack on D. H. Lawrence). A text *can* often accurately reflect a society's particular social/sexist divisions; yet its author may be deeply patriarchal. A good example here would be *Sybil, or the Two Nations* by Benjamin Disraeli. The novel gives us a very real sense of the tension between representations of class distinctions and injustices and Disraeli's 'patriarchal' representation of Sybil's sexuality (Disraeli, 1961). In other words, Marxist/socialist feminists do not use literary criticism as a substitute for political analysis, but look at a whole set of expressive literary features.

Rather than arguing that literary texts only 'reflect' social reality, Marxist/socialist feminists are interested in other key features as well as reflections. These include the ways in which literature interacts with other cultural forms (intertextuality); how literature interacts with readers as social beings (interpellation); and how literature is shaped by its own production processes. Nor do Marxist/socialist feminists always look at what is *there* in a text and try to resituate textual content in a political frame. Often they claim that literary texts distance themselves from internal ideologies and that literary texts can be understood by searching for internal contradictions and 'absences'. A text's 'unsaid' – the things about which it is silent – can tell us a great deal; 'absences' reveal ideological assumptions which an author finds hard to voice. Alternatively, textual contradictions can tell us a great deal about a text's 'moment' as well as what distinguishes a text from other contemporary texts or features of popular culture.

This is why the first objective of Marxist/socialist feminists, like many other critics, is to analyze the arrangement of intertextual relationships. While a Marxist/socialist feminist approach to the study of literature usually requires a critic to try to account for textual choices in relation to specific social and historical processes, these choices are often thought to be 'unconscious' or 'incoherent'. Since social processes often constrain (materially and ideologically) the production of meaning in texts, that constraint can best be highlighted by looking at the text *itself* as a gendered system. It is this focus on *gendered* contradictions which has been the particular contribution of feminist critics to Marxist theory. This concern allows Marxist/socialist feminist critics to disengage from a traditional Marxist subordination of literary/cultural superstructure to determining economic/social structure. In other words, where traditional Marxist critics argue that culture *reproduces* the social relations of production, and traditional literary critics argue that high culture '*rises*' above, or has an aesthetic superiority to social and political forces, Marxist/ socialist feminists argue that *sexual* ideologies are not always *functional* (because patriarchal ideologies often work *against* capitalism's best interests); but nor are they ever *absent* from cultural productions, however 'high'.

It is the *articulation between* different discourses (economic/ sexuality) *and* the consequent problematizing of cultural features which are of interest. The *lack* of effectiveness of literary images or narratives can be just as revealing as texts which create an intact picture of socialist or bourgeois ideologies. Subsequently, many critics have suggested that the *specificity* of a wider range of literary features needs attention. These might include the question of the unconscious as an effect in the text, as well as the impact of the implied reader on texts. Where the interaction between cultural representations and social mechanisms of women's oppression is a concern of all feminist criticism, and the shaping of cultural representations by material practices is the

concern of traditional Marxists, *Marxist feminists* add the understanding that gender constructions will be always fraught. Since
tensions between different ideologies are negotiated mainly
through gender, as in literary representations of motherhood,
marriage and reproduction, these representations will inevitably
be contradictory. Literature consists of forms, values and images
shaped by, reflecting and helping to *contribute to* social and
gender relationships. *Practices* of representation in which authors
and readers negotiate ideas about gender and society will
therefore be of particular concern to Marxist/socialist feminists.

Thomas Hardy's novels, and *Tess of the d'Urbervilles* in
particular, can be read as statements about a certain historical
moment in English rural life. As Raymond Williams has pointed
out, the major period of the late Victorian novel was also a period
of new social thinking by and about outside groups and women
(Williams, 1963). While Hardy was clearly not a left-wing
polemicist, most critics consider Hardy's novels to portray a
remarkably accurate picture of changes in nineteenth-century
sexual politics. The women's movement contributed to a general
cultural crisis about gender roles, and this crisis is a major feature
of many novels about 'new women', including those by Hardy.
From a Marxist/socialist feminist viewpoint, the relationship
between Hardy's 'realist' account of new women and the
ideologies of patriarchal capitalism is complex and contradictory.
Tess of the d'Urbervilles describes the ways in which contemporary
religious and social values deform women's economic roles and
social possibilities. Tess is a 'pure' and honest woman destroyed
by an unthinking and harsh society. The novel is a powerful
vision of the incoherences and contradictions Hardy saw in the
world around him. But the novel is more than a simple
naturalistic social narrative, not only because it reveals Hardy's
rich sense of society's double ethical standard but also because
Hardy reveals in the *processes* of representation his own
uncertainties about social and gender change.

The plot of the novel takes Tess across the rural landscape of
Wessex from harvesting to dairy farming and episodes of agricultural life at Flintcomb-Ash. Tess's rape by Alec d'Urberville,
her love for and abandonment by Angel Clare, and her 'death' at
Stonehenge are 'determined' in Marxist terms by the economic
dislocations and migration of the labouring rural poor, including

Tess's family. Issues and representations in the novel could be analyzed in a traditional Marxist way by studying the relationship between Tess's different work processes and the material conditions of late nineteenth-century rural England. But *Tess of the d'Urbervilles* also describes a contradiction between Tess's thoughtful, common sense *woman's* consciousness and the social roles chosen for her by male characters in the novel – her father, Alec, Angel and co-workers such as Dairyman Crick. From a Marxist/socialist feminist perspective it could be argued that Tess 'performs' rather than *inhabits* male constructs – 'siren', 'protester' and 'commodity' – but gradually discards those representations to gain her own womanhood by the end of the novel.

In the first part of the novel 'The Maiden', Tess fights Alec d'Urberville's feminine construct – Tess as a prettified henkeeper and lady companion. Angel Clare also 'refuses' Tess any autonomy by encouraging her to 'pick up' his fragments of knowledge. Tess becomes Clare's dear possession, a problem in grammar. Since thought and language are inseparable, any limits to Tess's linguistic expression necessarily involve limits to her thinking. Hardy makes a direct connection between descriptions of Tess's sexuality and economic events. There is a strong link between Tess's growing sexual/emotional maturity and the work available to her. The type of work Tess does influences the kinds of emotions she experiences, and therefore the kinds of actions and personal decisions she can make. The more equitable work of dairymaid allows Tess to develop her subjective 'common sense' understanding of nature and ethics and encourages her to consider a possible future with Angel Clare. Later industrial appropriation constrains Tess's gender roles as well as her social freedom, and Hardy specifically attacks the advent of threshing machinery for its inhuman and relentless mistreatment of women workers. Similarly Tess's final 'fall' from purity in 'Fulfilment' – her return to Alec and 'prostitution' – has an economic justification: to save her brothers and sisters.

Hardy never describes rural Wessex only as an *external* construct and constraint; he is concerned very centrally with how social forces are *perceived*. Necessarily, Hardy offers no single philosophic or cosmic explanation to account for social constraints and changes. A marked feature of the novel is the mismatch between differing historicized ethical assumptions and characters' perceptions of these and of each other. This is inevitably reflected in narrative form. One key focus for Marxist/ socialist feminists, then, would be on the ways in which Hardy 'avoids' an organized and comfortable realism when representing gender. The novel is a multigeneric mixture of naturalism, realism and melodrama. An unwillingness to choose one particular narrative form usually marks a writer's doubts about his/her own social values.

The multigeneric quality of *Tess* is not a sign of lack of writing skill but evidence of Hardy's changing ideas about social relationships between men and women and about literary representations. The text reveals an underlying uncertainty which is specifically focused on women characters and on the place, or lack of place, of women in English society. *Tess of the d'Urbervilles* offers a set of expectations, of conventional masculine views about sexuality, morality and marriage. For example Tess's rape makes her irredeemably 'impure' and she cannot formally baptise her dying infant or bury the baby in a churchyard. These expectations are shown to be brutal and harsh. They are also narratively represented in melodramatic episodes which sharply contrast with Tess's self-reflexive monologues. The clash of genres *as well as* the clash of ideologies suggests new questions about gender representation.

Marxist/socialist feminists would see such clashes and multigeneric mixtures as representing Hardy's views about social change, specifically changes in thinking about women. The focus here would be on the dialectical pitting of male attitudes and expectations (those of his readers as much as those of his characters) against women's representations and on the resulting mental and physical destruction of women. Like other heroines fighting to establish an individual and gendered identity against given social identities – Emma Bovary and Anna Karenina would be other obvious examples – Tess fights against being a mere appendage to men. This has immediate consequences for the narrative structure of the novel. A key focus for Marxist/socialist feminists would be on those 'awkward' structural moments when Tess's character development outpaces the plot. A good example here is the section of the novel set in the Talbothay's dairy. This contains an interesting series of episodes which are resolutely historical in depicting a nineteenth-century rural working dairy, but also *contradictory* in character representation. There is a dialectical pitting of dairy maid 'femininity' (the erotic jostling for Clare's attention) against Tess's intensively self-reflexive Gramscian 'common sense' intellect. The central concern of the Italian Marxist, Gramsci, was with what he referred to as 'peasant' ways of thinking. Much of Gramsci's political analysis in *Prison Notebooks* is devoted to describing this way of thinking as *philosophy* shot through with elements of 'common sense', which can be contradictory but equally very combative (Gramsci, 1971). Hardy never relinquishes his human-ist view of the universe, but Tess seriously challenges humanism in her Talbothay monologues. The struggle over gender identit-ies is foregrounded (in this chapter) by pitting the caring and supportive working-class dairymaids against the actions of Angel's less than supportive middle-class brothers. Hardy never offers Talbothay's dairy as a new *paradigm* of gender relationships but does describe women 'consciousness raising' collectively: sharing hard work and assisting Tess's relationship with Angel when Izzy declines Angel's invitation to Brazil.

'I don't-know about ghosts,' she was saying. 'But I do know that our souls can be made to go outside our bodies when we are alive.'

The dairyman turned to her with his mouth full, his eyes charged with serious inquiry, and his great knife and fork (breakfasts were breakfasts here) planted erect on the table, like the beginning of a gallows.

'What – really now? And is it so, maidy?' he said.

'A very easy way to feel 'em go,' continued Tess, 'is to lie on the grass at night and look straight up at some big bright star; and by fixing your mind upon it you will soon find that you are hundreds and hundreds o' miles away from your body, which you don't seem to want at all.'

The dairyman removed his hard gaze from Tess, and fixed it on his wife.

'Now that's a rum thing, Christianner – hey? To think o' the miles I've vamped o' starlight nights these last thirty year, courting, or trading, or for doctor, or for nurse, and yet never had the least notion o' that till now, or feeled my soul rise so much as an inch above my shirt-collar.'

The general attention being drawn to her, including that of the dairyman's pupil, Tess flushed, and remarking evasively that it was only a fancy, resumed her breakfast.

Clare continued to observe her. She soon finished her eating, and having a consciousness that Clare was regarding her, began to trace imaginary patterns on the table-cloth with her forefinger with the constraint of a domestic animal that perceives itself to be watched.

'What a fresh and virginal daughter of Nature that milkmaid is!' he said to himself.

(From *Tess of the d'Urbervilles*, Oxford University Press: Oxford, 1988, p. 124)

First we notice that Tess is presented here as a questioning outsider. Her thoughts are not *socially* constructed but work *against* other constructions in the narrative including those of gender. Specifically, her thoughts are *not* determined by physical appearance, by feminine qualities but emerge the further she *distances* herself from her body. Tess's independent, monologic assertions are given direct and have structurally more significance than either the authorial symbolic motifs ('gallows') or Angel and Dairyman Crick's masculine representations ('fresh and virginal'). Tess's future narrative outcome is indeed the gallows, foreshadowed here by the appearance of Dairyman Crick's knife and fork, which follows immediately after Tess's independent self-reflexivity. The dialectical juxtaposition of social/narrative constraints and women's independent mono-logic identity could not be clearer. Because Tess's speech is given a dramatic space, the speech works against other constructions of femininity – Dairyman Crick's failed attempt to humorously deflate Tess's vision as well as the inappropriate signifiers of 'domestic animal' and Clare's 'virginal daughter'.

Tess is not an intact stereotype – the fair dairymaid – but a proletarian worker forced to sell her labour in the winter when dairy work is unavailable. Hardy is not trying to represent Talbothay's as a rural retreat (although it is in these terms that Clare perceives dairy life) but as a functioning capitalist farm. Talbothay's is responsive to the exigencies of its customers who spot the 'twang' in butter caused by garlic-eating cows and it produces milk for urban centres. This harsh naturalism is at odds with Tess's coming to consciousness. Hardy does not choose one generic mode over another but positions Tess's self-awareness (and the attractions this might have for readers as well as Clare) against the social constraints which lead to her destruction. As Althusser argues, the imaginary ways in which we present to ourselves our relationship with the world create contradictions in language and literature.

Marxist/socialist feminists would want to explore the novel's attention to the displacement of agricultural workers (Poor Law legislation dictated that a parish's poor rate was lowered by having fewer houses) and the proletarianization of those remaining (like Tess) *in tandem with* Tess's struggle with identity. The narrative structure of this episode is shaped by that struggle represented by the ambiguities of narrator point of view. The fragmentation of point of view, the multigeneric form of *Tess of the d'Urbervilles* and the dialectical juxtaposition of gender representations are all important foci for Marxist/socialist feminist criticism. We might also agree with Virginia Woolf's comment about Hardy's novel: that she could not stop reading it (Woolf, 1944).

SECTION 6: SYLVIA TOWNSEND WARNER, *SUMMER WILL SHOW*

The main focus of Marxist criticism is on history. While Marxist theory has a wide range, Marxist literary criticism from Marx through to Althusser and Eagleton looks *to* history and historical representations for literary values and meanings. The vast majority of traditional Marxist literary critics share an involved attention to the historical contexts of literary texts and to texts in which historical events have a key narrative role. Many Marxist critics believe that gendered values and meanings are historically determined by class. Although the French Marxist Louis Althusser argued that literature both revealed and disrupted dominant ideologies, he agreed that textual contradictions were tied to material history (Althusser, 1971). While contemporary critics like Terry Eagleton acknowledge the difficulty of tying literary representations to historical determinations, earlier critics such as Georg Lukács made fictional realism a main focus of their critical attention (Eagleton, 1976; Lukács, 1971). The assumption here is that history is a shaping force of culture. Lukács paid particular attention to realism because he believed that realist novels could describe social institutions and relationships, while simultaneously revealing moments of political contradiction.

Traditional Marxist critics might pay attention to the ways in which the situations of female characters derive from a distinct set of historical and social dynamics. But distinct *gender roles* such as those of marriage and motherhood are more often described in terms of class issues than in terms of women's patriarchal subordination.

Sylvia Townsend Warner's *Summer Will Show* is a long historical fiction about the Paris Revolution of 1848; it therefore seems an ideal candidate for a Marxist/socialist analysis. The text is a seemingly coherent realist novel with a positive heroine, Sophia, with whom spectators can identify. But feminist critics would suggest that to discuss *Summer Will Show* only in terms of realism and class exploitations would be to ignore a more basic difference – that of gender contradictions. There are ideas about sexual politics in *Summer Will Show* which cannot fully be explained in terms of material and historical contradictions alone. But in most versions of traditional Marxist criticism gender is not assigned a central or even a distinctive role. Sexuality itself is never at the centre. What Lukács and earlier critics have in common is a blindness to the significance of gender. A key question for Marxist/socialist *feminists*, then, is how to utilize traditional Marxist paradigms to understand women's representations.

What can Marxism teach us about literary forms, and what is the utility of Marxist methods of literary criticism? What Marxism *can* give feminism, as I have described, is a way of understanding the historical contexts which produce literature and which, in turn, literature helps to produce. Marxist theory addresses social conditions and exploitations and how writers consciously or unconsciously transpose these issues into literature. What feminism adds to Marxism is an attention to the psychic, to the subjective in interaction with social formations, and therefore a greater understanding of the gendered *subjectivity* of political and historical representations and events.

In Britain Marxist/socialist feminism could be said to begin with Juliet Mitchell's key essay 'Women: the longest revolution' first published in *New Left Review* in 1966. In this essay Mitchell drew on the work of Louis Althusser to describe how literature and culture are *material* forces in patriarchy (see Mitchell, 1984). The four structures of capitalist patriarchy – reproduction, production, the socialization of children and, sexuality – are interdependent. Women's liberation will be achieved only if *all* four structures are radically transformed. The end of patriarchy would therefore need a cultural, as well as a social, revolution. In France the work of Julia Kristeva is one example of how feminism extends Marxist theory. Although refusing the label 'feminist', Kristeva has developed a materialist analysis into a psychoanalytically based theory of gender representations. In *Desire in Language* Kristeva draws attention to the ways in which women as subjects are constituted in language and literature (Kristeva, 1980). In America Tillie Olsen is generally acknowledged to be a major contemporary Marxist critic emerging from a socialist literary tradition going back to Charlotte Perkins Gilman. In *Silences* Olsen interweaves the voices of women workers, mothers and published writers to show the impress of history on women's culture (Olsen, 1978).

What methods have evolved from these ideas? The British critic Michèle Barrett, in 'Feminism and the definition of cultural politics', argues that Marxist/socialist feminism can focus on levels of aesthetic *skill* in the *construction* of works of art (Barrett, 1982). The essay contains an account of Judy Chicago's feminist art work *The Dinner Party* as well as an overview of feminist aesthetics; it makes literary *production* processes strategic to aesthetics. Other approaches, such as those introduced by the Birmingham Centre for Cultural Studies, focused on the *relation* between cultural practices and the lived experiences of readers and their ways of reading. Here Marxist/socialist feminism could be characterized as ethnographic because it analyzes the *reception*, as well as the *production*, of literary texts. Reception also involves the interpellation, or drawing in, of readers by texts (Davis *et al.*, 1982). Earlier accounts, like those first outlined by the Marxist-Feminist Literature Collective (MFLC) pay attention not only to what characters *say* but to what they *cannot* say – to the awkward moments in novels when speech is denied or repressed (MFLC, 1978). Like other Marxist/socialist feminists they address the relation of 'her story' to 'history' in novels like

Brontë's *Villette*, since it is women characters, above all, who reveal discrepancies between lived experience and material worlds. Historical novels not only can identify women's lived experience of social contradictions and exploitations in the *past*, but can also suggest the relevance of past values to the present.

In *Summer Will Show* Sylvia Townsend Warner describes the Paris Revolution of 1848. Townsend Warner published her novel during an intensely historical *contemporary* moment – the Spanish Civil War in the 1930s. She was an active member of the British Communist Party and other progressive and pacifist movements of that period. Sophia, the heroine of *Summer Will Show*, works with revolutionaries in Paris as a *déclassé* aristocrat who joins forces with the Left. Yet for a woman, and in Townsend Warner's case a lesbian woman, the 1930s' left-wing agenda was profoundly masculinist, reflecting the exclusive 'male club' quality of Oxbridge socialist intelligentsia. Left-wing writing was expected to be materialist and progressive, not to thematize sexual politics.

In all Sylvia Townsend Warner's novels women characters are thinkers and free spirits. One of Townsend Warner's main themes is the subjection of women in marriage and the forces ranged against independent women by institutions like the church, marriage and the city. *Summer Will Show* makes an obdurate analysis of the economic and gendered constraints of nineteenth-century marriage. Set in 1848, the novel traces Sophia Willoughby's struggle for a new identity which takes her away from the functions of motherhood and educator (after the death of her children from smallpox) to Paris where she gains a political consciousness. Sophia is the wife of Frederick, who has squandered her inherited fortune (his legally by marriage) and abandoned her for his mistress in Paris. Townsend Warner's sexual politics are very clear. In England Sophia is trapped by gender, by class and by history. She is deprived of her family estate by the injustices of the British legal system before the Married Women's Property Act, when women could not retain their property rights on marriage.

In this sense the novel's plot matches very well the concerns of Marxist/socialist feminism in that Townsend Warner presents Sophia's story as both typical of the novel's historical moment as well as sharing characteristics of all exploitative marriages past *and* present. Marxist/socialist feminists feel that historical novels can offer both general statements about historical issues as well as particular and individualized expressions of the *effects* of historical forces. In Paris, Sophia meets and begins to love Minna, her husband's mistress, joins the communards, and lives a *flâneuse* street existence. The valorization of communard and female street-walking is a metaphor of historical transgression. In *Summer Will Show* men are colonizers of psyche and purse. At first Sophia is ironic: 'in some ways men were essential. One must have a coachman, a gardener' (p. 76). Distance and independence bring an ensuing and new delight in her own and Minna's eroticism: 'since she had freed herself of Frederick nakedness was again a pleasure' (p. 176).

A particular focus of Marxist/socialist feminists is on the ways in which historical fictions achieve historical 'faithfulness' and make concrete social worlds. One of Townsend Warner's major techniques is describing the detail of public life. Sophia, like Minna, learns to speak out in public and acts as a courier for the revolutionaries. The *actual* historical accuracy of such episodes is irrelevant. What *is* important is the general atmosphere of historical specificity evident in the descriptions of striking workers and street markets. After Minna has been stabbed on the barricades, Sophia returns to their apartment and, in a forefronting of 'real' history, opens and reads Marx's *Communist Manifesto* as the novel ends. Marxist/socialist feminists would make a connection between individual tragic events (Minna's wound) and the 'real' world of political action and political beliefs deployed by Townsend Warner. From this perspective, the presence of the *Communist Manifesto* would be read as a grand finale authenticating the subjective desires of Sophia and Minna.

Yet the work can also be read as a lesbian novel. Sylvia Townsend Warner was a *lesbian* Communist and there is a strong element of fantasy in *Summer Will Show*. A good example is Minna's long monologic account of her early childhood in Russia; it could be argued that the novel is a multigeneric mixture of realism and fabulism. The stories in *Summer Will Show* reveal how women's heterosexual oppression involves repressing a consciousness which can be 'raised' not only through material change, but also through lesbian desires. Sophia and Minna share a 'desperate, calculated caress' (p. 250) and Sophia ruptures *both* bourgeois *and* sexual conventions. 'When I looked at the things I had stolen, it re-established me' (p. 229). Townsend Warner's *Summer Will Show* shares with Virginia Woolf's *A Room of One's Own* and *Three Guineas* an interest in the 'outsiders' of society, as well as the belief that lesbian women's perspective stands in a parodic relation to the 'realistic' moral values of society.

Marxist/socialist feminists would focus on moments which reveal partiarchal exploitation. Sophia's economic *and* sexual estrangements are clear in the following passage describing the inequities of nineteenth-century marriage laws.

> 'He has cut off my supplies. As he is entitled to do, being my husband. He has told the bank not to honour my signature, he has removed the gold fittings from my dressing-case. So you see, Minna, I am penniless, or soon shall be. I have what is left over from my ring, that will last a while. I have my clothes, for what they are worth. And my hair. I believe one can always sell one's hair. After that, unless I comply with Frederick's wishes, nothing.'
>
> 'You will stay? You must, if only to gall him.'
>
> 'I don't think that much of a reason.'
>
> 'But you will stay?'
>
> 'I will stay if you wish it.'
>
> It seemed to her that the words fell cold and glum as ice-pellets. Only beneath the crust of thought did her being assent as by right to that flush of pleasure, that triumphant cry.
>
> 'But of course,' said Minna a few hours later, thoughtfully licking the last oyster shell, 'we must be practical.'
>
> This remark she had already made repeatedly, speaking with the excitement of an adventurous mind contemplating a new and hazardous experience.
>
> (From *Summer Will Show*, Virago, London, 1987, pp. 273–4)

Frederick has cut off all Sophia's credits as well as confiscating her gold and jewels. The passage is, as Marxist/socialist feminists would argue, a good example of one concentrated and particular effect of patriarchal capitalism. Women had an ambiguous economic status in marriage until the Married Women's Property Act (1882) which prevented husbands from forfeiting their wives' property. Women were excluded from full participation in society by the patriarchal family – significantly here leaving

Sophia only her 'own hair'. Women were both men's property and banned from productive relations. Marxist/socialist feminists would point to Frederick's actions as an example of the ultimate patriarchal capitalist privilege: control over women as property. Capitalist patriarchy created a commodified domestic woman whose fictional figure here focuses on an issue central to Marxist/ socialist feminism: the link between economic possession and sexual exploitation.

The passage is in free direct speech, where the narrator's perspective is reduced. There are quotation marks but no inserted narrator comments about the characters. This gives Sophia's reporting of Frederick's savage actions a dynamic immediacy which increases their harshness. Townsend Warner's choice of free direct speech allows the characters of Sophia and Minna a dramatized and heightened significance. Their feelings are not immediately translated by the author for her readers.

Yet conversely, to be free of her wealth enables Sophia to be free of Frederick as a husband, and the passage ends in a hint of female bonding and lesbian transgression: 'a new and hazardous experience' which is symbolized by the eroticism of Minna 'licking the last oyster shell'. The passage moves into the third person and describes Sophia's subjective feelings. Rhetorically Townsend Warner sets up a basic opposition between the metonymic effect of Frederick's actions 'the words fell cold and glum as ice-pellets' and Sophia's internalized and potential lesbian desire: 'Only beneath the crust of thought did her being assent as by right to that flush of pleasure, that triumphant cry.'

The opposition is created through an imagistic contrast of 'ice' versus volcanic 'crust'. Even though the passage is in the third person a reader, inevitably, is attracted more to warmth than cold and therefore to sympathize with Sophia and Minna's relationship. The presence of these images acts as a form of focalization. The passage's shifting point of view highlights both Sophia's *conscious* material experience of patriarchy (in dramatized speech) and her *unconscious* deeper feelings 'beneath the crust of thought'.

In this way the novel suggests the characters are beginning to disengage from heterosexual patriarchy as well as from capitalist patriarchy. Sophia is able to liberate herself from the patriarchal family through her sensuous relationship with Minna. A later

passage illustrates how Sophia understands for herself the connections between her 'new' sexuality and her economic position.
Now, in addition to singing in the street she shopped in the street
also. The decent veil of shopping in a foreign tongue and under
conditions which made such shopping an adventure and a fantasy
had soon ravelled away. With her whole soul she walked from stall
to stall, countering the wiles of those who sell with the wiles of those
who purchase, pinching the flesh of chickens, turning over mackerel,
commenting disadvantageously upon the false bloom of revived
radishes. Her fine nostrils quivered above cheeses and sniffed into
pickle-tubs and the defencelessly open bellies of long pale rabbits.
Her glance pried out flaws, the under-ripe or the over-ripe, and her
tongue denounced them.

(From *Summer Will Show*, Virago, London, 1987, p. 287)

The passage is an example of Sophia's maximum disengagement
from patriarchal capitalism. She quickly learns to circumnavigate
street markets and choose cheap food. The 'decent veil' she
would need to wear as a rich woman has been lifted and she
bargains happily with the street vendors. The passage utilizes
the continuous active present – 'countering', 'turning' – as well
as a number of sensuous images. The 'sexuality' of food is also a
heightened feature of the passage. Rabbits have 'open bellies',
chickens have 'flesh' and radishes have 'false bloom'. Sophia
uses her body, 'her nostrils', 'her glance', 'her tongue' in effusive
descriptions of female eroticism. Placing the sexuality of Sophia's
body close to economic life makes visible the mutual determina-
tion of sexuality and politics. As Marxist/socialist feminists would
argue, both are major and interrelated features of patriarchal
capitalism. The symbolic appearance of lesbian desire in *Summer
Will Show* is a symptom of the absences in patriarchal gender
constructions and the need for fresh sexual, as well as fresh
social, thinking.

Sophia's 'sexualization' has taken place *outside* capitalist
production – metaphorically on the street among vendors here
and more significantly with Minna after Frederick 'disinherits'
Sophia. The narrative placing of Sophia's relationship with
Minna demonstrates Townsend Warner's belief that if women
are property they lack sexual freedom. The narrative movement
through lesbian eroticism to the reading of the *Communist*

Manifesto suggests the ideological force of 'free' sexuality. Only when the productive practices which determine class and gender interests are renounced or taken away, Townsend Warner suggests, can the political truly be contested.

A Marxist/socialist feminist project would focus on the micro-analysis of patriarchal capitalism which *Summer Will Show* offers the reader. *Summer Will Show* also uses parody and dreams to redefine gender representations in ways both historically determined and historically 'new'. Sophia's characterization and the heat of her desire for Minna oppose the economic *and* sexual mores of patriarchal capitalism. Sophia's skilled street marketing and gun running bear the marks of an emergent independent 'new woman' marked by the 'loss' of capitalist signs of exchange – jewels, rich clothes and her class status.

From a Marxist/socialist perspective, the novel can be read not simply as a reflection of economic and social forces current in mid-nineteenth-century England but as an example of alternative ideologies which question conventional realism. In this sense *Summer Will Show* is a good example of the contestations and contradictions which are the focus of Marxist/socialist feminists. In some ways the novel is closer to contemporary historical *metafiction* – exemplified in Salman Rushdie's *Midnight's Children* – in its celebration of a plurality of difference. *Summer Will Show* offers both the authority of historical events and the subversive politics of lesbian Communist alternatives to those events.

4   French feminism

SECTION 7: CAROLYN STEEDMAN, *LANDSCAPE FOR A GOOD WOMAN*

French feminist criticism offers, perhaps, the clearest critical account of the relationship between female subjectivity and forms of language. Whilst French feminism includes both the existential philosophy of Simone de Beauvoir and the materialist analysis of Christine Delphy, the psychoanalytic critiques of Julia Kristeva, Luce Irigaray and Hélène Cixous all focus on subjectivity and language. Despite their differences, these critics share a number of preoccupations. The first is that Western patriarchy is a symbolic order with a language/discourse characterized by objectivity and rationality. Changes in Western socioeconomic structures will involve linguistic changes in this symbolic order which might be stimulated by new models drawn from the maternal. Second, their writing shares similar characteristics: all develop closer links between literature and theory and interrogate literary languages in terms of complex metaphysical ideas. Third, these critics argue that with new and multiple psychosocial, linguistic constructs we might release the repressed Other, or femininity, into culture (Kristeva, 1980; Irigaray, 1977; Cixous, 1979). Hence French feminists are interested in texts which draw attention to *processes* of representation. French feminists believe that such processes often reveal gender-specific subjectivities and that it is the *processes* of meaning making which create gender misrepresentations, not only in literature, but also in the political world.

One danger, and a common attack on French feminism, is to

read gendered subjectivities as *essential*, as creating fixed and immutably different forms of literature. Another danger is that if traditional Eurocentred literary theory ignores difference – aiming to create a unified, organic critique – how then can the Other ever be represented at all? In the light of these issues, French feminism utilizes deconstruction to focus on the ideologies which produce literary meanings. Literature is a key focus of French feminism precisely because literature, above all the other arts, often incorporates the Other, either as the unconscious, or in dreams or linguistic slippages. We need to leave behind, these critics claim, our faith in 'schools' of criticism and ideas of sequential literary development and instead plunge into more plural questions about language, questions which could centre on the roles of Others. Julia Kristeva, for example, stresses that there should be no single language, or metalanguage, of criticism but rather a disruptive 'birthing' of ideas and feelings (Kristeva, 1980).

The major questions posed by French feminism are these. Given that literary language shapes our literary knowledge, how can we rethink literary perceptions and structures? Where does the 'feminine' appear in literature and what new representations of subjectivity might it suggest? For French feminists, new literary subjectivities are already operating in the 'maternal function' which precedes our entry into the symbolic and hence into literature. The material bodies of mothers, the relationship between mother and infant, create psychic, subjective images and rhythms which are never lost from our unconscious, although they may be forgotten. Aspects of literary style reinscribe this maternal moment in literature.

One key focus of literary criticism, then, would be on representations of mothers and maternal relations. Women's identities derive from an intensely problematic but reciprocal reproduction of our mothers. The mother is both Other and ourself and our memories of our mothers are in ourselves. Literary representations of the mother as a subject in process can be deconstructed in order to understand the maternal function. A number of non-literary theorists, most obviously Nancy Chodorow, agree that the reproduction of mothering especially the reproduction of those moments *before* our entry into the symbolic, or social language, might disrupt the symbolic

(Chodorow, 1978). Frequently this is described in terms of 'voiced breath' musical rhythms and other features of the mother-child symbiosis. In the Freudian model mothers have a specific function – to act as a 'castrated' being until birthing a son replaces the absent phallus. French feminists, on the other hand, argue that women's understanding of mothering has been symbolically, or socially, constructed away from the exciting and vibrant fantasy of maternal origin. A return to, or re-vision of, the mother and maternal rhythms and tones, of the semiotic element in language, could be a mechanism for subverting traditional literary representations.

The figure of a mother, or rather the difficulty of figuring mothers, is the theme of Carolyn Steedman's *Landscape for a Good Woman*. But before turning to a passage from that text it would be helpful to summarize the more specific maternal theories of Kristeva, Irigaray and Cixous. French feminist ideas about reproduction, nurturing or, in Carolyn Steedman's case, the *desire* for these experiences suggest a range of signifying processes.

Julia Kristeva claims that the existing symbolic order is challenged by the sort of formal linguistic experiments which conceptualize mothers in modernist literature (Kristeva, 1980). According to Kristeva, modernist literature brings together gendered subjectivities, the unconscious and social relations and explodes traditional representations of subjects or characters. In general, Kristeva maintains that linguistics, as in the work of Saussure, ignores the *subject* of writing, preferring to disassociate the structural value of a text from its inhabitants. Kristeva, on the other hand, argues that any theory of literature must include a theory of subjectivity, particularly maternal subjectivity. In *Desire in Language* Kristeva sets out her idea that an infant has no sense of self, of a subjectivity separate from the mother, in the first phase of his or her life (Kristeva, 1980). Taking the concept of *chora*, or enclosed space/cave/womb, from Plato, Kristeva suggests that this early moment can be defined as a *chora*, a state before subjectivity and hence language and representations. The *chora* is an all-encompassing concept which includes the totality of an infant's desires or drives. It is the foundation of any signifying process. Yet this moment, Kristeva argues, continues to exist *in* language. That is to say any literary representation of subjectivity is constantly being threatened or pressured by the force of that pre-Oedipal time. The semiotic is continuously at work *within* the structure of the symbolic.

This can be seen in rhythmic patterns of sound. In French 'la sémiotique' is 'semiotics', the science of signs and Kristeva starts by using 'le sémiotique' to refer to the organization of instinctual drives as these impact on language. Kristeva devotes a major part of *Desire in Language* to describing differences between the semiotic and the symbolic; here I will merely summarize the main themes. The semiotic and the symbolic are the two forms of language which a subject 'speaks' or signifies, with the semiotic being a pre-symbolic language. Kristeva argues that the semiotic is the time when children have an all-encompassing relation to the mother achieved through gestures, aural and vocal rhythms and repetitive patterns. Because individual subjectivity is constructed in a mothering relationship, women's close identification with mothers and mothering creates in us a more ambivalent relation to the symbolic or metalanguage.

If castration marks out the symbolic contract, what can be women's place, Kristeva asks, in such a sacrificial order of language? The answer for criticism will be to subvert the symbolic, its social codes and paternal function by attention to the body, the emotions and the unnameable repressed by the symbolic. A disruption of narrative or deviation in grammar, the absences or contradictions of literary texts, will be highly significant indications of the semiotic at work. Twentieth-century literature, in particular, reveals the pre-Oedipal, or semiotic, because it often incorporates, post-Freud, features drawn from the unconscious. Like the unconscious, semiotic patterns will resist making sense but can be made intelligible by analysis. We are *conscious* of the semiotic when we observe repetitions of vocabulary, rhythmic or musical sentences or a disruption of syntactical order. One way in which we can get access to our own semiotic is by investigating representations of mothering. According to Kristeva, this process may not necessarily involve actual images (although Kristeva does analyze Bellini's paintings of the Holy Mother) but can focus, for example, on the way in which poetry gives rhythmic patterns a power beyond conventional grammar.

Like many feminists writing about motherhood, Kristeva is

very aware of the danger of defining the feminine in terms of motherhood. Kristeva suggests, however, that the man-subject is as much a product of the interrelation of motherhood, the semiotic and discourse as is the woman-subject. Some male writers, like James Joyce, can also be seen as subverting the symbolic order. The most obvious examples of the presence of the semiotic, Kristeva claims, will be at moments when textual surfaces break apart, erupting into ellipses . . . or incorporating non-literary forms (*intertextualité*). Carolyn Steedman's *Landscape for a Good Woman* is a particularly good example of a text which directly addresses issues, of working-class mothering and bastardy, excluded from the symbolic order. These issues lead Steedman to think through how her text might *re*-produce her mother in order to challenge patriarchal *processes* of representation. Kristeva's work raises problems for feminist criticism, not least because she refuses the label feminist. She takes little account of the cultural and political structures impacting on literary texts. But the usefulness of Kristeva's ideas of mothering and the semiotic lies in her emphasis on the *materiality* of language itself.

The philosopher Luce Irigaray, like Kristeva, suggests that our entire system of Western writing is built on the idea that woman is Other (Irigaray, 1977). Like Kristeva, what Irigaray perceives more hopefully is that woman's position of exclusion or marginality enables us to see the faults in traditional representations. The role of the mother is crucial to this enterprise. To Irigaray the relation between infant and mother is an issue of fantasy. Fantasy does not mean 'illusion' but is part of an individual psychic reality. In *This Sex Which is Not One* Irigaray argues that dominant gender representations exclude M/Others and that women readers should focus on the relation of 'woman to herself' (Irigaray, 1977). What this might involve more precisely in terms of literary criticism is experimenting with a new syntax, by avoiding 'owning' proper names, or turning to texts like Steedman's which raise such issues.

These complex and innovative ideas are shared by Hélène Cixous, who claims that Western representations subordinate women. In order to find a 'truer' way of reading Cixous suggests we attend to memories of childhood and bodily rhythms (Cixous, 1976a). The early relationship with the mother is locked into our unconscious, which therefore carries images and experiences often revitalized in literature. Cixous suggests that we try to hear the different 'voices' in a text, sharing rhythms with an (M)Other and experimenting with new subjectivities. Cixous suggests that all forceful women writers give birth to words flowing in accord with the contractual rhythms of labour.

French feminist criticism, then, involves two critical processes. First there is a deconstructive activity aimed at breaking up 'given' arrangements of meaning. Second is a 're-visionary' activity aiming to find the forgotten 'syntax' of the semiotic present in juxtapositions, slips of language and intertextuality.

I propose to examine a brief passage from Carolyn Steedman's *Landscape for a Good Woman* as an example of what French feminism summarizes as *écriture féminine*. Throughout the 1970s and 1980s the publishers des femmes in Paris published a number of key texts of *écriture féminine*. The starting point of this criticism is that women's actual physical experiences, if represented, might constitute a counterlanguage. Building on Freud's notion that the unconscious is represented in disruptions of syntax (or slips of the tongue) critics argue that similarly women's unconscious might disrupt the ordered syntactics of traditional literary criticism, making writing turbulent and non-unified – what Cixous calls 'writing the body' (Cixous, 1979). Each critic draws from *écriture féminine* a different possibility. Kristeva argues in *Desire in Language*, as we have seen, that a kind of language exists in the pre-linguistic experience of early infancy. Irigaray prefers the term *parler femme*, (rather than *écriture féminine*) because *parler femme* is defined by its *mode* of address (speaking *to* women) rather than its *forms* (*what* or *how* one speaks) (Irigaray, 1977). Cixous aims to transform writing by mixing autobiography with sentence fragments and portmanteau words (Cixous, 1979). Similarly, Irigaray's *This Sex Which is Not One* has no one style but mixes analyses, body descriptions and occasional silences.

To write *écriture féminine*, or *parler femme*, is to disrupt the existing structure of language and attempt new formulations. One major danger is the problem of universalism. *Écriture féminine* has been attacked by Gayatri Spivak for effacing history and the material reality of Others (Spivak, 1987). But as this section makes clear, French feminists do address key questions of patriarchal power and the possibility of a women's language.

Landscape for a Good Woman sets out many of these ideas. The autobiography, powerfully and parodically, includes intertexts of Steedman's 'real' history and the explanations of psycho-analysis, literature, sociology, history and myth. In so doing Steedman contests the genre boundaries of traditional literature. Steedman continually dialogues, self-reflexively, with her own assumptions, making critical accountability a key feature of the text. The book is the story of Steedman's mother, her working-class life and Steedman's 1950s childhood. Daughter of a Burnley weaver, her mother moved south and became a manicurist. Steedman creates her mother as an interesting, eccentric outsider – a vegetarian who co-habited with Steedman's father and finally died of cancer where the book begins.

Landscape for a Good Woman is both a record of people who live on the 'margins' outside the accredited stories of sociologists and historians and an attack on the languages of dominant culture. The histories of Steedman and her family cannot therefore be written in a linear chronology as case studies but have to be *re*-performed – staged in the way that an analysand might talk to an analyst or a daughter to a mother. The book shares with *écriture féminine* the aim of breaking with traditional contexts by racing through the multiple discourses of psychoanalysis and history, deconstructing their interpretative devices and listening to different voices. Like Irigaray, Steedman attacks the authorita-tive explanations of psychoanalysis, because while psycho-analysis might explain Steedman's inability to be a mother herself it could never account for her mother's *class* journey.

> A little girl's body, its neat containment, seems much more like that of a man than it does that of a woman, especially if she does not really know what lies between his legs. His body was in some way mine, and I was removed from my own as well as his. Though I didn't feel the revulsion from my mother's body that Kathleen Dayus describes in *Her People* (indeed, my mother was an attractive woman who kept her figure, though she tended to put on weight very easily) I recognise the distance and distaste of the girl child from what has produced her, and what she might become:
>
> Suddenly, Mum shot up out of bed. I'd never seen her move so

quickly, nor look so misshapen as she did then, standing beside the bed with her calico shift all twisted up in front. I'd never seen her undressed before or without her whalebone stays . . . I never know how she got all that flabby flesh inside those stays. She looked so comical that I had to put my hand over my mouth to keep from laughing out loud[30].

This isn't an expression of 'the obscure bodily self-hatred peculiar to women who view themselves through the eyes of men'[31]. It is a revulsion based on some obscure recognition of a difficulty, an ambivalence. My refusal of my mother's body was, I think, a recognition of the problem that my own physical presence repres- ented to her; and at the same time it was a refusal of the inexorable nature of that difficulty, that it would *go on* like that, that I would become her, and come to reproduce the circumstances of our straightened, unsatisfying life.

Part of the desire to reproduce oneself as a body, as an entity in the real world, lies in conscious memory of someone approving that body. I have no evidence from the time when my mother did enough to enable me to produce my fantasy children, Joan and Maureen; but my conscious memory of much later years is of rarely meeting with this kind of physical confirmation and approval.

(From *Landscape for a Good Woman*, Virago, London, 1986, pp. 94–5)
[30 Kathleen Dayus, *Her People*, Virago, London, 1982, p. 81]
[31 Adrienne Rich, *Of Woman Born*, Bantam, New York, 1977, p. 219]

Steedman shares with French feminists a desire to look at the relationship between female subjectivity, mothering, and lan- guage. The passage beings with a statement about childhood sexuality from which the narrator is disassociated. We are presented with a self-reflexive exposition of the relations between and differences between the bodies of mothers and daughters. Steedman makes a 'French feminist', link between self-constructions of femininity 'the desire to reproduce oneself as a body' and a mirroring mother 'rarely meeting with this kind of *physical* confirmation and approval'. The run on from 'physical' to distanced 'approval' through quasi-religious legal 'confirma- tion' stresses the importance of the *material* body. The passage is replete with maternal images: her mother, Kathleen Dayus's mother and the mother Steedman will not become. The complexities of Kristeva's 'maternal function' are here in the way in which negation and identification operate in the mother–daughter symbiosis. The passage moves from negative statements 'I didn't feel' to the identificatory 'I recognise'. Steedman is unable at this point to come to terms with her mother as an abject figure (according to Kristeva a necessary stage on the journey into the symbolic) and places her mother's materiality, in parenthesis '(indeed, my mother was an attractive woman . . .)' while displacing abjection through quotation and Dayus's grotesquerie 'all that flabby flesh'.

As French feminists suggest, the driving force within the symbolic (Steedman's overt text) is the material semiotic rejection. Steedman is unable to relate to an (M)Other because the (M)Other is not yet within Steedman's own identity: 'My refusal of my mother's body'. Part of her difficulty is caused by her mother's refusal, in this passage, to operate the maternal function because of 'the problem that my own physical presence represented to her'. According to Kristeva what the child must abject is the 'maternal container' (here hugely parodied in reverse in Dayus's 'misshapen' mother's body without 'her stays'). The child does not need to abject the mother's body as a *female* body. In this sense Steedman's disassociation from reproduction and recognition of her mother as a 'woman who kept her figure' can be a basis for an alternative discourse of maternity. For French feminists all signification is driven by a dialectic between semiotic desires (here Steedman's desire to re-vision the materiality of her mother) and symbolic stages (becoming 'an entity in the real world'). Steedman agrees that the maternal calls into question the limits of the symbolic world, particularly since her own mother could be said to prefigure a new maternal ethics as a successful single parent.

The symbolic order is the order of signification, the social realm. In 'Women's time' Kristeva associates the symbolic with linear 'masculine' chronology, with the acquisition of language with its laws, boundaries and stasis (Kristeva, 1981). *Landscape for a Good Woman* deliberately subverts linear, logical argument by privileging plural voices (here the intertextual Dayus and Rich and fantasy: 'my fantasy children Joan and Maureen'). Yet, as Kristeva suggests, the semiotic is *in* the symbolic so

Steedman resorts to the epigrammatic, academic 'oneself as a body'.

Steedman's pronouns are constantly in motion (as Cixous suggests, refusing to 'own' a character or representative figure). The passage moves from third person to 'his' which is both an abstract anonymous girl's father as well as Steedman's own father to 'she' then 'I' (reinforced by the everyday conversational 'didn't') to 'my' (in relation to the mother's body), 'her' and 'oneself'. There is no symbolic, authoritative single voice. This is because the *process* by which a me becomes an I and confidently reproduces the mother is itself in question both as the *content* of the passage *and* in Steedman's *écriture féminine*.

Another example of Steedman's style is this later picture of her mother.

> Her presentation of herself as a good mother shows also with what creativity people may use the stuff of cultural and social stereotype, so that it becomes not a series of labels applied from outside a situation, but a set of metaphors ready for transformation by those who are its subjects.
>
> (From *Landscape for a Good Woman*, Virago, London, 1986, p. 103)

Here the pronoun 'she', unlike 'my mother' in the previous passage agrees with Steedman's *symbolic* creation of her mother as a product of cultural constructs. There is no self-reflexivity. In the first passage the psychoanalytic 'loss' of the mother's body triggers Steedman's semiotic desire to bond, which she deliberately poses as an issue of *écriture*, of pronominal slipperiness. The authority of symbolic social history is subverted by the memory of experience. The first passage's multigeneric, plural voices place the theoretical in play with the personal and the personal is constantly threatened by the canopy of the critical. Steedman's own position in the passage as 'I' immediately confirms her mother as Other, while simultaneously Steedman questions *society's* 'Othering' of her mother – the woman – *as well as* creating *herself* as Other 'removed from my own body'. As a bastard Steedman has no place in the symbolic, in patriarchy.

By describing the power as well as the problem of the maternal, *Landscape for a Good Woman* foregrounds French feminist ideas. The text addresses Irigaray's claim that daughters are in exile from the mother, an exile they need to resolve. Part of that resolution will be encouraged by testing out the ambiguities and absences in social constructions of mothering, as Steedman does so well. A key feature of *écriture féminine* is a new address to the reader. A reader is not 'taught' a specific message but remains open to a text, continually constructing and reconstructing her reading position. *Landscape for a Good Woman* offers a clear and exciting illustration of this process.

SECTION 8: VIRGINIA WOOLF, *TO THE LIGHTHOUSE*

French feminist criticism has been very prominent in feminism since the early 1980s. It was then that a number of writers began to focus on the sexism of *systems* of thought underpinning 'literature', not simply on the sexism of literary *stereotypes*. French feminist criticism drew on the psychoanalytic and linguistic analyses of Lacan and Saussure to question the very forms of writing itself, as well as representations of subjectivity. The term 'French feminism' applies to a number of critics, but the writings of Julia Kristeva, Luce Irigaray and Hélène Cixous have been more influential in Britain and America then the work of other critics such as Antoinette Fouque.

What links all three writers is a deconstructive belief that systems of language derive from systems of cultural power and that these reveal contradictions once the literary text is deconstructed, or taken apart. At the heart of this literary and psychoanalytic argument is de Beauvoir's idea that 'Woman is Other' to man. Like de Beauvoir, French feminists agree that female subjectivity is absent from, and repressed by, patriarchal language or the symbolic. Although none of these three critics was born in France and all three, like Virginia Woolf, refuse to be identified as 'feminist', what Kristeva, Irigaray and Cixous are rejecting is aspects of feminist politics, not the idea that criticism can explain women's repression. Following Lacan, French feminism argues that cultural and social languages and institutions (the symbolic) are shaped by linguistic laws which silence the Imaginary or the fluid world of early childhood. The feminine is identified with the Imaginary and is therefore a gap, an absence in the syntax of the symbolic. Critics study the ways in which

literary texts might 'reveal' the suppressed feminine. For
example, Cixous uses psychoanalysis to deconstruct formulations of gender (Cixous, 1976a). Irigaray suggests that the syntax
of the symbolic depends on metaphors of solids (one object
following another). Against this, Irigaray poses a syntax of fluids
– a smooth metonymic flowing narrative (Irigaray, 1977). Since
Kristeva's writing is described in more detail in my critique of
Landscape for a Good Woman I will simply note here Kristeva's
ideas, which specifically offer a helpful guide to features of
Woolf's writing. Kristeva argues that we can subvert the symbolic
and its social codes and paternal function by finding a discourse
closer to the body and emotions (the semiotic) which is repressed
by the symbolic (Kristeva, 1980). For example, Kristeva claims
that speaking subjects in literature often reveal ruptures of the
symbolic in deviations of grammar.

Modernist writing in particular (such as Woolf's novels)
depends on the semiotic in its irregular rhythms, self-reflexivity
and the incorporation of other forms of writing. Kristeva calls this
process of incorporation *intertextualité* which, following Bakhtin,
she defines as the way a text is a mosaic of references to other
texts, images and conventions. In his work the Russian formalist
Bakhtin claimed that literature struggles between languages and
is structured by 'dialogic' intercourse (Bakhtin, 1981). Kristeva's
main argument in *Desire in Language* is that literary texts are
heterogeneous, made up of elements of the semiotic and
symbolic and other texts.

Like Kristeva, Irigaray's main aim is to investigate the relation
between writing and subjectivity, specifically feminine sexuality.
Irigaray argues that symbolic or masculine language privileges
the visible, concentrates on finding the 'right' word or precise
meaning, and that this relegates 'woman' and the language of
female sexuality to absence. Irigaray's *Speculum of the Other
Woman* and *This Sex Which is Not One* argue that all the main
systems of Western knowledge are shaped by masculinity. The
title *Speculum* is a metonymy for women's language. Where
Lacan describes the acquisition of language in relation to self-
recognition in a mirror, Irigaray describes language as a
speculum – a *sexual* reflector. Irigaray examines polarities of
masculine/feminine represented by analogies, repetitions and
oppositions in language and weaves a feminine non-linear

argument through metaphors and associations. This is Irigaray's response to the exclusion of the feminine from symbolic representations. She mimes and mimics paternal language, which suggests that a woman writer's use of *mimicry* might equally displace the phallic. We can see all of these ideas at work in *To The Lighthouse*. Irigaray's writings have been accused of essentialism, but, in general, her notion of double syntax – the idea that under the 'masculine' logic of a sentence there might lurk a feminine 'unsaid', perhaps hidden in elemental *fluid* metaphors – is enormously relevant to Woolf.

Hélène Cixous, similarly, explores the relation between women's bodies and writing. Cixous's first task in 'The laugh of the Medusa' is to deconstruct masculine structures of knowledge. Cixous does this by focusing on the fluctuating representations of gender in texts as well as on the ways in which readers take up gender positions when reading (Cixous, 1976a). One key feature of women's writing which attracts Cixous is feminine myths. Cixous 're-visions' mythology by rereading traditional myths such as the story of Sleeping Beauty and discarding masculine metaphors in favour of feminine metaphors. The classic dualist/binary opposition between female passivity and male activity in a myth like Sleeping Beauty, Cixous points out, is a binary opposition at the heart of all symbolic systems. Cixous argues that biological differences between the sexes do relate to different forms of perception and to different ways to organizing knowledge and language. But the privileging of the male as active and the female as inactive, as Other, is a *social* not biological distinction and in turn this structures a gendered subjectivity and language. The poetic management of binaries in literature is therefore a key focus because this reveals issues of sexual difference. Other key foci include representations of the unconscious (which is linked to body signifiers), as well as interrogatives and the fluidity of women's writing. Cixous's account of James Joyce is a good example of this kind of critical approach; she argues that Joyce's main innovation was to represent subjectivity in a non-linear narrative (Cixous, 1976b). Cixous is similarly attracted to the work of Edgar Allan Poe because Poe disrupts conventional subjectivity by attention to the unconscious (Cixous, 1974). A key feature of Woolf's modernist style is its apparent endlessness.

Analyzing a passage from *To The Lighthouse*, using the

framework of French feminism, enables us to understand Woolf's unconventional uses of narrative shifts in perspective. Woolf seems to practise what could be called a French feminist approach to writing: one that exposes the binary oppositions of language, that mimics masculine language and attends to myth, fluidity and heterogeneity. Woolf began her writing career in 1904 at the age of 22 and throughout all her work, women are her centre of gravity. Gender identity, Woolf believes, is socially constructed and shapes literary constructions. In her writing Woolf continually circles around issues of gender consciousness, the body and the roles of literature and women. In her critical essays Woolf argued that the sex of an author was clear from the first words of a novel. Our feminine style, Woolf suggests, is shaped by our values and experiences, which are different from those of men (Woolf, 1929). A woman makes serious what appears insignificant to a man, and trivializes what is to him important. Far commoner for women writers than for men is the experience of the line and imagination running free. What prevents that unconscious self-revelation is that much of female experience – in particular the psyche and sexuality – must be hidden. *A Room of One's Own* is a history of the *psychological* as well as material constraints impacting on Jane Austen, Charlotte Brontë and the invented figure of Shakespeare's sister (Woolf, 1929). *To The Lighthouse* shows a similar interest in prevailing constructs of femininity and Woolf's attempt to overturn these with a non-linear narrative, irony and a direct address to a woman reader.

> Filled with her words, like a child who drops off satisfied, he said, at last, looking at her with humble gratitude, restored, renewed, that he would take a turn; he would watch the children playing cricket. He went.
>
> Immediately, Mrs Ramsay seemed to fold herself together, one petal closed in another, and the whole fabric fell in exhaustion upon itself, so that she had only strength enough to move her finger, in exquisite abandonment to exhaustion, across the page of Grimm's fairy story, while there throbbed through her, like the pulse in a spring which has expanded to its full width and now gently ceases to beat, the rapture of successful creation.
>
> Every throb of this pulse seemed, as he walked away, to enclose

her and her husband, and to give to each that solace which two different notes, one high, one low, struck together, seem to give each other as they combine. Yet, as the resonance died, and she turned to the Fairy Tale again, Mrs Ramsay felt not only exhausted in body (afterwards, not at the time, she always felt this) but also there tinged her physical fatigue some faintly disagreeable sensation with another origin. Not that, as she read aloud the story of the Fisherman's Wife, she knew precisely what it came from; nor did she let herself put into words her dissatisfaction when she realised, at the turn of the page when she stopped and heard dully, ominously, a wave fall, how it came from this: she did not like, even for a second, to feel finer than her husband; and further, could not bear not being entirely sure, when she spoke to him, of the truth of what she said. Universities and people wanting him, lectures and books and their being of the highest importance – all that she did not doubt for a moment; but it was their relation, and his coming to her like that, openly, so that anyone could see, that discomposed her; for then people said he depended on her, when they must know that of the two he was infinitely the more important, and what she gave the world, in comparison with what he gave, negligible. But then again, it was the other thing too – not being able to tell him the truth, being afraid, for instance, about the greenhouse roof and the expense it would be, fifty pounds perhaps, to mend it; and then about his books, to be afraid that he might guess, what she a little suspected, that his last book was not quite his best book (she gathered that from William Bankes); and then to hide small daily things, and the children seeing it, and the burden it laid on them – all this diminished the entire joy, the pure joy, of the two notes sounding together, and let the sound die on her ear now with a dismal flatness.

(From *To The Lighthouse*, Penguin, Harmondsworth, 1964, pp. 45–7)

The novel brings together in its title some of the issues posed by French feminists. With its co-ordinating participle 'To' the title indicates a *process* already begun. The title invites the reader to ponder the mode of address – is it directional or affirmative – as well as to supply a possible preceding place (before 'to'). The general image is one of a journey, indicating that novel writing as well as the experience of novel reading will be similarly topographical – a journey which is *towards* something but not completed and in process. What does *To The Lighthouse* tell us about issues of gender and writing? French feminist criticism, by tracing a text's operations of binaries and disruptions, helps us to understand that femininity is the repressed other of social language. This view assumes that the linguistic and psychic structures given to women characters will be different from the abstract rationalism associated with male characters. The passage reveals Woolf's interest in exploring these perceptions.

Mr and Mrs Ramsay have different 'languages'. His is the world of 'universities and people wanting him, lectures and books and their being of the highest importance' and hers is in continuous process with 'every throb of this pulse' making a 'rapture of successful creation'. Mr and Mrs Ramsay are 'two different notes, one high, one low' which *seem* to 'give each other as they combine'. The long continuous paragraph shows the different ways in which Woolf manages to mark the strength and creativity of Mrs Ramsay's perceptions against what the novel reveals to be the aridity of masculine intellect. First Mrs Ramsay is represented figuratively with 'one petal closed in another', 'like the pulse in a spring', understanding gender identities in terms of 'waves' which when they 'fall' diminish the 'joy of the two notes'. The continuous repetition of these images and Woolf's extended use of synaesthesia, or the mixing of sensations, from *within* Mrs Ramsay's point of view privileges the sensual over the symbolic. The syntactical structure of the passage privileges 'fluids' over 'solids', to utilize Irigaray's terms.

Woolf frequently reports to polysyndeton, or the repetition of conjunctions, such as 'and' which creates a continuous fluid, flowing syntax adding phrase to phrase without an obvious conclusion. Woolf's preference is for the semi-colon rather than the solid full stop. The account is deliberately non-linear, not *il-logical* but *anti*-logical, as Woolf delights in continuous paren-thesis, or phrases of qualification, indicating her valuing of cyclical, returning thoughts rather than chronological develop-ment. The everyday world of expensive greenhouse roofs can co-exist with major ethical judgements in Mrs Ramsay's percep-tions, while her husband more narrowly, and pretentiously, restricts himself to books. Woolf's continual use of attributive verbs like 'seemed' allows Mrs Ramsay's thoughts to float free of her social actions; Woolf's dominant narrative technique here is one of indirect speech.

Following Cixous, we can see the ways in which the movement of Mrs Ramsay's thoughts is closely related to the way she experiences her body. The passage develops organically from these sensations. Trying to encourage her husband makes Mrs Ramsay 'exhausted in body'; her awareness of his failures – 'not quite his best book' – tinges her physical fatigue with another 'disagreeable sensation'. As with Woolf's use of the figurative images of 'petals' and their connotations of female sexuality, Woolf subverts symbolic representations with the polyphonic thoughts of Mrs Ramsay. The passage has a circular movement organized not in terms of narrative *events* but in terms of feminine *melodic* movements. Mrs Ramsay is not presented as an external persona but acquires narrative status with each breath, each physical sensation which she recognizes. Like French feminists, Woolf avoids any rigid use of fixed propositions and authoritative point of view in favour of a fluid linguistic *process*.

In 1923, looking through her essays to prepare them for the *Common Readers* Woolf felt that she could devise a new method, 'some simpler, subtler closer means of writing about books, as about people' (Woolf, 1944, p. 177). It would need a 'theory of fiction. The one I have in view is about perspective' (*ibid*, p. 83). In her novels Woolf continually experiments with perspective, with the role of an aware, female observer. *The Waves* mixes soliloquy with narrative and lyric prose. In *The Years* Woolf uses the voices of different generations; *Between the Acts* mixes fiction and 'facts'. Woolf continually, as here, experiments with point of view to give shape to both the sensual as well as to the simultaneity of women's consciousness.

Woolf's complex interrelationship of the feminine with a new perspective, like Cixous's, explores the possibility of 'writing the body'. What both Woolf and Cixous refuse to conceal is the very material (body) of language. The *materiality* of words is a key focus of attention in the passage. The core of Mrs Ramsay's feelings originate in her perception of the *gender* differences between herself and her husband. This is described as a pre-verbal (erotic) sensuality with metaphor as its material expression. Woolf lingers in these moments of intimacy with Mrs Ramsay, and Woolf's metaphors ritualize the sensuous. Metaphors and metonymys abound: 'the pulse', 'the whole fabric fell in exhaustion', 'waves', and 'two notes', inviting the reader to contribute meaning to Woolf's vocabulary. The reader has to combine the vocabulary of the passage with more familiar or similar words. Irigaray and Cixous, in particular, place the relationship of reader and text at the heart of criticism – letting oneself be read by the text. Woolf subverts a rational progression, deconstructing Mr Ramsay's conceptual structure 'discomposed', and allows Mrs Ramsay's thoughts to flow freely through metaphoric associations. The flow of the narrative, in the passage, from one point to another point is controlled not by chronology, but by the metaphoric similarities of Mrs Ramsay's thoughts. In many ways, this method could be said to be Woolf's key device. Thoughts are Woolf's main mechanism of character-ization. We enter characters' minds in a flowing mixture of narrated monologue; 'Mrs Ramsay felt' with enclosed descrip-tion. Cixous, similarly, refuses to 'own' her characters, allowing her authorship to vacillate within a narrative (Cixous, 1979). Both Woolf and Cixous move between subjectivities by using third person pronouns: 'her', 'she', 'he'.

The lack of an assertive authorial presence, in French feminist thinking, creates room for the Other. In contrast to Mr Ramsay trying to complete his book by 'digging his heels in at Q' (p. 40), Mrs Ramsay is capable of a synthetic, anti-linear vision. These moments exceed the symbolic boundaries of patriarchal dis-course, as French feminists would argue. The recourse to multiple, indefinite pronouns, the use of silent graphic notations (here three dashes) allow Woolf to avoid an omniscient narrator. Nor are the events of the novel in chronological order. The discussion between Mr and Mrs Ramsay about the possibility of reaching the lighthouse begins the novel but it is not the beginning of the narrative in time. There are long passages, like this one, of subjective reflections which deviate from any linear plot. Textually the continuous use of long sentences and intense figuration produces a sense of irregular time. The net result is a slowing down of the heuristic, or learning process, whereby Mrs Ramsay, Lily and the reader 'appropriate' the world of *To The Lighthouse*. None of the characters is centred because Mrs Ramsay's house and garden are not described in spatial terms; space and time exist only *through* the woman subject.

This is one of the key gender differences described by Kristeva in her essay 'Women's time'. In the piece Kristeva notes several historical representations of sexual difference (Kristeva, 1981). The symbolic becomes 'masculine' history, which is linear time, and Kristeva equates the 'feminine' with cyclical or monumental time. All discourse, according to Kristeva, is sexually differentiated by time. 'Masculinity' retains, and indeed celebrates, logical connections and linearity (the symbolic). This singularity is challenged by the semiotic which contains the 'feminine' drives. So that changes to dominant histories will depend not only on new political practices (Kristeva discusses feminism, modernism and terrorism) but on new forms of language which value the feminine. *To The Lighthouse* works through these ideas, particularly Kristeva's idea of men's and women's time. As we have seen, the repetition of figurative metaphors, foregrounding of rhythmic syntax, indefinite speech and cumulative clauses in *To The Lighthouse* all combine to slow down linear time and to privilege 'women's time'.

The passage offers another construction which would interest French feminists. One meaning 'frame' is the 'Fairy Tale' (note the capitalization) – the story of the Fisherman's Wife which Mrs Ramsay reads aloud to James. In the story the wife uses her wishes 'inappropriately' by becoming more and more demanding. Her last wish, to become Pope, that is to achieve a symbolic status in a patriarchal world, is so over-reaching that wife and fisherman are reduced to their former poverty. Woolf's use of the story matches Irigaray's method of 'mimicry' very well. In essence Irigaray argues, like Woolf, that women are socially represented only as mirror images of men (Irigaray, 1977). In return, Irigaray exaggerates this mirroring, or mimicry, miming the masculine symbolic by incorporating extracts from Freud, Plato and other thinkers into her texts and exposing their 'excess'. Similarly the Fisherman's Wife parodies phallic avarice and the passage mocks Mr Ramsay's dependence on Mrs Ramsay's 'mirroring' technique 'filled with her words, like a child who drops off satisfied' by juxtaposing that independence with the tale. Mr Ramsay depletes and 'exhausts' his wife who begins to question patriarchal social relationships only 'as she read aloud the story'. Masculinity, and the mirroring of masculinity, Woolf here suggests, restrict women's creativity. All that is available to woman in patriarchy, Irigaray argues, is a silent and cryptic script of body language and amputated desires – a 'dismal flatness'. Woolf subverts partiarchal language from within by mimicking the abrogation of power by men. In *Desire in Language* Kristeva describes all of this heterogeneity as corporeal and signifiable, but also contends that *symbolic* social structures (she instances the family) are not able to grasp heterogeneity.

In the passage Mrs Ramsay's semiotic has disrupted the apparent stability of the symbolic family structure. The under-lying structure of the piece is based on a duality between the heterogeneous, subjective order of Mrs Ramsay and the semantic linear distancing of Mr Ramsay's order. *To The Lighthouse* could be characterized as a French feminist novel. By this I mean that the masculine symbolic is both mimicked and called into question by the semiotic. French feminists argue that a lack of linearity is the link with the pre-Oedipal maternal unconscious which allows writers to break with symbolic language.

Woolf experiments with binary structures more explicitly in her novel *Orlando* which reveals a similar privileging of the semiotic and the body. *Orlando* is about communication and the lack of communication across binaries – of gender, class and time. Related to this are sub-themes of exclusion and inclusion (involving gypsies and prostitutes) tied to ideas about ownership and power. Yet the novel is a fantasy, not a linear realist nar-rative. Woolf draws on body imagery to stand for metaphysical ideas. The whole narrative of *Orlando* is constructed around physical contrasts of summer and winter, of the earthy mixture in Orlando of Kentish earth and Norman fluid (Woolf, 1928). Woolf is equally attentive to what we can call the symbolic and the semiotic in her criticism. In *A Room of One's Own* she refuses to note down male ideas about women as *objective* information, but reads her source books *emotionally*, noting tone and point of view (Woolf, 1929). Woolf makes gender difference both part of the content *and* the syntax of her work. In her essay about the Duchess of Newcastle, Woolf uses an image of fluidity describing the Duchess flowing in and out of rooms as a metaphor for the Duchess's social freedom and literary style (Woolf, 1979). Similarly, in her essay about Madame de Sévigné Woolf rejected the past tense of literary historical time in favour of the present tense (Woolf, 1942). Many of the topics of Woolf's essays overlap essays written by her father, Leslie Stephen. Both write engagingly and accessibly about similar aspects of literary form

– autobiography and cultural constraints. The essays read very much like a dialogue with Woolf confronting and subverting each of Stephen's views (Woolf, 1979). Stephen argued that Charlotte Brontë's lack of cultural knowledge created mannerisms in her fiction; but to Woolf, Brontë's untamed ferocity is a protest against patriarchal authority (Humm, 1986).

There are many similarities between the ideas of French feminism and Woolf's writing. Both argue, in different ways, that 'feminine' and 'masculine' are constructed binaries and that we need to change representations in order to change society. Language determines the ways in which we perceive gender and come to know ourselves as gendered beings and the ways in which society perceives gender and creates gendered subjects. *To The Lighthouse* shows that the *female* symbolic can be a dynamic alternative to those existing representations.

5 Psychoanalytic criticism

SECTION 9: MAY SINCLAIR, *MARY OLIVIER: A LIFE*

The dialogue between feminist criticism and psychoanalysis has been hugely rewarding. Both share particular themes: the psychic relation of mothers, fathers and children; the relation between sexuality and its expression; the instability of identity.

Second, both share key methods: they treat their texts, whether the unconscious or novels as kinds of codes and as representing the 'unsaid' in everyday life. Both expect dreams, displacement and sensations to explain individual feelings. Psychoanalytic literary critics focus on authors' and characters' motivations and on the hidden areas of texts as well as on readers' responses to surface and sub-text. What psychoanalysis does is to offer a reading of the feminine rooted neither *entirely* in the social construction of femininity (which nevertheless organizes the feminine) nor *entirely* in biology, but in language and subjectivity. Pre-verbal experiences of the unconscious or the semiotic (the early moment of infant–mother bonds) are often described as language before being read as symptoms. Psycho-analytic cases, as well as literary criticism, have a tendency to be written as *texts*. Both openly reveal their status as 'fiction' without, of course, abandoning their search for a 'true' meaning in the discourse each examines. Psychoanalysis tries to read the 'text' of each subject in terms of her dreams and style of speech, among other things. To do this it focuses, in particular, on 'literary' forms – on absences, distortions and slippages – which may provide access to hidden parts of a subject's personality.

Literary criticism, similarly, confronts defensive actions in texts. By examining metaphors, similes and absences in the literary work, critics aim to reveal a hidden sub-text which may structure a text's 'personality'.

Various theorists have tried to explain such unconscious processes but the writing of Jacques Lacan on *gender* and the unconscious has been very useful to feminism. According to Lacan, the unconscious reveals the fictional nature of sexual categories, and formations of masculinity and femininity crucially connect to language. For Lacan, the difference between the sexes is not simply biological but takes shape in discourse or signification (Lacan, 1977). Lacan develops his account of subjectivity with reference to the idea of a fiction. Language, Lacan argues, is what identifies us as gendered subjects. The acquisition of identity, and hence subjectivity, occurs only as we enter into the symbolic (or social production of meaning). According to Lacan, we are not *born* as subjects but begin by making imaginary identifications. Such identifications will always be difficult and will often be fictive. For Lacan, it is with language acquisition that we 'gain' sexual difference. The pre-Oedipal infant lives in a maternal world of sounds and rhythms. With the sight of ourselves in a mirror we give up this bodily maternal warmth and enter social construction or the symbolic order, called the 'Law of the Father'. This is the moment of 'I' when we can create our identity as an 'I' as well as 'me'. According to Lacan, language privileges the masculine over the feminine because entry into the symbolic is Oedipal. That is to say, the infant has to search for signs, figurative language, and any language substitutes for the mother. In this sense literature as a figurative language is marked out as masculine.

Yet fortunately sexual identity is always unstable, it is susceptible to disruption by the unconscious and disruption manifests itself in discontinuities and contradictions in literary and everyday languages. More positively, the meaning of the feminine could always be open to redefinition because it is less 'formed' by the symbolic. Lacan's works are drawn on by feminist critics, including Juliet Mitchell, Jacqueline Rose and Mary Jacobus, to argue that gender is not a biological essence but a linguistic construct (Mitchell and Rose, 1982; Jacobus, 1986). Yet Lacan's theories also pose problems for feminist literary critics.

It is the Oedipus complex, Lacan agrees with Freud, which forces us into the symbolic order. If language is controlled by the Law of the Father then so is literary criticism. How can women gain entry? One answer came from object-relations psychoanalysis. The American feminist Nancy Chodorow turned away from the unconscious towards the social in her account of sexual differences in *The Reproduction of Mothering*. Chodorow's work has been very important to feminists because she claims that what marks our sexual difference is not the Oedipal mirror moment but the *pre-Oedipal* and intense infant–mother relation (Chodorow, 1978). It is this which shapes our fantasies, our words and finally our writing and reading. Chodorow introduced the possibility of a *valuable* female discourse.

Chodorow argued that woman's sexual difference stems from her identification with her mother. Because the infant's gender identity (of either sex) is shaped in relation with the mother, boys become men by learning to be 'not the mother' while girls become women and 'reproduce' mothering. Because it is women generally who 'mother', girls do not experience a sense of separation. Sons, however, have to learn to differentiate themselves from the feminine. As a result men often separate from others in the adult world, while women remain connected. The daughter does not lose the pre-symbolic world in the way that sons must. Chodorow argues that female identity grows in a fluid and symbiotic relationship with the mother which we yearn to 'reproduce' with our own children. Chodorow's description of the maternal world matches very well the opening chapter of May Sinclair's *Mary Olivier: A Life*, as we shall see in a moment. But in general, Chodorow's ideas are particularly relevant to women novelists writing, like Sinclair, about early family relationships. Daughters, according to Chodorow, carry with them into the figurative or symbolic world of language, the Other rhythmic, pre-symbolic language which sons have left behind with their mothers.

Women's writing can, then, incorporate much more varied figurative, semiotic, even literal, forms of language. There are important correspondences between the work of Chodorow and the fiction and poetry of women writers. Two critical texts in particular have drawn attention to these concerns. Marianne Hirsch's *The Mother/Daughter Plot* utilizes object-relations theory in order to analyze mother–daughter relationships. She argues that the maternal is continually being repressed in women's writing but if released it could validate the pre-Oedipal world of the semiotic (Hirsch, 1989).

Hirsch's text built on Sandra Gilbert and Susan Gubar's *The Madwoman in the Attic*. Describing the work of Jane Austen, Mary Shelley, the Brontës and Emily Dickinson, among others, Gilbert and Gubar claim that women writers strategically reveal their psychic and social anxieties in recurrent images of enclosure and doubles (Gilbert and Gubar, 1979). These feminist critics and others point to explicit parallels between studies of connection and affiliation in psychoanalysis and women's writing. They suggest that women writers replicate their own mother–daughter bonding in the development and realization of female characters' identities. Women writers frequently describe female identity as rooted in early and continual connection with a mother or a mother substitute figure. A good example here would be the relationship between Antoinette and Christophine in Jean Rhys's *Wide Sargasso Sea* (see Section 22).

The work of Nancy Chodorow is considered controversial by some feminist critics because Chodorow takes *existing* and *social* mothering relations to account for her male-separation, female-connection models. In this way Chodorow's theories can neither account, some critics would claim, for cross-cultural patterns nor for other psychic manifestations deriving from the unconscious and desire. Yet in various ways women writers frequently do create fictions in which mothers and daughters experience great connectedness.

Fiction often describes how the meanings of identity are created through and by representations in early childhood. May Sinclair's *Mary Olivier: A Life* illustrates many of these issues. Both *Mary Olivier* and much feminist criticism confront the coincidence between the engendering of daughters and mother–daughter affiliation.

May Sinclair was born in 1863 and studied briefly at Cheltenham Ladies' College under Dorothea Beale, one of Britain's pioneers in women's education. Sinclair's first novel *Audrey Craven* was published in 1897 and after the death of her mother she become involved in suffragette activity, fundraising and writing articles in support of the movement, which is

fictionalized in *The Tree of Heaven*. By 1919, the year of publication
of *Mary Olivier: A Life*, Sinclair was a leading London literary
figure associating with the modernist writers T. S. Eliot, Pound,
Dorothy Richardson and H. D. and maintaining friendships with
H. G. Wells and Galsworthy. May Sinclair died in 1946 but her
writing career finished much earlier, shortly after the publication
of *Arnold Waterlow: A Life*. Sinclair's critical essays, written for *The
Egoist* and *The Little Review*, reveal her great interest in modernist
themes and Imagism.

Sinclair's interest in psychoanalysis went even deeper. She
was a founder member of the Tavistock Square Clinic and
reviewed leading psychoanalytic texts for *The Medical Press*.
Sinclair's novels are among the first British fictional accounts of
many psychoanalytic themes including infant sexuality just as
her writing about Dorothy Richardson for *The Little Review* was
the first to use the words 'stream of consciousness' to describe
Richardson's narrative technique.

Mary Olivier: A Life utilizes a stream-of-consciousness technique to describe the relationship between Mary and her mother
and the growing maturity of Mary as a writer.

> One night she came back out of the lane as the door in the hedge was
> opening. The man stood in the room by the washstand, scratching
> his long thigh. He was turned slant-wise from the nightlight on the
> washstand so that it showed his yellowish skin under the lifted shirt.
> The white half-face hung by itself on the darkness. When he left off
> scratching and moved towards the cot she screamed. Mamma took
> her into the big bed. She curled up there under the shelter of the
> raised hip and shoulder. Mamma's face was dry and warm and smelt
> sweet like Jenny's powder-puff. Mamma's mouth moved over her
> wet cheeks, nipping her tears. Her cry changed to a whimper and a
> soft, ebbing sob. Mamma's breast: a smooth, cool, round thing that
> hung to your hands and slipped from them when they tried to hold
> it. You could feel the little ridges of the stiff nipple as your finger
> pushed it back into the breast.
>
>   Her sobs shook in her throat and ceased suddenly.

II
The big white globes hung in a ring above the dinner table. At first,
when she came into the room, carried high in Jenny's arms, she could

see nothing but the hanging, shining globes. Each had a light inside it that made it shine.

Mamma was sitting at the far end of the table. Her face and neck shone white above the pile of oranges on the dark blue dish. She was dipping her fingers in a dark blue glass bowl.

When Mary saw her she strained towards her, leaning dangerously out of Jenny's arms. Old Jenny said "Tchit-tchit!" and made her arms tight and hard and put her on Papa's knee.

Papa sat up, broad and tall above the table, all by himself. He was dressed in black. One long brown beard hung down in front of him and one short beard covered his mouth. You knew he was smiling because his cheeks swelled up his face so that his eyes were squeezed into narrow shining slits. When they came out again you saw scarlet specks and smears in their corners.

Papa's big white hand was on the table, holding a glass filled with some red stuff that was both dark and shining and had a queer, sharp smell.

"Porty-worty winey-piney," said Papa.

The same queer, sharp smell came from between his two beards when he spoke.

Mark was sitting up beside Mamma a long way off. She could see them looking at each other. Roddy and Dank were with them.

They were making flowers out of orange peel and floating them in the finger bowls. Mamma's fingers were blue and sharp-pointed in the water behind the dark blue glass of her bowl. The floating orange-peel flowers were blue. She could see Mamma smiling as she stirred them about with the tips of her blue fingers.

(From *Mary Olivier: A Life*, Virago, London, 1980, pp. 4–5)

We enter the world of the novel through the eyes and perceptions of the infant heroine whose sensations condition our views of her later life and development. A psychoanalytical study of the text's 'unconscious' could, following Freud, look at phallic symbols in the passage. My reading will rather focus on the *latent* content *within* the symbolic by pursuing images on which the later construction of female gender identity in the novel depends. What emerges in the passage is the infant heroine's acknowledgement of the power of the maternal, which she reveres and from which her consciousness develops.

Gender identity is not fixed here but still 'slippy', a slippiness that Sinclair reveals through shifts in point of view and different tenses. There is the indirect third person 'Mamma took her into the big bed' and first person stream of consciousness 'Mamma's face was dry and warm'. The passage is so saturated with a mother's presence and with the daughter's dependent reciprocal affiliation that it exemplifies Chodorow's theory of female libidinal development. The passage is replete with oral imagery of 'sobs' and 'whimpers'; with smells, tastes and other sensations – 'sweet', 'wet', 'smooth', 'cool' – which are replicated in the objects surrounding Mary, such as lights like 'big white globes'. The fluidity and mother/infant figuration are powerfully erotic: 'she curled up there under the shelter of the raised hip and shoulder'; 'Mamma's mouth moved over her wet cheek'; 'you could feel the little ridges of the stiff nipple', as mother and daughter co-exist in mutual arousal. It is the *sensual* world which Mary draws on for her 'symbolic' judgements rather than any dramatized or narrated moral episodes: 'You knew he was smiling because his cheeks swelled'. The symbolic field, represented by the father, is of less value than the semiotic.

Mary's feelings in the passage would be characterized by feminist psychoanalytic critics as a process of 'separation–individuation' and as a dramatization of the anxieties such processes entail. The passage moves as a narrative, only *through* the psychoanalytic: character movement and development are conveyed through psychic motifs. The run on from the paragraph describing her mother's breast 'smooth, cool, round thing' to the paragraph describing the dinner table over which 'the big white globes hung in a ring above' could be described, in psychoanalytic terms, as Mary's ambiguous and problematic sensation of boundary. In Mary's empathetic and sensual intimacy with her mother and their profound interdependence, the two identities seem to merge into one another. The process of separation from oneness with the mother, together with its complex and accompanying dangers to identity, is dramatized through the contrasting representations of globes/breasts as Mary confronts the phallic father. 'Broad and tall above the table, all by himself . . . one long brown beard hung down in front of him'.

In Freud's account of the acquisition of gender identity children wish to displace the *same sex* parent and take his or her place in the affections of the opposite sex parent. A boy fears that his father will castrate him and wishes for the return of the mother. The girl, recognizing her castration, wishes to leave the mother in her 'desire' for her father. In Freudian terms the 'tall' 'long' father would be an over-determined image representing Mary's complex feelings about her father. To be caught up in this scenario is to accept the phallic symbol(s) as always active and powerful. Yet what Mary senses is a *transgressive* revision of this symbolic scene. Her desire is for the *mother*, not the father. The passage also calls attention to the impossibility (within existing social constructions of gender) of this decentring of the male. Mary's desire for her mother is prefaced at the beginning of the passage by an ominous and prophetic dream of a man 'scratching his long thigh' showing 'his yellowish skin under the lifted shirt'. The dream introduces Mary's anxieties, which will undermine the symbolic union with the mother when the father's 'long brown beard' acts as a correlative for the man's 'thigh'. The wish for fulfilment with the mother is also and always a source of anxiety and fear psychoanalytically. Later in the novel May Sinclair describes Mary's struggle for emotional and intellectual freedom from her mother and from her mother's threats to Mary's individuality.

Yet at this moment the passage both enacts and thematizes Chodorow's description of female subjectivity. 'Her face and neck shone white above the pile of oranges'. The colour association 'white' between the 'white globes', white 'neck', which has led on from 'round' breast, works to distance the dream man with his 'white half-face'.

Her mother is 'making flowers out of orange peel . . . she could see Mamma smiling'. The image of the orange condenses maternal associations. An orange's texture, colour and juiciness are tactile and its shape takes up the earlier roundness of breasts together with something of their weight. Mary's desire for the orange is a projection of her desire for the mother. Projection is a psychoanalytic term for the process by which unconscious feelings are pushed out from the self on to another person or object. Mary is beginning her childhood and needs, psycho-analysts would argue, 'part-objects' in order to do so. The reality of the social world, the symbolic, can be integrated into the infant's world or 'introjected' if a child can invest objects with fantasies and feelings of love and hate. The orange is a 'part object' which can momentarily stand in for the mother. But it is also, perhaps more significantly, an *aesthetic* object. The orange can be read as a prototype for the art objects or writing which Mary will later want to create. In this way, psychoanalysts would claim, the artistic medium becomes the mother's body in adult life, just as the orange here begins to act as a part-object replacement for the mother in early infancy.

Sinclair often uses associations. The passage records every detail of Mary's experiences but does not do so sequentially, in a neat chronological order. Rather, Mary freely associates 'breasts' and 'oranges' or 'thighs' and 'beards', *herself* dramatizing connections rather than an omniscient narrator. This allows Sinclair a much fuller exploration of psychoanalytic themes. The orange could be read as a Lacanian fetish object because Mary certainly becomes fixated on every object her loved mother touches; it is as though the orange were a part of her mother's body. The psychoanalytic concept of the part or transitional object has attracted feminist literary critics precisely because it is an acted-out correlative of artistic illusion.

In short, *Mary Olivier: A Life* contests the symbolic with a powerful account of mother–daughter bonding. There is no historical or social introduction to the novel which begins in the cot just before this passage. Instead, we read an eye-witness account of the semiotic, and its fluidity and associations are our introduction to the 'life'. The orange could be dismissed as an insignificant object, but its circular breast-like shape, and blood imagery are clearly offered to the reader as a point of resistance to Mary's inevitable entry into the symbolic. It is also a startlingly prophetic image of Hélène Cixous's much later celebration of the 'maternal' orange in her homage to *her* literary 'mother', Clarice Lispector, in *Vivre l'orange* (Cixous, 1979).

Where Freud described femininity as a psychical *impasse*, feminist psychoanalytic criticism offers the exciting possibility that the feminine is constantly being reworked in relation to the mother. In May Sinclair's *Mary Olivier: A Life* the infant girl does not perceive her mother to be *castrated*, as lacking, but as plenitude and 'fruitful'. The feminist psychoanalyst Juliet Mitchell claims that psychoanalysis is an exemplary instance of Gramsci's optimism of the will precisely because the aim is to change will (Mitchell, 1974). With psychoanalytic tools, feminists can perhaps begin to deconstruct the gender hierarchies of society as ambitiously as feminist literary critics deconstruct the gender identities of literature.

SECTION 10: DORIS LESSING, *THE GOLDEN NOTEBOOK*

Both psychoanalysis and many feminist critics today examine the relations between the social constructions of 'women' and 'men' and psychic identifications. Psychoanalytic theory has joined deconstruction and other areas of feminist criticism to explain literary repressions and structures of desire. Psychoanalysis allows feminism to destabilize gendered fixities, a process which could lead to new cultural representations. The important contemporary association of psychoanalysis and literary criticism is, of course, not new. The first psychoanalytic critiques of literature were written by the founder of psychoanalysis, Freud, with his accounts of Dostoyevsky, Shakespeare, Ibsen and Goethe. In these essays Freud describes the workings of unconscious processes as a series of textual signs – as slips of the tongue or jokes (Freud, 1980). The mechanisms by which literature unwittingly reveals aspects of identity, Freud argues, are repetitions, silences and textual breakdowns. Where Freud examines texts as *encounters* between text and author the French psychoanalyst Jacques Lacan went on to examine the *forms* in which unconscious processes might be represented (see Section 9). In Lacan's essays about literary topics, like his essay on Edgar Allan Poe, Lacan searches for literary versions of psychoanalytic states such as 'primal' and 'repetitive' scenes (Lacan, 1972). Lacan extended Freud's accounts of individual perversions and objectifications to the signifying system as a whole.

The development of psychoanalytic theories about gender representations and literature has taken a number of directions. At least four different but interrelated concerns shape feminist criticism. First is a symbolic view of representation drawn from Freud's theories. This tends to examine plot and imagery as if these are functions of the individual psychologies of characters which in turn are assumed to represent the psychology of the author. Second, and related, is a Jungian approach which describes literary selves as split between *personae* or public selves and *shadows* or the dark side of identity. In this approach more emphasis is attached to dreams as representations of the unconscious. Third, there is an object-relations approach drawing on the work of Nancy Chodorow and Melanie Klein which examines representations of mothering and mother–daughter affiliations (see Section 9). Finally a Lacanian approach draws on Lacan's theories, which argue that while the *symbolic* texture of literature might reveal psychic processes such as narcissism, linguistic features such as metaphors frequently reveal a greater range of psychic desires. These theories provide the tools for feminist criticism's examination of gender difference. Feminist critics attend to specific features of difference: gender perspective and point of view; gender subjectivity (in representations of displacement), and gender *absence* involving reading against the grain of a text. In other words, feminist psychoanalytic criticism aims to discover *processes* of gender difference.

There are challenges which psychoanalysis and feminism together offer to traditional literary criticism. The greatest challenge both make is to the unity of the subject. Psychoanalytic critiques, like feminist criticism, involve accounts of many rich and random realities. Another, and crucial, challenge is to the traditional separation of art, politics and society. No one area has a more privileged status in explaining individual psyche or text, and both challenge hierarchies of value: women's magazines may be as useful as a modernist novel in offering representations of women's desires. Feminism itself, both as a political movement and as a literary practice, is analogous to psychoanalysis. Both use a model of repression. Feminists think that women's experience is often repressed or 'unconscious'. Consciousness raising in feminist groups is like the bringing up of the repressed into consciousness in therapy or the raising of the sub-text in literary criticism: they are both ways of learning about the previously unexpressed effects of patriarchy.

Feminist psychoanalytic criticism is thus very diverse. It includes the study of the psychodynamics of female characters and their authors; psychoanalysis of textual metaphor; and study of the psychodynamics of gendered readings. One good example of some of these concerns is the work of the British critic Juliet

Mitchell. Her key work *Psychoanalysis and Feminism* was published in 1974 and had a major impact on feminist criticism. Mitchell argued that we cannot do without Freud's descriptions of the psychical operations of gender representations, even if psychoanalysis *was* patriarchal. Mitchell was one of the first feminists to make constructive use of Freud's theories, arguing that Freud describes patriarchal society at a particular stage (which still exists) rather than biological universals. Hence Freud's ideas *did* explain the consequences for women of penis envy and the Oedipus complex in patriarchal culture (Mitchell, 1974).

In her literary essays Mitchell offers two kinds of psychoanalytic insight. The first is that women's style is often 'imprisoned' in traditional discourse and can be 'critically' released. The focus here is on syntactics. The second is that narrative *form*, as much as character representation, defines gender and that literary characters can be described in terms of stages of composite psychic crises. Here Mitchell makes a psychoanalytic critique of textual structures (Mitchell, 1984).

All of these concerns and theories are hugely relevant to the study of Doris Lessing's *The Golden Notebook*. Lessing is preoccupied with the psychic subjectivity and experiences of the central character Anna Wulf. In addition, Lessing directly introduces many ideas and concepts from psychoanalysis, including those of Carl Jung and R. D. Laing. Laing was a major guru figure among intelligentsia in the 1960s. His work develops from an analysis of split subjects, or the 'divided self', to a study of splits between individuals and social institutions such as the family, encapsulated for Laing in the figure of the schizophrenic. *The Golden Notebook* was published only two years after the appearance of Laing's *The Divided Self* (1960).

Psychic states are at the centre of the novel. *The Golden Notebook* is about Anna's search for identity and her psychosis. Anna experiments with many social personae – mother, political activist, writer and lover – and throughout the novel is unable to integrate these or her past life in South Africa. The novel, fabricated as it is from descriptions of women's psychological experiences, attracted a large constituency of women readers. Anna continually discusses how social language constructs women in fixed subjectivities and roles. One of the ways in which

Anna exposes these constructions is by creating an alternative record – a diary of her every emotion and every experience on one day, 17 September 1954. Lessing's technique of installing and then subverting the empirical in favour of the intense minutiae of psychic life is one example of her attention to the psychoanalytic. Another is the multiplicity of the novel's structure. Anna is writing five books, not one, each with a different form of perception sometimes figured as an alternative character, Ella. *The Golden Notebook* propels the reader into Anna's fragmented consciousness as each notebook fails in turn to adequately represent women. The Black Notebook is Anna's African autobiography; the Red Notebook is her activism in, and resignation from, the British Community Party; the Blue Notebook is a psychoanalytic explanation of Anna's fragmented daily life; and the Yellow Notebook is Anna's self-reflexive account of her psychosis and creativity.

The Golden Notebook draws an analogy between a fragmented female identity and fragmented writing. Like psychoanalysis the novel is never complete but always in process. R. D. Laing also draws attention to the significance of contradiction and inconsistencies in personality formation. The theme of the novel is Anna's struggle for unity through the multiple perspectives she creates. One of the most distinctive themes of second wave feminism is its attention to female consciousness. Lessing insists, throughout her work, that women's thought processes are different from those of men. Consciousness raising has to do with the nature of feminist perception just as the 'mad', according to Lessing, have a double consciousness: current communication and future information. To Lessing, psychosis is a method of getting in touch with powers beyond 'normal' comprehension. By accepting the authenticity of her 'mad' as well as her 'normal' selves, Anna is able to finish the Golden Notebook.

Anna begins the novel as a psychoanalytic interpreter. In this short passage she describes her political activity and the political groups she knows in South Africa.

> Inside a year our group was split, equipped with sub-groups, traitors, and a loyal hard core whose personnel, save for one or two men, kept changing. Because we did not understand the process, it sapped our emotional energy. But while I know that the process of

self-destruction began almost at birth, I can't quite pinpoint that moment when the tone of our talk and behaviour changed. We were working as hard, but it was to the accompaniment of a steadily deepening cynicism. And our jokes, outside the formal meetings, were contrary to what we said, and thought we believed in. It is from that period of my life that I know how to watch the jokes people make. A slightly malicious tone, a cynical edge to a voice, can have developed inside ten years into a cancer that has destroyed a whole personality. I've seen it often, and in many other places than political or communist organisations.

(From *The Golden Notebook*, Michael Joseph, London, 1962, p. 65)

Here Anna begins to see the need for a new kind of political behaviour, a kind which may very well have analogies with therapy. Anna does not locate this behaviour in *events* but in *signifiers*. She describes voice 'tone', 'jokes', a 'cynical edge', as opposed to describing the content of speeches or political activism. In psychoanalytic criticism signifiers reveal meanings before these are even understood by characters. Anna's attention to signifiers enables her to read the unreadable in behaviour and later in texts. Psychoanalytic critics would draw attention to another feature of the passage – Anna's 'projection'. In projection subjects cast off their own negative traits on to others. Here Anna is splitting the negative feelings *she* has about political activism on to others.

Anna also reveals another psychoanalytic trait described in the behaviour observations of R. D. Laing's *The Divided Self*. Laing's main theme is that split selves, or schizophrenics, are often the chosen 'scapegoats' of their families. Laing argues that creativity often surfaces in schizophrenic psychosis. Schizophrenia represents a moment of resistance to what Laing called 'mapping'. Mapping occurs when experiential structures like the family (A) engage in public events (B). The function of social rituals is to map A on to B at critical moments like births, marriages and deaths. Lessing incorporates Laing's concept into Anna's strategies. Throughout the novel Anna tries to engage in 'mapping', most famously when equating the significance of the start of her period with her resignation from the Communist Party. But Anna is rarely successful and loses faith in those centralizing social explanations in favour of 'split' perceptions.

A central feature of Anna's behaviour which would interest psychoanalytic critics is, of course, her dreams. Dreams are often juxtaposed with key events in the novel. Lessing was very interested in Jung's psychological theories. In the novel Anna goes into Jungian therapy and Lessing clearly believes that Jung's ideas offer a system for analyzing fictional constructs of the unconscious. Carl Jung, like Laing and Freud, believed that the mind was the holder of split forces and that psychic energy was represented in particular symbols. Self-identity comes, according to Jung, from a process of 'individuation' which is the subject's struggle not only with his or her own unconscious but with 'primordial' or archaic images. Often this struggle manifests itself via imagistic fantasies (Jung, 1976).

Jung describes the unconscious in terms of universal archetypes which seem to manifest themselves in all individuals. These archetypes, Jung claims, emerge in the themes and imagery of dreams and some are frequent and recurring. Jung grouped his archetypes into paired opposites, like light and dark, which, to Jung, represent a balance between rationality and irrationality (or the *persona* and the *shadow* selves). Although many feminists demur at the *universal* quality of Jung's archetypes, particular Jungian symbols have attracted feminist artists and writers: images of rebirth (transcendence), primeval time (mother), circles and treasures and spirit symbols of energy and renewal.

Anna's dream descriptions bear close similarities to those in Jung's work. As Jung suggests, Anna uses her dreams as *regulators* which alert her to imbalances of the mind. Anna's frequent descriptions of her psychic states seem to stimulate her into action, just as many psychoanalytic critics interpret dream displacements in literature, such as condensations and metonyms (figures of speech which stand for objects), as if these have some predictive narrative power. In the Blue Notebook, Ella, the fictional Anna, dreams of how to cheat businessmen. She gives them a box containing shards of imperialism and the flesh of people killed in the Korean War, which when opened turns into a green crocodile whose frozen tears in the form of diamonds satisfy the businessmen. Ella notices, in her dream, that the crocodile's malicious grin resembles her own wry look. At that moment Ella ends her psychotherapy.

By following Jung's catalogue of archetypal images, we could argue that Ella has become 'whole' and therefore ceased to need treatment since she is in dream transference the treasure box. Ella combines Jung's binary opposites of dark and light by uniting the darkness of public life with the light of diamonds through an animal image – the crocodile – which, in Jungian terms, represents the mother or origin.

Let us consider another of Ella's dreams.

> Ella had a dream which was unpleasant and disturbing. She was in the ugly little house, with its little rooms that were all different from each other. She was Paul's wife, and only by an effort of will could she prevent the house disintegrating, and flying off in all directions because of the conflict between the rooms. She decided she must furnish the whole house again, in one style, hers. But as soon as she hung new curtains or painted a room out, Muriel's room was recreated. Ella was like a ghost in this house and she realized it would hold together, somehow, as long as Muriel's spirit was in it and it was holding together precisely because every room belonged to a different epoch, a different spirit. And Ella saw herself standing in the kitchen, her hand on the pile of *Women at Home*; she was a 'sexy piece' (she could hear the words being said, by Dr West) with a tight coloured skirt and a very tight jersey and her hair was cut fashionably. And Ella realized that Muriel was not there after all, she had gone to Nigeria to join Paul, and Ella was waiting in the house until Paul came back.
>
> (From *The Golden Notebook*, Michael Joseph, London, 1962, p. 194)

According to Jung a house is the archetype of the unconscious. Because Ella's 'shadow', or 'sexy piece', the dark side of her personality overwhelms her persona, the dream culminates in disintegration. The dream reveals Ella's inner fissures as well as the impossibility of a heterogeneous, whole self-identity because this cannot be achieved at the expense of the inner self. The assertion of identity can only come through a unification of *differences*.

One final short passage, from Anna's Golden Notebook, shows Lessing's concern with the psychoanalytic origins of individuality.

> I have only to write a phrase like 'I walked down the street', or take

a phrase from a newspaper 'economic measures which lead to the full use of . . .' and immediately the words dissolve, and my mind starts spawning images which have nothing to do with the words, so that every word I see or hear seems like a small raft bobbing about on an enormous sea of images. So I can't write any longer. Or only when I write fast, without looking back at what I have written. For if I look back, then the words swim and have no sense and I am conscious only of me, Anna, as a pulse in a great darkness, and the words that I, Anna, write down are nothing, or like the secretions of a caterpillar that are forced out in ribbons to harden in the air.

(From *The Golden Notebook*, Michael Joseph, London, 1962, p. 407)

This would be interpreted in psychoanalytic terms as a mind/ body split. Anna has lost her sense of self – her individuality as a writer – and is invaded by a flow of associated images 'caterpillar' and 'ribbons'. She has disassociated herself from her body and become 'a pulse in a great darkness'. There is a proliferation of symbols with words as 'rafts' in a 'sea of images' which 'swim' all representing fluidity and Anna's uncontrolled phantasy which may, or may not, lead to creativity. Anna's descriptions would be interpreted psychoanalytically as evidence of dissolving personal boundaries, particularly because she has lost any sense of time. Only if Anna adopts a process which Jung called 'amplification' (the comparison between symbolic images and structures and existing mythical structures) can she explain her anxieties to herself. In Laingian terms, Anna has already begun to achieve a 'healthy' state by exploring the depths of her subjectivity.

A traditional reading might dismiss this passage as evidence of Anna's sterility; she is now a writer to whom words mean 'nothing'. Feminist psychoanalytic critics would note more positively Anna's self-reflexive sensitivity and the way in which she searches for identity *through* feminine images of the 'sea', 'pulse', 'ribbons'. Like the caterpillar (in Jungian terms an animal/ origin/mother image), Anna might to be able to spin a chrysalis from her primeval fluid darkness. The passage encourages an interplay of opposites ('sea'/'air') indicating support for Anna's insight that her writing *could* allow psychical material to surface. The signifiers 'nothing', 'no sense' are then not negatives but represent the gap many women experience between psychic experience, 'pulse', 'darkness', 'the sea', and symbolic, public language. As Lessing suggests earlier in the novel '"if we lead what is known as free lives, that is, lives like men, why shouldn't we use the same language?" "Because we aren't the same. That is the point"' (p. 43).

6 Poststructuralism

SECTION 11: IRIS MURDOCH, *THE UNICORN*

One of the most fundamental challenges to literary realism and bourgeois liberalism comes from poststructuralism. Some of the confusion surrounding the term comes perhaps from its very usefulness. Poststructuralism must be one of the most over-worked but under-focused of contemporary critical terms. A helpful beginning might be to separate out poststructuralism and structuralism. *The* major difference between structuralism and poststructuralism lies in their very different views about the nature of discourse. In very simple terms structuralism, growing largely out of linguistics as it did, involved itself in finding patterns (structures) and systems in language (discourse) which could articulate or represent larger forms of knowledge. Post-structuralists argue that structuralism has a very limited notion of signification. For example, while few structuralists ever claim to be able to explain a text's meanings in *full*, a structuralist analysis does attempt to explain narratives in terms of their similarities to, or deviations from, particular linguistic or literary *norms*. For this reason structuralism is often linked to formalism, the Russian literary movement, because both tried to codify writers' techniques in a 'science' of language. Poststructuralism fissures, or breaks *apart*, systems of representation rather than celebrating structures.

Poststructuralism grew out of *two* closely related disciplines: linguistics *and* psychoanalysis. In addition, there are obvious connections between poststructuralism and second wave feminism, both in terms of chronology and in terms of their challenges to the *bases* of language. Both date from approximately 1966–70 with the publication of work by Roland Barthes, Jacques Derrida, Jacques Lacan and Michel Foucault. It was these critics who radically questioned the view that literature actually says what it means. The deferral of meaning in texts, as well as absences or marginalities, are inescapable features of all language. Similarly, feminism focuses on women's marginality – on the absence of women in social institutions as well as in texts. Other key issues which each addresses are the construction of subjectivity as well as the position, or lack of position, of the author.

Poststructuralism focuses on how literary representations work within, and *in spite of*, particular cultural frameworks. Poststructuralism 'deconstructs' or debunks structuralism's faith in measuring, and any isolation of systems from the power structures which control those systems. In other words, post-structuralism has made us aware of the ways in which men and women are absent from, or included in, representations, depending on who owns or speaks the language of representation. Poststructuralism makes a radical jump across the boundary between a text and the reading of a text by focusing on how linguistic processes (discourses) 'construct' readers.

It may seem paradoxical to describe *an* approach of poststructuralism while claiming that poststructuralism criticizes existing systems. Yet what poststructuralism questions is the belief that language has a *transparent* system and instead suggests that there are many textual determinants of meaning. What interests poststructuralists in language is not only its functioning but also its *failure*, those moments when meaning is suddenly non-existent. What precisely is questioned by poststructuralists? First of all style has come under scrutiny. Poststructuralists argue that literary style is not 'natural' and does not flow from some innate individual genius. Instead, literary styles and conventions are products of particular cultural and historical contexts as much as they are freely chosen by authors. This argument suggests that literary value might derive not so much from a *fixed* place in the canon but from a text's ability to offer constantly changing meanings.

One particular focus of poststructuralists is therefore on the narrative voice(s) and on the ways in which narrative voices sometimes escape their authors. For this reason poststructuralists are intensely interested in mixtures of autobiography and literature and in mixtures of genres. Moving beyond formal genres, poststructuralism attends to hybrid texts and popular fictions such as romance and the Gothic. As well as narrators and genres, another key focus is on other representations of difference, in particular the construction of binary opposites such as men/women, black/white. These oppositions hide hierarchies of value which often make woman into the negative and opposite of man.

The reason why poststructuralists are so concerned about binaries in literature is because of the parallels between social ideologies and literary forms. If you believe, as structuralists do, that literary representations (signifiers) have some relation to the signified (or referent), then signification becomes a kind of 'unhappy marriage' between ideology and representation. Poststructuralism prefers to problematize all signifiers including 'author' and 'reader'. If structuralism argues that there is some direct (if not necessarily causative) relation between author, signifier and social reality, poststructuralism fiercely attacks this closed system of meanings. Poststructuralism asserts that every text is made up of other textual discourses which carry with them their own meanings and contexts. An author is only *one* meaning among many others.

One of the key arguments of poststructuralism is its assertion that the author can never be the *source* of textual meaning. In some ways this same issue also surfaces in everyday life. While I have a female identity I know that this identity has been socially, psychoanalytically and self-consciously constructed. Depending on what others seem to think of me, what everyday roles I have to play, my femininity will constantly vary. But even this identity is hardly stable since appearance, age, health, weight and so forth all make their mark on my 'discursive' representations. I am never the author of my life. Poststructuralism recognizes this fluidity of authorship.

One influential essay by Roland Barthes in the late 1960s articulated this new thinking very clearly. In 'The death of the author', Barthes claims that the 'author' is as much a product, a construction of the text as characters or plot. Traditional criticism, Barthes argues, unites author and work and this unification stems from a bourgeois belief in individualism. The notion of an author 'pre-ordaining' all interpretations of his/her text should be replaced, Barthes suggests, with a 'scriptor', a term meaning the writer of the text who does not exist outside the text (Barthes, 1986). By radically overturning the idea of authorial *authority* and the concomitant practice of trying to discover an author's intentions, poststructuralism allowed texts to be more interactive processes with readers. As Barthes claimed, the death of the author allows the birth of the subject as well as the birth of the reader.

If we apply Barthes's idea to Iris Murdoch's *The Unicorn*, this would mean that if we went to interview Murdoch to ask her thoughts about *The Unicorn* we would be wasting our time. Not only is it a fallacy to trace textual meanings direct to their authors, but it would also be extremely unwise. Authors are very elusive beings who constantly reconstruct their own books every time these are discussed. Rather than listening to a real-life author, poststructuralism describes the author as an *authority structure* within the text itself. Poststructuralism attends to the signifying processes of the text rather than trying to find a text's creator.

If we can never, strictly speaking, know an author's intention but only an *implied* and constantly shifting intention (depending on the reader) does it follow that all readings are as good or as useful as each other? To many feminists the gender of the author *is* of crucial importance if only because we know that texts are differently received by critics and readers *depending* on the gender of the author. In addition whether a text is written by a Black woman or a white woman is of crucial importance. Yet there are ways in which texts can be read poststructurally as *processes*, and also in feminist terms, if we think of the author as a figurative representation in the text. To study textuality need not involve a complete erasure of the author. The shift from the notion that the text 'belongs' to an author to the view that it might belong to a reader was enormously productive. Criticism could now focus on the similarities and differences *between* processes and between significations. Indeed, texts may be unreliable, they may not 'authorize' or construct a particular meaning at all. In some ways this allows critics to be more flexible, less uncertain of their views. Women are often made to feel outsiders in particular academic discourses and, following Barthes, could use poststructuralism to open up such discourses.

This is not to say that *all* reader responses are of equal significance to poststructuralists. The critique of reading contexts undertaken by Janice Radway and other critics came to be known as reader–response criticism (Radway, 1987). But where reader–response criticism focuses on the *ethnography* of a reading situation, poststructuralism looks at *texts* in terms of *how* texts address readers. For example texts may use direct address (provocative questions) or be indirect (self-reflexive). The key issue in poststructuralism is to bring the *processes* of writing and reading closer together. Poststructuralism gives a new significance to those features of a text which invite or reject a reader: absences, ellipses (. . .), parody (which depends on reader recognition of the genre), interruptions (giving a reader breathing space) and repetitive syntax. These are features which might be regarded as textual failures by traditional critics. A poststructuralist critic would notice immediately Iris Murdoch's love of punning character names, for example, Martin Lynch-Gibbon the military historian of *A Severed Head*.

It is clear, I hope, why feminist critics are attracted to poststructuralism. First, it seems to offer the promise of a reading process unhampered by universal or predetermined values. Second, it challenges the linguistic institutionalizing of social power. Terms such as 'nature' and 'womankind' should not simply stabilize or eradicate difference. Feminists could use poststructuralism to expose the gendered constructions of these terms. Feminist criticism of the early 1970s – texts such as Kate Millett's *Sexual Politics* – had exposed gender stereotyping in literature. Now poststructuralists could move on to analyze how gender categories are less likely to be the chosen stereotypes of individual authors and much more likely to be cultural products. If this project of deconstruction seems too negative, poststructuralists could retort that mechanisms of gender construction are so pervasive *and* persuasive that any powerful tool is of use. Even a writer like Iris Murdoch, who writes a more traditional fiction of moral philosophy, might be susceptible to a poststructuralist critique.

Iris Murdoch began writing in the 1950s with her first published book *Sartre* (1953). A philosophy professor at Oxford, Murdoch's fictions are frequently described as novels of ideas. Murdoch has published over fifteen works which incorporate metaphysics, fantasy and contemporary satire. *The Unicorn* tells the story of Marian Taylor's arrival at the desolate Scottish Gaze Castle. Marian has been employed as a governess for a 'prisoner' Mrs Hannah Crean-Smith, the eponymous unicorn. With its rococo plot, the novel traces the lives and sexual experiences of other inhabitants of the castle and Effingham, neighbour and civil servant, who adores Hannah from afar. In some ways the novel adopts many of the conventions of British mystery fiction as well as the Gothic by promising that the impressionable observer, Marian, might discover dreadful truths in the violent Gothic setting of Gaze Castle. In turn the novel's theme is an *allegorical* quest.

Murdoch's deliberate use of conventional genres and her evident moral preoccupations might seem to exclude *The Unicorn* from a poststructuralist analysis. Clearly Murdoch is not considered a poststructuralist writer. She has specifically attacked contemporary novels as being either crystalline or journalistic. Her novels avoid avant-garde experiments and she often deliberately turns to traditional literary genres in order to examine important moral truths or messages. In very simple terms genre is a form or type of fiction, for example thriller, romance, Gothic. The choice of label can be made from looking at content, and genres create specific expectations in readers. The organization of books in multichain bookshops into westerns, romance and so forth is an indication that readers perhaps have a large body of understanding about the conventions and forms to which they are attracted. In this sense genre, by its nature, affirms the importance of readers as much as authors. As poststructuralists would point out, genre consumption suggests that readers are very expert in seeing conventions in texts rather than reading texts as transparent windows on reality. As well as appealing to particular readers, Murdoch's choice of several genres also allows her to avoid an obvious authoritative narrator. *The Unicorn* has no single style and can be read as a series of almost epigrammatic comments about the difficulties of realism. In any case the notion of genre implies interaction *between* texts and affinities *across* texts. By merging the conventions of the thriller with the Gothic, Murdoch signals her interest in pastiche which undermines any notion of a single authoritative point of view.

Characters in *The Unicorn* are grouped into binaries which, in good poststructuralist fashion, are parodically exaggerated. For example, Hannah simultaneously represents Sleeping Beauty, a unicorn, a phoenix, even Christ, while Marian is her 'faithful' maid. Murdoch's concern with intertexts takes the novel from the fictional to the ideational. One example of some of these issues can be seen in the opening to Chapter 6. Openings are important and crucial moments in Murdoch's novels because it is here that significant aesthetic patterns are laid out.

'That suits you, Marian, look!' said Hannah. She held up the big hand-mirror which they had brought out with them on to the terrace.

It was a warm still evening, after dinner but not yet very late, and they were sitting out at one of the little white iron-work tables, sipping whiskey and trying on some of Hannah's jewels. An unclouded sun, very soon to be quenched in a level golden sea, had turned everything on the land to a brilliant saffron yellow. Marian felt as if she and Hannah were on a stage, so violent and unusual was the lighting. Their hands and faces were gilded. Long shadows stretched away behind them; and the big rounded clumps of wild sea-pinks which grew in the cracks of the pavement, having each its shadow, dissolved the terrace about their feet into a pitted, chequered cloth. The sense of play-acting was increased too by the fact that they were both in evening dress. At last Marian was wearing the blue cocktail dress which Geoffrey approved of, and Hannah was wearing a long dress, one which she had selected from the collection which came on approval. It was a light mauve dress of heavy grained silk with a tight high bodice and vaguely medieval air. With a golden chain about her neck she looked, thought Marian, like some brave beleaguered lady in legend or like some painter's dream of 'ages far agone'.

Hannah had suggested that they should have, tonight, to inaugurate the dress, a little celebration, with some champagne and a better wine than usual, and that Marian should dress up to match. Gerald Scottow and Violet Evercreech had joined them for the champagne, and conversation had been animated though singularly impersonal and polite. They had dined *à deux*. Hannah had complained playfully the Gerald was neglecting her, and Marian had had the thought that Gerald was avoiding her. She did not know what to make of this thought. She had enjoyed the novelty of the little dinner, but it had had somehow a slightly forced pathetic air.

(From *The Unicorn*, Panther, London, 1977, pp. 50–1)

Poststructuralism undercuts our ability to believe in 'realism', particularly in realism's addiction to good/bad oppositions and colour coding. Similarly, the passage here represents the evening both as a moment of reality 'it was a warm still evening, after dinner but not yet very late' and simultaneously foregrounds *the activity* of representing reality by a parodic structuralism. That is to say the passage appears to be a transparent description, full of detail, annotated by an omniscient narrator but it also calls into question the link between realism and meaning. Murdoch does this by an exaggerated use of binaries – Marian/'blue cocktail dress', Hannah/ 'light mauve dress' – which 'overflows' into other vocabulary choices. A chain of binary opposites is suggested in light/dark polarities. Properties of 'golden', 'saffron', 'gilded' contrast with 'shadows', and a soon to be 'quenched' sun. These binary oppositions, however, are brought into play by the characters themselves, as it were, not the omniscient author. It is Hannah who suggests that Marian 'should dress up'. Murdoch, poststructuralists would suggest, creates a signifying surface full of binaries *only* to draw attention to the operative opposition of the sub-text in which Hannah is a mythical 'brave beleaguered lady' and Marian has more quotidian qualities, knowing 'little about jewels'. The boundary between oppositions and colour binaries is hard to maintain and is continually threatened by 'wild sea-pinks' and 'violent' lighting.

One other marked feature of interest to poststructuralists is Murdoch's mixing of registers. Feelings of strangeness and intimations of violence are metaprosaic expressions brought into the opening. The description of a relatively commonplace scene – drinks on the terrace – in the register of melodrama, invites us to anticipate the likely and rhythmic significance of the Hannah/ Marian pairing. Yet the passage is 'made strange', is defamiliarized by Marian's 'naivety'. Usually reporting clauses in genres frame speech; we would expect paraphrased speeches in melodrama to have character attributes such as 'Hannah had suggested *with chilling intent*' or 'Marian felt *alarmingly*'. Such adverbial phrases are freely used in genres as touchstones for readers, to encourage recognition. Instead Marian gives the reader no clues as to how to place the narration. In other words her actions and appearance are allowed some significance without mediation from an omniscient author.

Murdoch's 'over-use' of multigenres could be regarded as a poststructuralist undermining of narrative certainty. The repetitive imagery and binaries call attention to the difficulty of narrating in itself as well to the impossibility of simple dualisms (sexual or character). There is no single authoritative meaning. All may well be 'play-acting', 'inaugurations' and 'celebrations'. The dinner is both a 'novelty' and 'forced', in a contradictory antithesis.

While no one could claim Murdoch is a feminist there is a way in which the scene is 'feminized'. The use of negative adjectives 'unclouded' and vague and imprecise time 'not yet very late' is conventionally characterized as a woman's signature. Yet at the same time, of course, Murdoch is playing with, and parodying, this conventional and stereotypical association for a particular artistic effect – to highlight Marian's lack of power/knowledge and hence destabilize and unsettle the reader. Murdoch's undermining of binaries, her parodic echoing of genres, her 'weak' protagonist all combine to embrace poststructuralism's negation of universal truths.

SECTION 12: CHRISTA WOLF, *THE QUEST FOR CHRISTA T.*

One of the major problems in defining poststructuralism arises from the frequent conflation of poststructuralism with other theories which succeed it, including deconstruction and postmodernism. Not only does this delegitimize the model as a theoretical framework but creates difficulties for critics trying to describe particular critical tools and methods. The very prefix 'post' suggests that poststructuralism must relate to earlier practices. Many critics use 'poststructuralism' to define a historical moment – the break with structuralism – but then go on to apply the term to any writing which incorporates nonrealist features. Sometimes 'poststructuralism' appears as an additional adjective to 'experimental', 'contradictory' or to any other label attached to contemporary avant-garde writing. Often critics slip carelessly from poststructuralism to postmodernism when describing texts although, rather curiously, they rarely return from that more fashionable concept. With the arrival of postmodernism on the critical scene, many critics have simply adopted the formulae of *this* theory, utilizing terms such as 'parody' to describe writing which ten years before they would happily have described as poststructuralist. As well as careless and superficial readings, there are additional problems of definition. Poststructuralism cannot simply be used as a synonym for experimental. Although structuralism, as I suggested in Section 11, is primarily European and North American drawing on the theories of Ferdinand de Saussure, poststructuralism is a more general contemporary phenomenon.

Poststructuralism may have appeared at a particular time and place – the late 1960s in France – but, like all theoretical movements, it cannot be easily *differentiated* from other schools of criticism. Most major contemporary theories are complex transformations of other theories often working within and alongside similar frameworks, ideas and concepts.

However, some of these ideas and concepts are graspable as indications of a particular practice. For example, poststructuralists, as we might expect, are less interested in totalizing critiques and prefer to focus on a writer's own self-questioning. Supporters of poststructuralism claim that critics should no longer, if they ever did, produce objective and universal accounts of literature. Poststructuralists further claim that the discipline of literary criticism has no overarching power to explain cultural features, but can learn a great deal from psychoanalysis, philosophy and anthropology.

The early 1970s witnessed a widespread feeling in the Western academy that large-scale literary explanations were limited and inappropriate, and a growing sense that multiple and different voices needed to be heard. Psychoanalytic theories were explored by Julia Kristeva, Luce Irigaray and Hélène Cixous, to recover unknown and unrepresented forms of the feminine (see French feminism). The single most important contribution of *feminists* to poststructuralism was this attention to the existence or absence of gender in critical thought. Feminist critics warmed to poststructuralism because at last there seemed to be a critical movement which attacked literary *structures* of power, such as women's fictionalized quests for self-identity which always ended in marriage or death. Poststructuralism showed that *readers* can contribute to textual messages as much as authors. We can go beyond ('post') an author's given structure. In this way feminist poststructuralists could reject existing definitions of 'women' as well as reject the possibility of ever defining 'women' at all. Poststructuralists argued that representations of 'women' draw on existing social constructions produced through literary language as well as on the interaction of other discourses such as the law, medicine or the media. One problem, probably too metaphysical even to solve, is how to attack critical practices while at the same time borrowing existing tools. How can you claim to be staging a break in critical theory while at the same time writing recognizable criticism?

Yet if this seems a contradiction, what we call poststructuralism does have specific features. The institutional recognition of poststructuralism is usually dated from the publication of Roland Barthes's *S/Z* (1970). Barthes's career is paradigmatic of the key shift from structuralism to poststructuralism. Where Barthes's 'Introduction à l'analyse structurale des récits' (1966) focused on the *structure* of narrative, by 1970 Barthes's focus switched to differences *between* texts rather than similarities *across* narrative. That there was a general climate of political and cultural change in the late 1960s, coupled with new political demands largely stemming from the women's movement, is not in doubt. One of the first British celebrations of poststructuralism – Catherine Belsey's *Critical Practice* – praised the liberating effects of the death of structuralism in gendered terms, although Belsey at that stage indexed poststructuralism as 'post Saussureanism' (Belsey, 1980). In very simple terms, if we try to differentiate the foci of various critical approaches, it could be argued that structuralism focuses on anagrams and systems, psychoanalysis focuses on dreams and parapraxes or slips of the tongue and poststructuralism focuses on marginalized phenomena, local 'histories' and multiple subjects.

It was this emphasis on multiple subjects which marked a major break, too, in feminist literary criticism. The first phase of second wave feminist criticism has been called the moment of the 'resisting reader'. Feminists like Judith Fetterley and Kate Millett argued polemically that female stereotypes in male fictions were a mimesis of patriarchy (Fetterley, 1978; Millett, 1970). Poststructuralists, on the other hand, argued that this view was essentialist and untheoretical. Representations of sexual difference, poststructuralists claimed, were produced in multiple ways: through readers, through language as well as through textual messages. Indeed, this break is often polarized as a debate between essentialism and difference. The concentration on *difference* encouraged feminist poststructuralists to explore a greater variety of forms of femininity *and* masculinity in cultural texts. One result of poststructuralism's interest in difference was new thinking about literary identity. Signifiers of 'women' rarely refer to actual women, as second wave feminists had already proved. Poststructuralists went on to argue that all identities are constructed within systems of difference. The general feminist attack on social constructions of gender and biological givens was compatible with a poststructuralist interest in deconstructions and different discursive representations.

What poststructuralism offered was not without problems for some feminists. If literary signs could be endlessly different they could be endlessly replaced and endlessly irrelevant to women's social needs. If 'woman' is merely a signifier with no relevance to women as such, then feminist arguments about women's oppression, whether literary or social, would seem pointless. A poststructuralist answer might be that 'difference' opens up the possibility that at last a range of women's experiences would have some relevance to literary readings. The notion that texts are not 'fixed' by authors or critics and that meanings can be constructed 'differently' by differing audiences allows for far more flexible readings.

In other words, feminism shares with poststructuralism its antagonism to universal values and its desire to explore multiple kinds of writing. Both examine literary or social texts, not only in terms of what these texts *describe* but in terms of what they do to *hide* their own ideologies. To feminist poststructuralists the question of literary value, of choosing great books by great writers (the canon), is not a self-evident question and the answers which traditional literary criticism provides are a matter of class-, race- and gender-based forms of control. Because the canon is too powerful a hierarchy to be undone simply by adding texts by women or by creating an alternative canon (useful though this activity can be in raising the status of women writers), feminist poststructuralists looked to other practices of deconstruction. Challenges to the idea of a unitary literary identity came from several directions, French feminists, for example, discovered a maternal language (the semiotic) lying underneath the symbolic or written surface of literature.

Since the 1970s then, feminist poststructuralists have made radical breaks with essentialism and structuralism. What emerges from that decade are two key concerns: the highlighting of *processes* of literary production (discourse); and the examination of differences of gender (the many 'I's' to be found in some novels). Feminists draw on several influential critiques. Lacan, Derrida and Foucault are often cited as forerunners, even if their work is very disparate. Although coming from different disciplinary directions, all agree that if literary subjects have no fixed identities then the study of discourse is crucial. Since Derrida and Lacan are considered elsewhere (Deconstruction and French feminism), let me quickly summarize Foucault's ideas about power and language. The concept of discourse which Foucault developed in *The Archaeology of Knowledge* focuses the reasons why languages take certain forms. Discourses are formations of knowledge sometimes called 'fields'. Foucault argues that we read and speak only what we are allowed to read or speak since institutions control the formation of discourses. A good example would be the term 'hysteric' frequently given to obstreperous women.

Discourse analysis examines the implications of such vocabulary choices for women and thus tackles head on issues such as essentialism and historical misconstructions. Poststructuralists attend to general formations of knowledge and this allows critics to explore shifting gender representations. One powerful example of poststructuralist discourse analysis is in Afra-American writing. Black critics attack essentialism – such as the concept of a universal Black 'woman' – by describing the different verbal powers and perceptions of Black women writers. Hortense Spillers, in particular, describes ways in which the discourse of slavery 'deconstructed', degendered and destroyed Black women's bodies (Spillers, 1984). Foucault's main trope is 'the body', and he argues that sexual representations change from era to era not because bodies themselves change but because 'political' authorities change the conventions of body representation. Similarly Spillers argues that the politics of racism throughout history depends on a complex use of body signifiers, for example Caliban/Cannibal.

The second and equally radical feminist poststructuralist concern is to deconstruct differences of subjectivity. Critics are intrigued by texts with multiple narrative voices and by dialogues between narrator and readers. Again critics make much of apparent mixtures of fiction and non-fiction and novels which refuse an omniscient third person. Toni Morrison's *Beloved*, which describes multiple memories, is often called a poststructuralist novel.

All of these concerns come together in Christa Wolf's *The Quest for Christa T.* Wolf's career parallels that of the German Democratic Republic. Born in Landsberg/Warthe (now Poland), Wolf completed her Arbitur in 1949 (founding of the GDR). After her Diplomarbeit and marriage she worked in factories and as an editor becoming famous with her novel *Divided Heaven* (1963). The book was banned initially as anti-realist, just as her later book *Cassandra* was cut because of Wolf's support for the dissident Wolf Biermann. *Nachdenken Uber Christa T. (The Quest for Christa T.)* is triggered by the life history of a friend of Wolf who studied with her at the University of Leipzig and who, like Christa T., wrote a thesis on Theodor Storm. Yet the German title of the novel means remembrance not quest, and with its shared character/author first name the book is as much a fictionalized autobiography as a fiction biography of a dead friend.

The novel focuses on *processes* of reconstruction in which the narrator's responses become as important as the events of Christa's life. It is both a book of mourning and of deep epistemological uncertainty. Like another famous GDR author, Bertolt Brecht, Wolf 'defamiliarizes' identity by showing the constructed quality of her thoughts and shares Brecht's love of gnomic maxims – 'when if not now when' (p. 69) – and interrogatives. A poststructuralist critique would focus on Wolf's break from 'official' history writing signalled by a self-reflexive narrator. The process of literary construction is discussed by the narrator at the same time as she comments on political representations. In other words Wolf clearly has a poststructuralist aim:

to construct a new and gendered life history while problematiz-ing the construction of gender as a social category.

One can't blame them for not being able to describe a smile. It must suffice to mention that the dentist's wife spent more than a day reconstructing her tidy life to fortify it against this smile, telling herself she's a respectable housewife and spouse and occupies her position in the moral order of the world – and not the lowest position either. She doesn't say anything malicious about Christa T.; altogether she's an amiable woman, unable, also, to find the precise expression for her feelings. Otherwise she'd have probably called Christa T. 'not a very serious young woman'. When she thinks of a particular look that Christa T. can give, she even murmurs to herself: 'Weird, that's what it is'.

For to many people wonderment is weird. One shouldn't, especially when visitors are present, look around one's own living room as if it had suddenly become a foreign place, as if the tables and chairs could suddenly walk away on their own feet and the walls suddenly sprout holes.

Nevertheless, the dentist's wife and the principal's wife can simply stay away, can speak ill or be amiable and silent. We cannot stay away when things get difficult, and we must speak of her. There are several possible approaches here, even if the framework is firm and cannot be expanded much. The first testimonies would be the occasional letters we exchanged. Second, the scraps of paper with jottings about her children. For when Anna was three, Lena was born, in all respects the opposite of her sister: dark and delicate and sensitive. If I've complained about the disorder and volatility of her papers up till now – what am I to say about this bundle of papers. It's as if she never had a notebook within reach these days, not even a writing pad, but only envelopes, the backs of bills, memoranda – cast-off scraps from her husband's desk.

The third possible approach to these years would simply be memory. It seems easy to picture Christa T. walking up the stairs, a bundle wrapped in blankets on her arm – Anna – and her calling out to us from the stairs that she's terribly tired, and then our sitting there together, half the night, even if it's only because we think we're making the most of the time. – This would be the picture I see.

Everything points to transience. Nothing stays as it is. The signs we make are provisional; if one knows it, well and good.

(From *The Quest for Christa T.*, Virago, London, 1982, pp. 141–2)

Poststructuralists would draw attention to one obvious feature of this passage: the narrator's own interest in language. She questions the value of one-dimensional or linear chronology as a method of recording history – 'occasional letters' . . . 'scraps of paper with jottings' . . . 'the third possible approach to those years would simply be memory'. The narrator is open to subjective experience (to the memory of a smile) and questions formal narration: 'the signs we make are provisional'. The narrator cannot separate past from present or personal experience from historical record. She cannot make a coherent distanced framework for Christa's life.

Out of this discontent with the structure of traditional biographies arise further poststructuralist features. The first is a deliberate flouting of the normal *ways* of recording speech and writing. Both Roland Barthes and Jacques Derrida argue that speech and writing are opposed forms of communication and that patriarchy has privileged writing precisely because writing *is* 'closed', literally here as 'cast-off scraps from her husband's desk', (Barthes, 1970; Derrida, 1976). In the passage only the narrator's written record *can* make any sense from the fragmentary scraps which face her. Yet paradoxically Wolf allows the very fragmentation to challenge the nature of written records, to challenge narrative closure and the representation of Christa T. The second poststructuralist feature, then, is Wolf's deliberate crossing *over*, stepping across the boundary between speech and writing. The passage incorporates direct recorded speech 'Weird, that's what it is'; reports assumed interior thought as dialogue 'not a very serious young woman'; and uses interior monologue and self-reflexive interrogatives. In addition even the continuous report of the narrator's interior musings reads *like* conversation as if *spoken* to a reader for example in her use of a plural first person 'the signs *we* make'.

One favourite intertextual mixture chosen by many poststructuralists is texts which incorporate letters. The artificiality of literature is addressed when 'real' letters are presented as more 'real' than an author/narrator's account. As an example, Alice Walker's *The Color Purple* plays with an epistolary genre continually challenging the possibility of a happy ending because letters have no value without a reader. This passage foregrounds the problem of all women's relation to literary language when our letters about personal experience have a greater 'volatility' than formal narrative. Christa's letters problematize the traditional notion of an omniscient record by suggesting that the reader not the author can produce meaning. However, unlike the letters of modernist writing, for example E. M. Forster's opening letters in *Howards End*, Wolf is not hinting at, or privileging, superior 'artistic' sensibilities. Rather, Christa's letters involve the reader and narrator in a shared search for authenticity. Shifts in writing are there to *encourage* an engagement not to refuse one.

Christa Wolf also addresses the central poststructuralist conundrum I mentioned above; how do we *construct* a woman subject while *de*constructing existing representations of women? Wolf poses this as a question about time. The passage's 'time' is the time the narrator takes to assemble her thoughts, fragments and secondary evidence. This is described as a movement through the three possible approaches to recording life history. Yet this present time itself has different forms. The narrator's descriptions, in the present, of found fragments are conventional, linear, 'realistic'; but her own recollections, also in the present, are experiential and anti-linear: 'chairs could suddenly walk away on their own feet'. Even recorded memory – the *past* – is presented as an active part of the present through Wolf's choice of verb tenses: 'walking up', 'calling out', 'our sitting there'.

In her epigraphs to the novel Wolf reveals how much the novel consciously creates its own history. 'This coming-to-oneself – what is it? Johannes R. Becher' and 'Christa T. is a fictional character. Several of the quotations from diaries, sketches, and letters come from real-life sources' (frontispiece). The poststructuralist critic Julia Kristeva calls this 'women's time'. In her essay of that title, Kristeva describes women's time as cyclical, repetitive, embodying monumental time (Kristeva, 1981). Men's time, Kristeva suggests, is the time of history – linear, chronological and rationally ordered. In *The Quest for Christa T.*, events do not happen in a rational ordered way since key plot 'events' – Christa's death, the completion of her house, her children – all occur very rapidly near the end of the novel. Poststructuralists would agree that attention to the production of *meanings* of 'woman' might be as significant as events.

Finally, poststructuralism favours interrogative texts which unfix the idea of a stable viewing author/narrator. If 'authors' are *in* these texts at all, it is as interrogative (questioning) voices which are often self-contradictory. Interrogative texts refuse to have narrators who order the reader into a particular viewpoint and instead bring different points of view into the text, however contradictory these might be. What interrogative texts do, in other words, is cast doubt on single social beliefs by exposing the uncertainty of any firm grasp of history.

The passage's changes in personal pronouns are a mark of instability and an interrogative text. The passage begins with an indirect third person – 'it must suffice to mention' – and Christa is safely 'she'. Swiftly the *process* of writing is interrogated when the narrator becomes 'one': 'one shouldn't, especially when visitors are present, look around one's own living room' and equally swiftly is transformed into a dialogic relation with the reader 'we cannot stay away'. The narrator becomes 'I' and fails to sustain the third person just as Christa could not write her own autobiographical 'I'. Yet the narrator cannot order even her own memories. 'For when Anna was three, Lena was born, in all respects the opposite of her sister: dark and delicate and sensitive.' Clauses work by association, a random musing, rather than categorized life moments. The narrator, is humble, self-effacing: 'what am I to say'. As Roland Barthes claims, poststructuralist writing sees the 'death of the author' (Barthes, 1986). Here Wolf demystifies authorship by refusing to let her narrator be an objective authoritative speaker, and instead allows the process of recording to flow from relationships between narrator, Christa and the reader. The narrator becomes a historical subject only by constructing multiple *fictional* subjects. Christa Wolf refuses 'history' with descriptions of women's time; and she tries to break with the gender representations of patriarchy by turning to experiential perceptions. A more vivid example of poststructuralist narrative would be hard to find.

7 Deconstruction

SECTION 13: MAXINE HONG KINGSTON, *THE WOMAN WARRIOR*

Deconstruction calls into question the notion that a text has one single meaning which is reached when you find that images, characterization and plot have some structural unity. The idea that there is one single competent *critical* reading is also questioned by deconstruction. Rather than believing that a novel's surface and hidden levels can be decoded unambiguously, deconstructionists celebrate ambiguous and contradictory readings.

Deconstruction has had a huge impact on literary criticism in general, as well as on feminist criticism. This may be due to its playful experiments with fixed social roles and because it can grapple with multiple levels of discourse. A deconstructive analysis looks at how messages in novels are only able to be understood in relation to those elements which the messages attempt to cover over. That is to say, if we read a novel as if it represents the intention of the author and find that plot or characterization has significance only in relation to intention, we ignore the alternative literary signifiers (such as repetitions and discontinuities) which may help us understand the more complex levels of a text.

The consequences of deconstruction for feminism are particularly appealing. Deconstruction attacks hierarchies of value and single 'truths' and hence supports feminism's claims that some forms of knowledge, some claims of objective truth about gender identity, can be overturned. Feminist critics use deconstruction in order to subvert patriarchal discourses and knowledge claims. For example, feminist deconstructionists point to figures of speech which make the generic masculine a positive and the feminine a negative or subsidiary.

Deconstruction refers to those techniques and methods practised by critics who have been influenced by the French philosopher Jacques Derrida. In France Luce Irigaray and Hélène Cixous and in America Barbara Johnson and Derrida's translator Gayatri Spivak have been involved in this complex enterprise. In *Of Grammatology* (1967, translated 1976), his most significant work, Derrida focuses on the *Confessions* of Jean-Jacques Rousseau to examine the hierarchies of 'nature/culture' and 'speech/writing' which structure Rousseau's writing. Rousseau believed in the nobility of nature and in the notion that *l'enfant sauvage*, or wild child, might have a natural or direct form of knowledge. To Rousseau writing was merely representative, a less direct form of communication than speech. Derrida deconstructs or dismantles the *Confessions* to expose Rousseau's contradictory views about writing, speech and representations. Derrida argues that the effect of the literary is to do with its *multiple* meanings.

An attempt to impose a single meaning on the *Confessions* or any work of literature, the refusal to allow contradictions, Derrida argues, is a particular feature of Western logic. Derrida gives the term 'logocentrism' to Western philosophy's fusing of meaning with words (or logos). Along with its logocentrism Derrida attacks two other features of Western philosophy – its phallocentrism, or belief in unitary male values – and its dualism, or belief in binary oppositions. Derrida developed a critical practice of close reading looking at key metaphors such as 'difference' and 'woman' and the metonymys which writers choose, such as the use of proper names to stand for associated meanings.

According to Derrida, Western belief systems are totalitarian in several ways. First, Western thinking is very attached to the notion of an originating cause or meaning for actions or beliefs. Derrida deconstructs such ideas by reading texts subversively for their problematic hidden thoughts. Second, Derrida argues that originating meanings only derive their value from being placed in opposition to other terms or meanings which act as a negative.

Opposing terms which are of great interest to feminists are, of course, masculine/feminine, rational/intuitive, culture/nature. Feminist critics want to explore and expose the privileging of the masculine as a central or transcendent truth. Third, Derrida claims that 'logos' or logical meaning is always privileged over free association or the alternative play of differences in texts. Texts can have a myriad of signs, which might reveal meanings: the fairy story 'The Fisherman's Wife' which Mrs Ramsay tells her son James in Virginia Woolf's *To the Lighthouse* or the letters written by the Schlegels in E. M. Forster's *Howards End*.

Feminist critics argue that these literary signs can be deconstructed to reveal connections between culture and political beliefs. The fisherman's wife is an over-reaching avaricious woman – a typical patriarchal stereotype. Alternatively she can be 'differentiated', since Woolf might be presenting the wife as a seeker after knowledge and power. Derrida suggests that all language is constituted by *différance*, a term he chose to pun on the French words meaning 'to differ' and 'to defer'. By deconstructing a text not only in terms of what is offered, or as Derrida would say 'differentiated', but also in terms of what the positive term has substituted, that is the absent term or sign, we can supplant particular political beliefs or concepts with terms and concepts which have been devalued – those usually associated with the feminine.

One good example of this process would be to 'differentiate' the representation of women characters in Jean Rhys's *Good Morning Midnight*. In the novel women are frequently represented as sado-masochistic victims of male lovers. These are the socially constructed surface representations of women. Poverty inevitably leads to a form of prostitution which may involve violence or a kind of personal degradation. But there are suppressed representations in the novel indicated by signifiers of time and syntactical ellipses (. . .) where women characters reveal their dreams in internal monologues. Rhys does not impose on her characters what deconstructionists call an 'oppositional hierarchy' where one form of behaviour is right and another wrong. The novel, like the interpretative situation, *has* no single or unified view of women, who may be poetic, intuitive exponents of Caribbean myths as well as people with marginal social status. Destabilizing the preferred meanings and organized belief systems of literature by looking instead at *slippages* of meaning, deconstructive feminists have produced not only very sophisticated readings of canonic texts (for example, Gayatri Spivak's analysis of Wordsworth's poems (1987)), but also proved the value of non-canonic texts (see Jane Tompkins' deconstruction of Harriet Beecher Stowe's popular novel *Uncle Tom's Cabin*, 1985).

This brief summary cannot do justice to Derrida's complex and sophisticated arguments; but it is important to have some understanding of Derrida's ideas in order to know what is involved in a deconstructive reading, and also why deconstruction has proved so attractive to feminist criticism. Derrida makes it clear that metaphors of 'woman' and 'difference' are used in texts phallocentrically, to reinforce a masculine perspective. This is because such metaphors are hierarchically ordered. But deconstruction shows that such hierarchical oppositions are unstable and can be contested. Like feminism, deconstruction focuses on those areas of meaning which traditional literary criticism regards as less significant, such as metaphors of gender, and, like feminism, deconstructive critics work together with the reader in a shared uncovering of the ideological patterns shaping forms. Deconstruction has been accused of ignoring human agency. Yet French feminism, for example, informed by deconstruction, focuses on linguistic constructions precisely *because* language is one mechanism by which women have been 'de-authorized'.

Does this mean therefore that anything goes? If deconstruction argues that texts cannot be read in terms of an author's *intended* meaning and that the idea that there is a single correct meaning in a text is itself a product of logocentric thinking, then how can we ever explain a novel satisfactorily? This question ignores two basic features of a deconstructive analysis. Precisely *because* deconstruction enables us to discover the ways in which a text struggles for meaning (which may include historical struggles over language) a deconstructive analysis can itself be part of the struggle for meaning. Deconstruction tests to the limits any formal system of meaning by highlighting a text's conflicts and ambiguities. As a form of analysis, deconstruction can therefore function very creatively. Deconstruction reveals the *limitations* of formal genres and the canon and thus helps writers as well as readers to broaden literary possibilities.

Not all novels, of course, *are* authoritative accounts of social issues whose superficial messages have to be deconstructed in order to find hidden 'unconscious' meanings. Not all authors exclude difference and eccentricities. Some novelists take delight in deconstructing for themselves the surface meanings of their work. For example, Virginia Woolf often, and self-consciously, subverts the possibility of single or authoritative readings of her fiction. Woolf frequently exposes her narrators as unreliable figures. In *The Waves* Woolf interweaves multiple narrative voices as if to subvert the surface of the novel from within. To adopt a famous Woolfian synonym it is as if fish were constantly breaking the surface of the novel in order to angle the reader. *Orlando* could be called a deconstructive text. The character Orlando changes gender and survives from the Elizabethan period to Woolf's contemporary moment. Ostensibly writing his/her autobiography Orlando frequently stops the *process* of writing in order to digress about the *reality* of writing and literature. Woolf wanted, she claimed in a letter to Vita Sackville-West, to revolutionize biography so that the fictional world would seem more real than real life. Hence Orlando constantly deconstructs the formal genre of autobiography not only by changing gender from male to female, but also in addresses to the reader, all of which displace or deconstruct the logos of fixed gender roles.

As well as scrutinizing a text deconstructively as a *critical exercise* it can also be helpful to look at *creative* texts such as *Orlando* which *themselves* question writing deconstructively. There are several deconstructive novels which explicitly contest the power of Western logic and its concomitant need for narrative causality. In her fiction/autobiography *The Woman Warrior* Maxine Hong Kingston utilizes tropes of contradiction and self-reflexivity to question Western constructions of gender and race. Self-reflective texts often contain interesting and revolutionary ideas about the literary forms which they are busy deconstructing. *The Woman Warrior* is a very good example of a book which deconstructs the connections between referential language and self-identity and specifically attacks the binary opposites of Western thought. Born in America to Chinese immigrant parents, Kingston's own search for self-identity necessarily involved questions about language. The nameless narrator first enters her family history by describing an 'unspoken' family episode – the hidden story of her aunt's postpartum suicide.

The memoir is immediately positioned, then, as a battle between family history and family fiction, between surface and sub-text. Several chapters test the extremes of realist narrative by incorporating amalgams of archetypal Chinese myths, in particular the story of Fa Mu Lan, the mythical woman warrior, who herself contested gender identity by training as a fighter and taking the place of her father in battle. Interweaving these myths with her mother's memories of medical training in China, the memoir moves with the mother to California and becomes a humorous and realist account of American adolescence. These stories come to represent a battle of (binary) opposites between mother and daughter, between speech/writing and between autobiography/myth. The issue of the particular versus the universal is an integrated part of character formation. The mother, Brave Orchid, is both a stereotypical Chinese American, loud of voice as well as an individual, independent and knowledgeable doctor.

Assigning any single characteristic to a Chinese female self is for the narrator fraught with jeopardy. In order to immigrate into America at all, the Chinese were forced to learn long, elaborate 'stories' about their family histories complete with real or fabricated names and places. In addition, Brave Orchid uses stories to ironic ends. The stories she tells both reflect and create a Chinese past and are frequently in contradiction with each other. Only by the end of the memoir does the narrator realize that the narrative issue is not *which* stories are true and which are not, but why lies are lies. Chinese women have a particular deconstructive role, since it is their story-telling which creates culture as a complex and indecisive world. The Chinese translated term for story-telling is 'talk story', and this contradictory juxtaposition is both the subject of *The Woman Warrior* (in the stories of Chinese and American girls' childhoods) and a deconstructive metaphor of the impossibility of one causative past. The very contexts of 'talk story' constantly remind the reader of a potential feminist perspective, with their strong location in mother/daughter socialization. The narrator's father speaks but does not narrate or 'talk story'. Derrida argues that in

Western culture the symbolic law, or the privileging of writing, is a patriarchal system of representation. The female stories subvert a paternal view. By questioning the reality of Western sociosymbolic difference, by calling representatives of American institutions 'meter-reading ghosts' or 'garbage ghosts', in a continuous reworking and retelling of family history, Brave Orchid and her daughter could be said to engage in feminist deconstruction.

Maxine Hong Kingston's linguistic devices, her contradictory stories and open fragmented structure all call into question the *solidity* of discourse. The very organization of *The Woman Warrior* – its suggestive mixture of myth and *faux naive* adolescent narrative – challenge the possibility of mastery, of a progressive developing plot. The organization has a deconstructive design. Such narrative complexity aims to show how the past is constructed, or deconstructed by the present as much as the other way around. The text does not describe a liberal humanist evolution towards a golden future of anti-racism since the text has no 'master' voice. Each female narrator is her own author. Let us take a pair of passages which demonstrate the multilayered quality of *The Woman Warrior*.

> I saw two people made of gold dancing the earth's dances. They turned so perfectly that together they were the axis of the earth's turning. They were light; they were molten, changing gold – Chinese lion dancers, African lion dancers in midstep. I heard high Javanese bells deepen in midring to Indian bells, Hindu Indian, American Indian. Before my eyes, gold bells shredded into gold tassels that fanned into two royal capes that softened into lions' fur. Manes grew tall into feathers that shone – became light rays. Then the dancers danced the future – a machine-future – in clothes I had never seen before. I am watching the centuries pass in moments because suddenly I understand time, which is spinning and fixed like the North Star. And I understand how working and hoeing are dancing; how peasant clothes are golden, as king's clothes are golden; how one of the dancers is always a man and the other a woman.
>
> (From *The Woman Warrior*, Alfred A. Knopf, New York, 1976, p. 27)

The lack of personification in the passage is immediately striking. Perhaps the most obvious way in which 'autobiographical' observations begin is 'I saw', and they customarily end with 'I

understand'. Yet the customary association between the authoritative I and narrative point of view is not sustained. The narrator
merely records. She has no overt project or message and
therefore inserts no authorial qualifications or comments, for
example the traditional 'I saw in wonder' or 'disbelievingly'.
Narrator subjectivity is problematized when viewpoint is uncertain – an effective way of deconstructing a traditional realist
account of subjectivity. Despite the presence of a single observant
narrator – a woman who can both report the beginning of history
and make history into a convincing and detailed set of
observations – she is displaced from the *activity* of history.
Similarly, elsewhere in the memoir, the narrator's search for
meaning – the 'real' history of her family, her own chosen
identity – is constantly frustrated. Vital adjectival or adverbial
qualifiers are missing and therefore the text deconstructs a traditional representation of female subjectivity. It also deconstructs
the traditional form of autobiography, which is usually a non-
contradictory progressive revealing of family/public history.

The other marked feature of the passage is a deconstruction of
gender hierarchy. The two dancers who are creating the world
are not represented hierarchically or sequentially, with one
character superior to another, but are beyond characterization,
beyond social contexts: 'They turned so perfectly'. Hong
Kingston puts gender issues, but not gender *difference*, at the
heart of history here. The dancers carry no conventional gender
associations – they are their own construction. 'They were light;
they were molten'. The reader is given precious little sense of
chronology but a great many fragments of colour and religious
symbols: 'high Javanese bells deepen in midring to Indian bells'.
The passage offers a tantalizing picture of a world beginning to
exist without a morality of black and white oppositions although
'one of the dancers is always a man and the other a woman'.
Cultural symbols and objects – 'bells', 'royal capes', 'golden
tassels' – do not reinforce characterization, as they do in a
traditional realist narrative. Everything may or may not be
significant. Meaning is not created by difference. Like the rest of
the memoir, the passage refuses an in-depth, rounded psychological portrait in favour of a discontinuous chronology. Hong
Kingston juxtaposes wide-apart cultural fragments – 'Javanese',
'Hindu', 'American Indian' – but does not integrate these into a

single generic framework. The plural cultures highlight Hong Kingston's deconstructive rejection of binary and hierarchy. As Derrida argues, masculine and feminine should not be adversary parts but like the dancers, 'the axis of the earth's turning'.

This scene of the dancers is followed by subsequent scenes of pedagogical instruction about transmigration, humorous tableaux, quotations and ironic uses of non-standard English which all corroborate the view that a deconstructive narrative is unresolvable. The narrator knows about myths, fiction and histories and herself continually crosses the binary divide between Chinese and American English. It is only the Western symbolic order which devalues the dynamic quality of the oral tradition. Hong Kingston plays and puns with binary idioms. That is to say she utilizes the non-standard linguistic features of Chinese and stylistic cadences where syntax reproduces the emphatic structure of Chinese. Hong Kingston 'enables' American English to 'release' a story which is conceptually Chinese by transferring vocabulary from one side of the binary divide to the other (as in 'meter-reading ghost').

The memoir ends with the story of another woman warrior captured in battle – Ts'ai Yen – whose beginning belongs to Brave Orchid and whose ending belongs to the narrator.

> Then, out of Ts'ai Yen's tent, which was apart from the others, the barbarians heard a woman's voice singing, as if to her babies, a song so high and clear, it matched the flutes. Ts'ai Yen sang about China and her family there. Her words seemed to be Chinese, but the barbarians understood their sadness and anger. Sometimes they thought they could catch barbarian phrases about forever wandering. Her children did not laugh, but eventually sang along when she left her tent to sit by the winter campfires, ringed by barbarians.
>
> After twelve years among the Southern Hsiung-nu, Ts'ai Yen was ransomed and married to Tung Ssu so that her father would have Han descendants. She brought her songs back from the savage lands, and one of the three that has been passed down to us is 'Eighteen Stanzas for a Barbarian Reed Pipe', a song that Chinese sing to their own instruments. It translated well.
>
> (From *The Woman Warrior*, Alfred A. Knopf, New York, 1976, p. 209)

On a formal level the passage continues to hold in tension myth and family history. The main narrative structure is a foregrounded account of Ts'ai Yen's history which comes to represent the subtextual history of Brave Orchid moving to the 'savage land' of America where she lives among the 'Barbarians'. The narrator 'translates' her mother's story and the memoir is itself in 'eighteen' sections. Both mother and daughter continue to 'talk story' about their sadness and anger. The contradictions between past and present, between myth and reality are held in ironic tension, and the ending is open.

The Woman Warrior shares with critical deconstruction an urge to interrogate the ethnocentric nature of language difference. The legend *represents* differences not resolution. Hong Kingston has spoken of her affinity with the American writers William Carlos Williams and Gertrude Stein because both writers use 'intertexts' or parodic, juxtapositional fragments of literature (Rabinowitz, 1987). The song for a 'Barbarian Reed Pipe' illustrates the special power of women translators but it also illustrates the value of deconstruction. *The Woman Warrior*'s anti-canonic, fragmented representation of gender and cultural differences is a superb model of deconstructive criticism.

SECTION 14: ELIZABETH ROBINS, *THE CONVERT*

Deconstruction, like other criticism, argues that the meaning of any text is not necessarily transparent. Novels have multiple features, genres have multiple themes and these constituent elements may not smoothly dovetail one with another. There will be a network of codes in any text, some of which may not be visible at all to particular readers. The work of all literary critics is to tease out the hidden and less obvious aspects of literary texts in order to enlarge the reading experience. However, deconstruction, unlike other critical techniques, analyzes texts not to reveal to the average reader a coherent, hitherto invisible unity, but to show that unity is always nonexistent. Where Marxist criticism, for example, might give the text's author a subsidiary place among the other determinants of a text (social context or historical moment), the idea that a text *has* some overall, cohesive shape is still intact. And, of course, traditional literary criticism, especially the humanist approach, would argue that the *value* of a work of art, indeed, lies in its cohesive *organic* unity.

Deconstruction, on the other hand, argues that texts are frequently contradictory and that it is the *silences* of texts, those things an author *cannot* say (consciously or unconsciously), which are as important to the meaning of a text as what is transparently *there*. Often these contradictions and silences cluster around representations of women and feminist deconstructionists are particularly interested in the ideological constructs of gender which influence absences and stereotypes in texts. Hence a major focus of deconstructionists is on opposed concepts such as Black/white, woman/man, nature/culture, since often the use of a single one of these terms implies the absence, or inferiority, of the other. In addition the *forms* of representation of a single term – say 'true manhood' – depend on, or are shaped by, a series of negatives, of what manhood *is not*, that is womanhood. Hence texts can offer particular and misogynist constructions of women without even repeating gender stereotypes in any detail. It is these concepts (or binary oppositions) which must be teased out and taken apart (or *deconstructed*) in order for readers to understand that texts are multidimensional processes. Contradictions, absences and slippages do not mean that a text has less *value* (although it might mean that a text is less 'traditionally' pure and organic). Indeed, as deconstructionists demonstrate, literary qualities are *enlarged* by including social theories and gendered positions and therefore have a greater plurality of meanings.

The object of deconstruction is, first, to deconstruct those processes of literary production, like vocabulary choices, which appear to naturalize particular values (true womanhood would be a good example) and, second, to deconstruct the ways in which readers have come to think that certain cultural constructions *are* superior to others, particularly when superiority is often equated with the generic masculine. Patriarchal society, feminist deconstructionists argue, naturalizes values and meanings in culture – that it is natural for women to be heterosexual and want to bear children – and therefore these values will inevitably be represented in, and in turn constructed by, literature, even unwittingly. Since these naturalized characteristics are often quite unrelated to the actual characteristics of women, the deconstruction of literary identities and processes can make an active contribution to the undermining of social stereotypes. The ways in which readers respond to texts may be hugely altered if they see the contradictions, slippages and sheer tensions generated in a text's attempt to hold to particular gender misrepresentations.

These ideas are central to feminist deconstructionists. Gayatri Spivak, Barbara Johnson and Catherine Belsey all point to the ways in which women's representations often throw into relief the hidden patriarchal ideology of a text. In *Critical Practice* (1980) Catherine Belsey draws attention to the contradictory tensions in Arthur Conan Doyle's Sherlock Holmes stories, between a rational world of bourgeois science and the dark and magical women who appear to threaten this world. Written as classic realist texts the stories reveal their own limitations, she argues, by their elusiveness concerning women's identities and natures. The French feminists Julia Kristeva, Luce Irigaray and Hélène Cixous utilize deconstructive techniques to analyze the gendering of language and subjects. These techniques include a focus on binary images. They argue that women are often represented by images of hysteria and darkness while men are represented by fixed terms. Luce Irigaray, in particular, goes on to develop a deconstructive stance, not by arguing that particular readings of culture are wrong but by developing a deconstructive critical *style* herself. Irigaray parodies and pulls apart the opposites shoring up meanings in the work of Freud, Hegel, Plato and other philosophical and psychoanalytical writers. By rejecting oppositions such as myth/realism, empirical/transcendental, materialist/idealist, Irigaray shows how in these oppositions 'woman' is usually the inferior, associated or understood term. Similarly Gayatri Spivak, in her collected essays *In Other Worlds* (1987), examines Virginia Woolf's use of copula, or coupled words, such as picture/womb, lighthouse/phallus in *To The Lighthouse*. Spivak 'deconstructs' these terms to show how Woolf allegorizes systems of power and knowledge as feminine and masculine. Instead of a single system of values an either/or (either female 'good' or masculine 'bad'), *To The Lighthouse* reveals a more complex use of neither/nor evident in the coming together of Mr Ramsay's successful visit to the lighthouse and Lily's successful completion of her picture of Mrs Ramsay.

Through an analysis of Western forms of representation (and in the work of Gayatri Spivak Western *imperial* forms of representation) feminist deconstruction focuses on the rhetoric of gender statements and the ways in which that rhetoric is subverted by texts themselves syntactically or structurally. The major deconstructive technique is to point to juxtapositions in texts between dramatized statements and 'uncomfortable' adjacent vocabulary or descriptions. In this way deconstruction offers readers multiple signifiers to search for: strong adjectival or adverbial *reinforcers* of nouns or verbs which the author has chosen to grant primacy to certain feelings as well as strong personification of particular ideas; and grammatical breaks or semantic rhetorical figures which work against those adjectives or personifications.

The movement from surtext to sub-text, from statements to contradictions, has obvious consequences for critical readings. By focusing not so much on what a text claims to be about (content), and focusing more on syntax as an entity in itself, deconstruction offers readers a whole range of fresh literary marks. A deconstructive reading does not destroy the text's structure of meanings but reads the text against its own stated logic by searching for elements which may be marginal or incomplete. In this sense deconstruction resembles the approach of American New Criticism in the 1950s in which critics pursued the minute detail of texts; but unlike New Criticism deconstruction does not seek for a text's unity.

For these reasons Elizabeth Robins's *The Convert* (1907) may seem an odd text to deconstruct. The novel is a strong, coherent piece of social history rather than a modernist 'masterpiece'. Based on its first shape as a play *Votes for Women!*, the novel gives a documentary account of Vida Levering's 'conversion' to suffragism and suffrage campaigns at the turn of the century. *The Convert* could be described as a work of popular culture, following the commercial success of *Votes for Women!*, and its feminist ideology is matched by Robins's striking sociological and realistic detail of the day-to-day life of suffrage politics. The novel tries to *create* a feminist reader by portraying Vida's conversion as a necessary outcome of the sexual brutality she experienced at the hands of her former lover. No reader can miss the fact that Robins gives an accurate picture of the material and economic background of urban London politics.

To an unusual degree the novel grounds Robins's own political views by rippling the surface of episodes and scenes with far from hidden authorial views, transmitted through the actions and speeches of Vida Levering. *The Convert* does not exist in a social vacuum since Robins firmly identifies the sexual politics of representatives of the ruling class (aristocrats and MPs) as a patriarchal ideology. She also encourages her reader to understand that any women characters who hold anti-suffragist views are holders of a false consciousness. Such women are simply responding to ideas formulated by, and in the interests of, the ruling patriarchal class, and women could (like an apolitical reader) be 'converted'. The topic of suffragism was a lively one for literature, since the suffrage struggle, as Sandra Gilbert and Susan Gubar point out in *No Man's Land* (1988), was one of the most ferocious battles occupying the attention of politicians and thinkers between 1847 and 1920. The battle was also the 'moment' when the 'new woman' entered the public domain and Robins's novel is a harsh satire on the futile rage with which patriarchs greeted women's literary and political achievements.

Of course, any critical account of the impact of politics on literature is in danger of anachronism. In other words, there is always a danger of attributing to past authors and past readers a wider, deeper feminist consciousness than actually existed at the time. But between the 1880s and 1920s the suffrage campaign united writers and activists both in Britain and in America more wholeheartedly than any other political issue before or since. More important, by transforming women's social and political roles, the period transformed women's cultural representations. Trained as an actress in America, Robins struggled to introduce Ibsen to English theatre. She helped to organize the Actresses' Franchise League and Women Writers Suffrage League with the actress/writer Cicely Hamilton, and was a committed activist for the suffrage cause. *The Convert* could easily be read only against this background, that is as a propagandist and polemical text. From this critical perspective, Robins's articles for *Votes for Women*, the Women's Social and Political Union newspaper, her work for the Women's Trade Union League of America as well as her militant speech making would be important – a critical social context shaping the formal structure of the novel.

In this sense *The Convert* would be read as an ideologically charged text which addresses its readers in certain specific ways to win their support for suffrage. But *The Convert* also goes beyond political campaigns into a whole new evaluation of male and of female psychology. The period from the late 1880s to the 1920s witnessed a massive change in attitudes to masculinity and sexuality. In *The Great Scourge and How to End it* (1913) Christabel Pankhurst, Robins's friend, detailed the effects of venereal disease and protested against sexual inequities. In *The Convert* Robins makes a direct connection between personal and public sexual politics and her fictional accounts of the 'sheer physical loathing' of men for feminist women describe a more intense sexualized battle (p.145). For these reasons *The Convert* is open to a deconstructive reading which can rather highlight the text's more varied, more heterogeneous qualities, than simply confirm it as a realistic, didactic argument for suffragism. Deconstruction radically questions the easy assumptions we might make about a writer when we think we know her politics.

After receiving a few preliminary kicks, the subject had fallen, as a football might, plump into the very midst of a group of schoolboys. Its sudden presence there stirred even the sluggish to unwonted feats. Everyone must have his kick at this Suffrage Ball, and manners were for the nonce in abeyance.

In the midst of an obscuring dust of discussion, floated fragments of condemnation: 'Sexless creatures!' 'The Shrieking Sisterhood!' etc., in which the kindest phrase was Lord John's repeated, 'Touched, you know,' as he tapped his forehead – 'not really responsible, poor wretches. Touched.'

'Still, everybody doesn't know that. It must give men a quite horrid idea of women,' said Hermione, delicately.

'No' – Lord Borrodaile spoke with a wise forebearance – 'we don't confound a handful of half-insane females with the whole sex.'

Dick Farnborough was in the middle of a spirited account of that earlier outbreak in the North –

'She was yelling like a Red Indian, and the policeman carried her out scratching and spitting –'

'Ugh!' Hermione exchanged looks of horror with Paul Filey. 'Oh, yes,' said Lady John, with disgust, 'we saw all that in the papers.'

Miss Levering, too, had turned her face away – not as Hermione did, to summon a witness to her detestation, but rather as one avoiding the eyes of the men.

'You see,' said Farnborough, with gusto, 'there's something about women's clothes – *especially* their hats, you know – they – well, they ain't built for battle.'

'They ought to wear deer-stalkers,' was Lady Sophia's contribution to the New Movement.

'It is quite true,' Lady John agreed, 'that a woman in a scrimmage can never be a heroic figure.'

'No, that's just it,' said Farnborough, 'She's just funny, don't you know!'

(From *The Convert*, The Women's Press, London, 1980, p. 58)

The passage clearly depicts connections between representations of women and male sex antagonism. A feminist deconstructive reading would focus on the binary oppositions in the passage which construct men and women as distinct and different. It would examine how registers of discourse ironize the patriarchal characterization of women as deficit and men as superior. Activist women are unnatural creatures, almost apocalyptically 'primitive', 'yelling like a Red Indian, and the policeman carried her out screaming and spitting –'. The male speakers use stereotypical codes of sex difference. Suffragists are 'sexless', 'touched', that is hysterical, 'half-insane', as well as 'just funny'. The dangers of sex role transgression are rendered by the extremity of 'horror', 'disgust'. Borrodaile, Farnborough and Filey assume the full force of patriarchal authority denoted by the masculine metaphors of their discussion whose subject is a 'football, plump into the very midst of a group of schoolboys . . . everyone must have his kick at this Suffrage Ball'.

By depicting suffrage as a sexualized battle between the savage and the 'sane', across the boundary of the 'civilized', Robins poses dramatically the question of women's representation. The passage appears to be characterized less by heterogeneity than by a rather heavy-humoured and laboured ironic explicitness revealed in the adjunctive tropes 'gusto' and 'delicately'. The passage has a number of semantic redundancies. Robins uses the rhetoric of expletives to describe men's insistent and untiring hatred of thinking women. The powerful depictions of masculine fears of invasion 'sudden presence there' wanting to 'carry out' suffrage woman as well as the metaphoric castration of women 'sexless' and 'deer-stalkers' have their roots in a fear of the disruption of patriarchal authority. In this sense the passage is a good example of the hierarchical opposition male/female which is a major focus of feminist deconstructionists. As Derrida argued in *Of Grammatology*, the privileging of particular terms as positive and others as negative cannot be disentangled from a privileging of authority (Derrida, 1976). A feminist deconstructive reading would also want to examine the *limits* of such patriarchal authority. The passage centres the male voice and privileges that voice by the use of masterwords – 'shrieking sisterhood'. Patriarchal authority depends on the repetition of such masterwords which it attempts to use as general and naturalized representations of women.

Feminist deconstructionists argue that such masterwords are catachreses, that is they have no *actual* referents and function awkwardly. Catachreses indicate an improper meaning, a term used to describe something which does not belong. It would be hard to find examples of *actual* shrieking Red Indian-like suffragettes in the real life surroundings of *The Convert*. Deconstructive readings are particularly interested in the use of catachreses because these reveal the *limits* of patriarchal authority. That is to say, the constant use of a vocabulary without any real objects, a technique beautifully ironized here by Robins, reveals the ideological, rather than realistic, construction 'suffrage women'. Deconstructionists are also interested in interpreting a passage's *latent* meaning as well as the *explicit* rhetoric of catachreses. Deconstruction attempts to refuse obvious references in order to find another 'scene' below the superficial scene.

One marked feature of the passage is the way in which each male voice simply confirms, rather than qualifies, another male voice. As Robins satirically suggests, masculine language reveals its own limits. But there is also an absence, a silence in the passage which suggests another or latent meaning. Feminist deconstructionists would focus on what the passage tacitly implies, what it *does* not say as well as on its 'excess' of catachreses. The 'vanishing point' of the passage is the rhetoric of suffragism itself as well as an *explicit* narrator/authorial viewpoint. The *silence* of Vida Levering is as important as the *speeches* of her opponents.

Derrida argues that the tendency to privilege speech is part of the Western tradition of logocentricism. Deconstruction focuses on the gaps between signifiers and signified which are often represented in novels as a gap between speaking and silent characters. In the passage this is present as a mixture of direct speech and indirect speech. An authorial/narrator presence is implied, that is *latent*, in Robins's use of backshifting – the phrases 'manners were for the nonce in abeyance' – as well as in the way in which the male antagonists do not really listen to women and therefore extend no sympathy to women characters.

Feminist deconstructionists would argue that Robins's creation of the male as other, combined with the removal of a suffrage self, or spoken viewpoint, from the centre of attention reveal a deep anxiety about the representation of independent, activist women. As Derrida argues, it is often *outside* the apparent frame of knowledge, in the margins and borders, that politics reveals its vulnerability. The passage can be read deconstructively against its own politics, its own logic by noting the *absence* of Vida because it is the *lack* of a centre that is exactly inside or outside the passage which creates unity. To read deconstructively is to argue that Vida's 'absence' not only acts against the politics of *The Convert* but is also an 'unconscious' absence.

The critical issue is complex but not complicated. Feminist deconstructionists do not search for single critical explanations, or for the origins or causes of particular representations, but set up multiple questions and ways of analyzing texts so that readers can read and *reread*. In this sense a feminist deconstructive criticism can be more open, more accessible, more *comprehensive* than traditional or ideological critiques.

8   Postmodernism

SECTION 15: FAY WELDON, *FEMALE FRIENDS*

For over a decade, postmodernism has been a key term of literary theory as well as one used to describe a whole epoch in the arts, media and architecture. There is a huge critical debate about the meanings and characteristics of postmodernism, but one customary explanation for its *appearance* is the socioeconomic development of late capitalism into consumerism. The 1960s witnessed an expansion of capitalism on a global scale which led to the creation of new forces: superstructural credits, mass consumerism and multimedia spectacles. As Fredric Jameson argues in 'Postmodernism or the cultural logic of late capitalism', whereas modernism played an oppositional and marginal role within Victorian and Edwardian bourgeois society, postmodernism attends to all the new fashions of contemporary consumer society (Jameson, 1984). We have arrived in a *post*-industrial world in which cultural signs are constantly being manipulated and recirculated. A form of criticism which is *post*modernity sums up very well this sense of a momentous break. Postmodernism's loss of faith in single philosophies and in the progressive progress of modernity registers the current mood of much of Western culture. For Jameson, this loss, and its characteristic expressions of pastiche and apocalypticism, are a negative.

Jean-François Lyotard, on the other hand, resists this negativity. Lyotard's *The Postmodern Condition* is regarded as a key text of postmodernism. The essay offers economic and cultural explanations for the new dissolution of boundaries between high and low culture and for the way in which culture apparently can endlessly synthesize and reconstitute art forms (Lyotard, 1984). Lyotard's central claim is that the grand narratives, or theories, of Marxism and humanism have ceased to function because these 'metanarratives' do not help us to understand such endless cultural revisions. Indeed, Lyotard chooses an incredulity to metanarratives, or single, causal explanations of culture, as a key feature of postmodernism. Lyotard replaces metanarratives with an examination of cultural *contexts*: he argues that the meaning of culture derives both from its processes, like canon formation, and from the social contexts in which these processes take place.

Yet it is precisely this loss of faith and *place* which makes postmodernism seem a somewhat elastic term. Like any of the 'isms' which have surfaced post war (and the renewal of feminism is a good example here), postmodernism is a very general term for both a way of thinking *and* a form of critical praxis. In addition all 'isms' are expected to offer some historical thinking as well as ideas for aesthetic practice. In terms of literature what postmodernism tends to celebrate are the processes and *fictionality* of the text. Critics like to focus on how characters work with whatever languages and fragments of culture are available to them and on challenges to the centred and totalizing features of the West.

One way of understanding postmodernism is to see it not so much as a *negative* – an attack on the grand narratives of the West, such as humanism – but as a *positive* proliferation of fictional and critical forms and expressions. All theories of postmodernism, however, agree that whether postmodernism stems from the history of ideas, aesthetics or culture, or is negative or positive, the movement *has* certain dominant features and concerns. One is that postmodernism is self-reflexive; postmodern literature is often an eclectic mixture of literary constructs. While all the arts offer examples of postmodern practice, literature has been a significant source of ideas and themes for postmodernism. This is because contemporary fiction in particular encompasses many postmodern characteristics: a reworking of everyday contemporary culture and a self-awareness about gender and historical constructs.

Feminism's contribution to postmodernism is more problematic; but feminist critical texts about postmodernism are flourishing. Most agree that feminism and postmodernism share some characteristics: a concern to challenge the barriers between the dominant and the marginal as well as to challenge canonic genres. Both have undermined modernism's and capitalism's celebration of great artists and the universalization of white, middle-class masculine values. For both gender is a historical and shifting construct. In other words, art is not a separate and superior realm from life. Literary institutions are as likely to *construct* values as much as they are to *reflect* truths. The first postmodern analysis of gender and aesthetics was Rosalind Krauss's 'The originality of the avant-garde: a postmodernist repetition'. Krauss, much influenced by French theory, was sceptical about art history's celebration of 'originality' and argued that the author or creator was as much a symptom of the work as characters or plot (Krauss, 1981). Because post-modernism, according to Krauss, questions the concept of origin, of masculine individualism, it offers progressive possibilities for women.

Feminist critics share a postmodern perception that any destabilizing of 'ownership' challenges political certainties. If the meaning of literature exists in its relation to other works of literature and culture and not simply as defined by an author's intentions, then literature cannot be understood outside the culture which produces it. Many feminist critics such as Alice Jardine, Meaghan Morris and Rachel Blau Du Plessis, are attracted to postmodernism's textual 'democracy' as well as to its involvement in both high art and low. Not only does post-modernism refuse to give overarching explanations for literary representations but, by mixing high and low, it cuts across the one major boundary affecting women throughout history – the boundary between the domestic zone and the public world of men, so crucial to modernism (with its great street *flâneurs* like Leopold Bloom), and so antagonistic to women, is broken down in postmodernism's involvement in consumer culture.

Following certain key postmodern themes, Alice Jardine argues, in *Gynesis*, that discursive models of 'women' are frequently utilized by male modernist writers to describe marginality in general (Jardine, 1985). The potential essentializing of women is a very worrying feature of modernism. Meaghan Morris's *The Pirate's Fiancée* is another and major feminist postmodern critique. Gender representations, Morris argues, can be understood only in terms of the complex and contradictory ways in which contemporary culture interacts with the arts and produces and institutionalizes cultural languages (Morris, 1988).

Finally, postmodern writing is marked most of all by 'self-reflexivity', by the interweaving of autobiography, theory and literary criticism. Rachel Blau Du Plessis 're-visions' the *process* of literary criticism itself in this postmodern way. Her essay 'For the Etruscans' has an open, fluid surface in a typically postmodern style (Du Plessis, 1980). The essay is ostensibly a piece of literary criticism about Virginia Woolf and the literary tradition, but Blau Du Plessis interweaves this criticism with her own diaries and accounts of Freud as well as with Etruscan history. In this way we come to understand that the literary text/author is a cultural construct. The Etruscans are a grand metaphor for the exclusion of women in this process of construction. The Etruscan script can be *read*, just as women's writing now has some place in the canon, but we know very little still about the language's private and subjective contexts. In these examples postmodern feminist criticism contests traditional literary theory's faith in great works of art.

One of the few common denominators which many contemporary women writers share is a use of postmodern techniques. This is because women writers such as Margaret Atwood, Angela Carter, Alice Walker, Toni Morrison as well as Fay Weldon all self-consciously comment on their own meaning making process as part of the *content* of their fiction. These writers are often self-reflexive, utilizing fragments of contemporary culture and past history and delight in intertextuality and parody. Alice Walker's *The Temple of My Familiar* is a postmodern reworking of Western white history. In the novel Walker allows individual histories to include the possibility of many previous incarnations, both human and animal, as well as drawing on many cultural languages. One good example of the way in which post-modernist writing can 'de-centre' gender constructions is Toni Morrison's *Tar Baby*, which parodies the notion of an essential 'feminine' by giving the male character, Son, a feminine 'fluid' identity. Similarly, feminism is itself drawn from a mixture of contradictory languages – the language of liberal humanism with its underpinning assumption of individual freedom and self-determination for women, as well as the pre-symbolic language of mothering (the semiotic). It could be argued that the female experience in general is close to postmodernism. Women have almost always been marginal to the social order and frequently had to understand 'double' languages – the language of the home and the language of institutions such as schools.

Postmodernism is known most of all for its hostility to totalizing discourses, or master languages. What is significant for literary criticism in all of these ideas is that the literary canon, like literary criticism, would need more complex analysis. To be a woman writer is constantly to confront a canon which only recently admitted women in any numbers. Fay Weldon is a contemporary woman writer whose work constantly questions the certainties of high art and low culture on which the canon depends. Weldon's very style, a use of parodic, contrasting genres and anti-linear plots, is preeminently postmodern. In her work Weldon constantly plays with 'authoritative' narratives and deprives individual histories (particularly those of men) of an authorizing cause and effect. Actions can be caused by magic and witchcraft in some of her novels as much as by individual psychology. Postmodern writers, like Weldon, question any separation of literature from culture.

Fay Weldon has written over seventeen novels as well as television scripts, plays and short stories for magazines. Her work centred on women long before 'women's writing' became a centre of feminist criticism. Typically her novels describe a woman, or group of women, over a long time span and address concerns at the heart of feminism, like domestic violence and economic discrimination against women.

In *Female Friends* Weldon shows her concern for the specific conditions of women's oppression with her choice of topics: childbirth, marriage, domestic violence and poverty. The novel suggests a coincidence between these issues and masculine power and ideologies, particularly the ideology of heterosexual romance. The eponymous three female narrators – Grace, Marjorie and Chloe – tell their stories from both third person and first person perspectives. Their life histories begin as stereotypical women: a man's woman, a career woman and a mother respectively and the novel episodically and systematically challenges these representations. *Female Friends* is postmodern because it problematizes enunciation and subjectivity. Characters are shown to be 'spoken' by the languages which they speak. In this passage Marjorie allows herself to be seduced by Patrick (who misogynistically simply wishes to live rent free in Marjorie's large house) because Marjorie seeks companionship as well as a kind of psychic freedom from the internalized demands of her absent mother.

> Marjorie is fascinated rather than insulted. That the state of the mind and the state of the body might be inter-related is something that comes to her with the shock of truth.
>
> *Marjorie* How do I stop being unhappy and depressed?
> *Patrick* You get me to move in as the lodger.
>
> Patrick smiles at her. How broad, strong, young and healthy he appears, and how simple, sensible, and straightforward his requests. You would think he was a farmer's son and not a criminal's.
>
> *Marjorie* Mother doesn't like strangers in the house.
> *Patrick* Your mother's in South Africa.
>
> True, thinks Marjorie, with a flicker of, what, spite?
>
> *Patrick* And I am not a stranger.
>
> True. Patrick kissed Marjorie once, in 1946, leaning his strong hands against her small ones, pinning her against the trunk of a poplar tree, and who's to say what might not have happened if it had not started to rain, or indeed if it had been a different tree, and not a poplar, with its upstretched, unsheltering branches. How Marjorie had trembled. Patrick Bates, grown man, in His Majesty's uniform, and she nothing but Helen's plain and awkward daughter. 'Never mind,' he'd said then, as if he knew more about her than she did herself, and what can be more erotic than that. 'Never mind.'
>
> (From *Female Friends*, Picador, London, 1975, p. 117)

The passage looks ostensibly like a romance. Patrick leans 'his strong hands against her small ones'. Marjorie 'trembled . . . nothing but Helen's plain and awkward daughter'. This vocabulary draws on a potent feature of romance – the dream that a strong man, asserting his masculine superiority will save and raise the social status of a poorer and usually plainer woman. Romances stress a heroine's naivety – 'Marjorie is fascinated rather than insulted' – and she must not understand the nature of sexual desire 'as if he knew more about her than she did herself'. Typically, a romance heroine's extreme passivity is encouraged by the use of third person point of view, as in this passage. Romance does not overtly question the myth of male superiority or the primacy of heterosexual relationships. Similarly, here Patrick's selfish demands become 'simple, sensible and straightforward' requests.

Yet the passage is characteristically postmodern because it undercuts and challenges all of these assumptions. Patrick's strong masculine authority is parodied 'you would think he was a farmer's son and not a criminal's'. There is a strong authoritative narrating voice 'the state of the mind and the state of the body might be inter-related' which gently and ironically deflates the norms of romance along with its hero. The varied generic tones are registered by a splitting of the narrative between direct discourse '*Marjorie*: Mother doesn't like strangers in the house' without narrator intrusion, and indirect discourse 'true, thinks Marjorie'. The event has a history '1946', 'His Majesty's uniform' but in postmodern fashion undermines the historical reference and coherent subject with witty authorial asides: 'what might not have happened if . . . what can be more erotic than that'. The very design of the passage with its fragmented paragraphs and multigeneric movements (including dramatic couplets, third person narrator, paraphrased character monologue) makes the *process* of writing part of the *content* of the passage. This deliberately skewers any modernist notion of firm aesthetic distinctions. Weldon does not privilege one genre above another, nor does she privilege any single voice. Tenses in the passage are similarly unstable, moving from historical present 'Marjorie is fascinated' to the preterite 'might be inter-related'. The manipulation of perspective and form makes it hard to know exactly *who* is speaking. Certainly *Female Friends* shares postmodernism's challenge to single moral authority.

The condensed duration of time (the exact diachronic or chronological relation between 1946 and 'who's to say what might not have happened' is very unclear) summarizes and abbreviates important psychological characteristics which in more traditional fiction would have some extended description. Events are told rather than shown – a key device of parody. In postmodern fashion the passage makes characters seem very uncertain, in contrast to the firm interior monologues of conventional realism. Weldon exploits, while simultaneously contests, generic fixities particularly the ideological package which comes with romance.

Female Friends is a *feminist* postmodern novel. That is to say, this passage, like the rest of the novel, blurs narrative distinctions very precisely in order to throw into question constructions of women's sexuality and supposed lack of moral authority. Patrick has a certain comic status, a knowing authority, but this is immediately defamiliarized (along with its misogynist notions of heterosexuality) with mannered and intrusive third person commentary. Elsewhere in the novel Weldon wittily foregrounds her views about patriarchy and its effect on women.

> 'Well morality is for the rich, and always was. We women, we beggars, we scrubbers and dusters, we do the best we can for us and ours. We are divided amongst ourselves. We have to be for survival's sake.' (p. 194)

In the earlier passage Weldon makes a skilful use of diegesis mixing dramatic couplets with parodic metanarrative to give her women characters some narrative control even if they cannot yet, in the social script of the novel, control their finances. Marjorie is allowed a measure of self-reflexivity to set against the aggressive solipsism of patriarchy. Weldon's highly stylized satire refuses the script of conventional femininity as she refuses the narrative of conventional realism. Weldon's is a typical postmodern achievement.

SECTION 16: SYLVIA PLATH, *THE BELL JAR*

By its very prefix, postmodernism is not a *new* area of criticism but its ideas advance existing theories of gender, culture and capitalism. Feminist postmodernists agree that gender constructs are culturally variable and unstable. A major aim is to explore a variety of these cultural constructs both at high and low levels. Critics argue that the paradigmatic quality of postmodernism comes from its attack on totalizing explanations (such as Marxism) because these limit literary and social worlds. What this means for postmodern critical *techniques* is an increasing attention to the surface complexity of languages (discourses).

Currently postmodern criticism includes the arts as well as

philosophy and politics, and postmodernists take delight in writing which parodies historical beliefs (humanism), mixes genres (realism/pastiche) as well as paying intimate attention to popular culture. Cultural critics turn to postmodern ideas because these help to explain major changes in twentieth-century culture. The many arguments and critiques include the now classic accounts of Jean-François Lyotard and Fredric Jameson as well as the literary criticism of feminists such as Alice Jardine and others (see Section 15). While many forms of contemporary culture could be called postmodern – from parodic advertisements to architecture – literature's main examples are works which play with representations of the social world as well as with art itself. Postmodernism's special draw is precisely its comprehensiveness, its *post*modernist refusal of tight periodization. In literary history postmodernism first made an appearance in America in the 1950s and 1960s. Critics vigorously celebrated popular culture not just the literary canon and created a powerful sense of changing literary frontiers, as the title of Leslie Fiedler's book *Waiting for the End* suggests (Fiedler, 1965). Along with the celebration of popular culture, postmodernism often parodies discourses. A major preoccupation is to re-examine cultural forms and perspectives ironically and with some playfulness in order to highlight the futility of single critical frameworks. Critics focus frequently on 'self-referent' texts which characteristically subvert realism in favour of fictional/critical intertexts and narrator knowingness.

In case this postmodern attention to self-reflexivity is thought to be too non-political, defenders are quick to point out that subverting from within, challenging by parodying, and exposing the unreality of realism could be called 'political' criticism. Demystifying partriarchal reality is the basic strategy of feminist writers. We see this vividly in the work of Toni Morrison, whose utopian women's household in *Song of Solomon* parodies William Faulkner's *Absalom, Absalom!*.

Sylvia Plath's *The Bell Jar* foregrounds many of these issues very clearly. The novel is generally regarded as a key text of contemporary feminist literature.Both formally and thematically *The Bell Jar* critiques patriarchal institutions through an exploration of sexual politics and psychoanalysis. Beyond this, Plath offers an incisive critique of women's exclusive identification with marriage and motherhood. Most feminist criticism critiques the novel in psychoanalytic terms, for example as a study in cultural self-division. That is to say, the novel is often interpreted as a representation of female schizophrenia, or the divided self, caused by a masculine world. While acknowledging these insights from psychoanalysis, *The Bell Jar* could be equally critiqued in terms of more recent feminist postmodern scholarship.

The Bell Jar describes Esther Greenwood's failed suicide and attempts to come to terms with the world. The narrative is told by herself in first person. Many critics have been tempted to read the novel as Plath's autobiography. What a first person, autobiographical narrative should do is to offer a transparent window on the reality which Esther sees around herself. In a conventional realist autobiography many points of view may be expressed but the narrator's voice will be authoritative and her descriptions will seem to have a strong relationship to the commonly perceived worlds of her readers. Postmodern fiction, on the other hand, is much more self-conscious and critical about the act of self-reflexivity. Plath similarly often seems to flaunt the demands of a realist autobiography, parodying Esther's obsessive attempts to accurately reflect her social world.

The novel is *ostensibly* autobiographical, based as it is on Plath's own experiences as a student at Smith College, Massachusetts. It was completed in 1961, although not published until later, and details Esther's breakdown and 'recovery'. Esther wins a guest editorship on a New York magazine and meets and leaves misogynist Marco. Returning home she rejects her bourgeois all-American medic boyfriend Buddy Willard. Failing to get a place on a short story writing course, and to write a novel, Esther is taken to hospital after her failed suicide attempt by her wealthy benefactress, a best-selling novelist. The novel is also about Esther's complex relationship with her mother and has often been read as a conflict novel about mother–daughter symbiosis. Esther is always aware of *difference*, of her own marginal or border existence which would be thought eccentric by conventional readers. The same respect for difference is at the heart of postmodernism and this concern draws postmodernism in the direction of parody. A sense of transgression, of difference from the norm and the assertion of difference through parody and multigeneric devices informs both postmodernism and Plath's *The Bell Jar*. Esther's depression is *caused* by her confrontation with the literary tradition. Rejected by the writing course, Esther tries to begin her honours dissertation on James Joyce's *Finnegan's Wake* – the high priest of male modernism. Plath puts Joyce's text, and hence the values of modernism into question, when she finds that the book is 'an alphabet soup of letters' (p. 130). Plath ironically 'contaminates' the canon with a vocabulary of popular culture – with a favourite snack of American children. Plath reveals not only contemporary culture's loss of faith in modernist values – the letters are in 'fantastic, untranslatable shapes, like Arabic or Chinese' – but a loss of faith in traditional Joycean critical techniques. 'I counted the letters. There were exactly a hundred of them. I thought this must be important' (p. 130). A great deal of Joycean criticism is indeed devoted to this kind of detailed exegesis. Esther decides 'to junk my thesis' and 'the whole honours programme'.

The implication of Esther's lack of interest in literary models of the past is that modernism's élitism, its obscurity, are parodied and deflated. Esther, the surrogate critic, cannot adopt the aesthetic stance of objective distance from a text. She sees herself not above, but directly subject to, *Finnegan's Wake*'s 'funhouse mirror'. What Plath clearly focuses is Esther's self-reflexive parodic recontextualization of Joyce, taking him away from the ivory walls of academia and reading him ironically from the vulgar suburbs. In this way *The Bell Jar* could be called postmodern. The greatest contribution of postmodernism has been the devaluing of great traditions (whether literary or the arts) like the formalism of much of modernism. Feminist postmodernism deliberately undermines such principles as 'great masters', 'the literary canon', 'universal manhood' in favour of interrelating high with popular culture in terms of gender *effects*.

A persistent motif in *The Bell Jar* is Esther's commentaries on cultural divisions and on cultural productions such as magazines and universities. The problem of reproducing cultural values – the 'right' clothes to wear in New York, the 'right' books to write about at university – are a major part of the content of the novel. Where the locus of meaning shifts to the *problems* of enunciation, rather than the *products* of a belief system like liberal humanism, then writing can be said to be characteristically postmodern. Plath constantly draws attention to cultural differences in her writing, describing the way culture discriminates against average readers by making *Finnegan's Wake* into 'a heavy wooden object falling downstairs, boomp boomp boomp'. The *parodic* juxtaposition of cultural differences is highlighted, throughout *The Bell Jar*, by Plath's extensive use of references. Contemporary cinema, magazines, fashionable clothes and aspects of daily suburban life styles mingle with Joyce, Shakespeare and Dylan Thomas. The negotiation of this multiplicity is a key technique of postmodernism. It could be argued that the first publication of *The Bell Jar* under a pseudonym (Victoria Lucas), a standard publishing technique in popular fiction, reveals Plath's interest in non-canonic literary voices, which would now be considered postmodernist.

That's one of the reasons I never wanted to get married. The last thing I wanted was infinite security and to be the place an arrow shoots off from. I wanted change and excitement and to shoot off in all directions myself, like the coloured arrows from a Fourth of July rocket.

I woke to the sound of rain.

It was pitch dark. After a while I deciphered the faint outlines of an unfamiliar window. Every so often a beam of light appeared out of thin air, traversed the wall like a ghostly, exploratory finger, and slid off into nothing again.

Then I heard the sound of somebody breathing.

At first I thought it was only myself, and that I was lying in the dark in my hotel room after being poisoned. I held my breath, but the breathing kept on.

A green eye glowed on the bed beside me. It was divided into quarters like a compass. I reached out slowly and closed my hand on it. I lifted it up. With it came an arm, heavy as a dead man's, but warm with sleep.

Constantin's watch said three o'clock.

He was lying in his shirt and trousers and stocking feet just as I had left him when I dropped asleep, and as my eyes grew used to the darkness I made out his pale eyelids and his straight nose and his tolerant, shapely mouth, but they seem insubstantial, as if drawn on

fog. For a few minutes I leaned over, studying him. I had never fallen
asleep beside a man before.

(From *The Bell Jar*, Faber and Faber, London, 1963, pp. 87–8)

Why is this passage postmodern? It is postmodern because
popular culture is a major part of Esther's means of experiencing
the world. Esther's rejection of marriage and her sense of self-
identity are imaged by very positive, phallic images of a 'Fourth
of July rocket' which is immediately juxtaposed with the
formulaic writing of detective thrillers. A prototypical 'feminist'
identification with such an exciting positive object uncontami-
nated by the false 'infinite security' of a suburban marriage is
followed immediately by a pastiche of tough guy writing. Plath's
use of contradictory voices and parodic genres is thoroughly
postmodern. Plath both utilizes the types of popular culture
enjoyed by most readers and adopts a contestatory stance to
challenge their representations of gender identity.

Traditionally, the male detective is an isolated man with no
emotional involvement in the crime he investigates. Victims of
crime frequently have no psychological or epistemological
complexity. The reader has to identify only with the detective's
sense of value, his sense of time and of place and, most crucially,
his sense of himself. This is because detectives affirm the
continuity of social institutions by dealing with any opposing
values. In detective fiction action is constant and often violent,
described with an emotional charge which avoids psychic or
social contradictions. All these are characteristics historically
signified as masculinist even if they are not characteristics of
all men.

The traditional detective may be self-critical but he is equally
and notoriously misogynist. Raymond Chandler's Philip Mar-
lowe is a tough 'hard-boiled' emotionally contained individual.
Women characters in hard-boiled thrillers are conspicuous as
erotic triggers of criminality or as victims. The detective hero is
himself often a marginal professional surrounded by continual
threats to his security and status. But sexual identity is a
masculine certainty which, although it is often tested, is
inveterately affirmed. His masculinity stems from self-mastery
and because he is a free agent. One layer of that certainty is his
urbanity. The detective controls and polices the public streets,

dealing with threats to legality, to ethnic purity or to traditional gender roles. All characters, other than the detective, are at a loss how to understand their situations and it is the detective who sees the solution to moral disorder. The question of who sees what is at the heart of detective fiction. Traditionally, the detective is able to see as much as the criminal, and cognitively much more. The detective is traditionally an 'eye' in a fiction about seeing. All these formulae maintain in fictional form a culture's ongoing consensus about the nature of morality. The values endorsed in detective thrillers are those of objectivity, a belief in power and the distancing of human emotions.

Plath makes a complex and extended parody of many of these features. Conventional detective stories depend on a comforting certainty about time. Where clues and events are disordered, the detective replaces them in a neat linear, chronological order for the reader. Here time is anthropomorphized: 'a green eye glowed'. Esther's arbitrary sense of time 'divided into quarters like a compass' is marked by her arbitrary sense of place. She has no 'eye', no single knowing perspective nor is she a strong manipulating narrator. Everything is 'ghostly', 'exploratory' or 'drawn on fog'. In place of a tough assertive hero, we find someone who does not even know the sound of her own 'breath'. Esther is not a traditional moral centre, certain of her own values and her sexual identity. Instead she is literally the product of her surroundings, who had 'never fallen asleep beside a man before'. Plath problematizes the issue of gender roles by means of her parodic choice of a genre indifferent to, or actively hostile to, women. By swerving from a classic detective formula, Plath can address issues of power to 're-vision' that masculine confidence in a moral and gendered value system. As Patricia Waugh and other critics argue, the paradigmatic archetype of postmodern literature is the anti-detective story, the intended purpose of which is to frustrate a reader's attempt to psychoanalyze or identify with a heroine/hero (Waugh, 1992). Plath's parody, her smooth ironic iconoclasm 'with it came an arm, heavy as a dead man's, but warm with sleep', both challenge the prescriptive and masculine moralism of detective writing as well as, paradoxically, by *incorporating* popular culture, suggesting that novels can be more culturally aware, hybrid (postmodern) forms.

The relations between events, language and identity are

always problematized by postmodernism. If we turn to one of the more famous passages in *The Bell Jar* – its wonderful opening – we can see how Plath is able to describe multiple features of contemporary culture.

> It was a queer, sultry summer, the summer they electrocuted the Rosenbergs, and I didn't know what I was doing in New York. I'm stupid about executions. The idea of being electrocuted makes me sick, and that's all there was to read about in the papers – goggle-eyed headlines staring up at me on every street corner and at the fusty, peanut-smelling mouth of every subway. It had nothing to do with me, but I couldn't help wondering what it would be like, being burned alive all along your nerves.
>
> I thought it must be the worst thing in the world.
>
> New York was bad enough. By nine in the morning the fake, country-wet freshness that somehow seeped in overnight evaporated like the tail end of a sweet dream. Mirage-grey at the bottom of their granite canyons, the hot streets wavered in the sun, the car tops sizzled and glittered, and the dry, cindery dust blew into my eyes and down my throat.
>
> I kept hearing about the Rosenbergs over the radio and at the office till I couldn't get them out of my mind. It was like the first time I saw a cadaver. For weeks afterwards, the cadaver's head – or what there was left of it – floated up behind my eggs and bacon at breakfast and behind the face of Buddy Willard, who was responsible for my seeing it in the first place, and pretty soon I felt as though I were carrying that cadaver's head around with me on a string, like some black, noseless balloon stinking of vinegar.
>
> I knew something was wrong with me that summer, because all I could think about was the Rosenbergs and how stupid I'd been to buy all those uncomfortable, expensive clothes, hanging limp as fish in my closet, and how all the little successes I'd totted up so happily at college fizzled to nothing outside the slick marble and plate-glass fronts along Madison Avenue.
>
> I was supposed to be having the time of my life.
>
> (From *The Bell Jar*, Faber and Faber, London, 1963, pp. 1–2)

The tone of the passage is characteristically postmodern by commenting on cultural contradictions 'all I could think about was the Rosenbergs and how stupid I'd been to buy all those uncomfortable, expensive clothes'. The run on is very revealing by equating the Rosenbergs' execution with mistaken consumerism. Plath creates a shockingly distorted and exaggerated social disjunction. The narrator is distanced from what she observes while at the same time fiercely exaggerating aspects of her environment: 'queer, sultry', 'goggle-eyed', 'cadaver's head'. The function of an introductory passage is to introduce. The symbolic prefiguring of the novel's motifs is ambitious. The most explicit features of Plath's prose style, her special vocabulary and syntax are all present: an ironic transmission of the literal to the symbolic (streets at the bottom of their granite canyons); the descriptive parody of political positions (I'm stupid about executions); the exploitation of devices of association ('peanut-smelling mouth' of subways to suggest both a literal smell as well as the narrator's *faux naivety*). All the details which reflect the novel's main themes are scrupulously included: abortion/aborted life ('cadaver'), electric shock treatment and psychotherapy ('being burned alive all along your nerves'), as well as Esther's lack of self-identity ('I didn't know what I was doing').

A basic feature of postmodernism is a parodic citing of intertexts both of the real world and of high art and popular culture in order to contest generic boundaries. What Plath does here is to equate the sexual politics of abortion with the Cold War politics of the Rosenbergs' execution . The third paragraph attests to Plath's elegant ability to manipulate metaphor 'fake, country-wet freshness that somehow seeped in overnight evaporated like the tail end of a sweet dream'. Plath's amazingly precise means of expression is customarily direct: 'it was', 'I thought', 'New York was bad enough' and popular slang – 'goggle-eyed headlines' – figures large. The reader is forced to acknowledge not only the inevitable inability of any single cultural language to account for the world but also the limitations of politics.

The opening shows a postmodern, self-conscious playing on the status of the 'master narrative' of left-wing politics. Ethel and Julius Rosenberg were accused of passing secret material about the atomic bomb to the Russians. Although the evidence against Ethel was vague, both went to the electric chair in 1953, causing a worldwide storm of protest, particularly among the American intelligentsia. To make an ontological link between this event, in itself a *cause célèbre* of American post-war culture, and late adolescent angst is itself to underline (and very daringly) that no discourse 'owns' the truth, as well as to link the private with the public in very gendered terms. In this way Plath links the issue of the Rosenbergs' directly to the issue of writing itself. The particulars of narrative generate a double voice. The extremes of vocabulary; Esther's inability to experience *except* through extremity ('dust blew into my eyes and down my throat'), as well as the collision of discursive opposites (left-wing *cause célèbre* with peanut subways) is powerfully postmodern. The modulation from obvious comparisons ('mirage-grey' street with 'granite canyons') to less obvious ones ('cadavers' with 'balloon stinking of vinegar') generates a tone at once ironic but also hugely powerful.

In *The Bell Jar* issues of fictionality and cultural place are traversed by those of gender. *The Bell Jar* continuously explores the relation between ways of perception, gender and cultural languages while it equally continuously ironizes masculinity. By redefining the conditions of literary value Plath's novel is resolutely postmodern. For feminists, Plath's doubts about self-determination and self-expression could raise problems. Feminism has and *needs* a coherent politics and coherent identities to support that politics. To date postmodernism has been a very masculine enterprise. Postmodernism ignores the crucial differences of ethnicity and homosexuality as historically constituted and in living speakers. Postmodernism's call for language games, for parody is often cut off from *agency*, from social reforms and institutions. Postmodern writing makes no serious consideration of women's subjective and social experiences of mothering, nor of the emancipatory needs of different ethnic groups.

Yet postmodernism does make clear that all accounts are cultural constructions. Similarly, Sylvia Plath's *The Bell Jar* is clearly informed by a sense of what has become known as postmodernism because the novel plays with female identity, and social constructions of femininity as well as politics. I have given a very curt survey of some of the issues of postmodernism and how its techniques can be applied to contemporary fiction. Postmodernism can offer a complex exploration of stylistic motifs ranging from the metahistorical to parodic self-reflexivity. In addition, postmodernism offers a dynamic departure from traditional criticism's monocular attention to the canon. All texts struggle with meaning, particularly with the meaning of 'woman', and postmodernism offers the opportunity of opening up fixed binary terms (man = culture) and moving beyond.

9 Black feminisms

SECTION 17: ZORA NEALE HURSTON, *THEIR EYES WERE WATCHING GOD*

Black feminist criticism argues that both criticism and fiction are narratives which represent race in particular ways. How the critical establishment addresses, or does not address, Black representations and Black literary history is as much a fictional construct as the fictions on which criticism focuses. A crucial concern of many Black feminist critics is to make historical understanding a significant part of critical understanding. Black feminist critics to an unusual extent focus on representations of *memory*. Zora Neale Hurston's *Their Eyes Were Watching God* is a stunning example of how a Black woman survives by means of what Toni Morrison calls 'rememory' – the continual movement to and fro between past and present (Tate, 1983). In the 1970s, Black feminist critics began to expose how traditional criticism systematically wipes Black women out of literary history. The key Black women writers such as the Grimkés, Harriet Jacobs and Zora Neale Hurston were ignored. In addition, because Black experience is frequently represented in oral culture as much as in literary texts, memory plays a pivotal role in crystallizing identities and subjectivities. Even today, this historical thinking only receives adequate attention in the work of Black feminist critics.

Afra-American feminist criticism could be said to begin with the contemporary 'recovery' of Zora Neale Hurston's writing. Two key events in 1974 mark the moment: the publication of a special issue of *Black World* containing essays by June Jordan and

Mary Helen Washington, which carried on its cover a photograph of Zora Neale Hurston, and the reclamation essay by Alice Walker 'In search of our mothers' gardens', published in *Ms* magazine. Until the 1970s Black women were misrepresented or marginalized in most critical texts. Anthologies, even as late as 1979, either did not mention the work of Black women at all, or casually dismissed writers like Zora Neale Hurston from an exclusively masculine literary tradition starting from W. E. B. Du Bois. The writings of Afra-American women are simply absent in Black literary histories written by men. The crucial reclamation work built on Walker's pivotal essay. 'In search of our mothers' gardens' sets out many of the central issues of Black feminist criticism. What is a Black female aesthetic and what is its literary shape? What is the true history of Black women's artistic and literary past? Walker's answer is that an extensive Black cultural heritage exists outside the academy with its own very special interactive epistemology and deep roots in African culture, such as Afra-American 'call and response' or testifying dialogue (Walker, 1984). Walker argues that the oral stories told by female ancestors have equal value with written texts. Many of Walker's key images of women are themselves drawn from African oral cultures and myth; 'womanist' has links with the Yoruba deity Osun. 'In search of our mothers' gardens' answers the question of a Black aesthetic by enlarging definitions of art to include quilt making, baking and gardening. Walker's argument is that Black women are great artists and thinkers, skilled in cultural production, precisely because slavery and a racist post-bellum society denied Blacks access to formal education.

In her essay written directly about the work of Zora Neale Hurston, Walker takes up many of these themes. 'Zora Neale Hurston: a cautionary tale and a partisan view' contests any idea of a detached objective critique by substituting one of 'performance' criticism. Walker tests the value of Hurston's writing not only by comparing Hurston's work with other Black or white writing but also by reading Hurston aloud to Walker's own Southern kin in a form of oral criticism (Walker, 1984). Certainly Hurston herself thought story telling was a crucial part of Black identity. Hurston's accounts of Eatonville, Polk County and Haiti in *Mules and Men* display a variety of dialects and demonstrate the inapplicability of traditional critical categories.

The polyphonic stories, proverbs and hybrid narratives demand textual and thematic attention to the *process* of dialogue as much as to its content (Hurston, 1978). In *'One* child of one's own' Walker describes her own tussles with white and Black feminist criticism (Walker, 1984). The essay is an autobiographical account of Walker's entry into an identity as a professor, mother and writer and describes issues of integrity and creative freedom in Black culture and the frequent lack of these features in academic curriculae. The essay models Black cultural diversity with its own attention to dialect, puns and Black humour.

The same kind of self-conscious attention to the cultural contexts in which criticism operates can be found in Barbara Smith's pioneering essay *Toward a Black Feminist Criticism* (1977). In this much anthologized piece Smith created a Black aesthetic. Smith *named* Black feminist criticism and described its tasks. First, criticism must challenge the centred and centring male Western tradition with readings of difference, as Smith demonstrates so effectively by reading Toni Morrison's *Sula* as a lesbian novel. It could be argued that before Smith's essay appeared, Black lesbian criticism did not exist. Second, Smith defined a Black feminist standpoint. This is one which builds on a notion of autonomy but not on separatism. Smith went on in later essays to create the term 'simultaneity of discourse' to define Black feminist criticism. This is a way of reading which focuses on the interrelation of discourses – of race, gender and sexuality (Smith, 1983).

The issue of audience focuses these concerns. Black feminist writing, both critical *and* creative asks: who do we speak to – Black women, white women? From what sources do we construct our language? Do we interpret or do we create? The specific pragmatics of a largely white-owned publishing industry insist that Black writers consider issues of translation and double languages. In *Mules and Men* Zora Neale Hurston both invokes Black slang and dialect yet places this inside a text of academic ethnography. Hurston's rich mixture of Southern folk allegories and contemporary political analysis was truncated by her white editors. The issue of audience becomes a discursive issue in any textualized questioning of point of view, the role of the narrator and vocabulary choices.

Their Eyes Were Watching God takes up these issues of enunciation and identity. There are a number of reasons why

Hurston's work is of interest to feminist critics. First, and most obviously, Hurston is seen as the 'mother' of twentieth-century Black women's writing. Between 1934 and 1948 Hurston wrote four novels, two books of folklore and an autobiography. Second, her texts reflect those tensions of audience and self involved in tensions of race, sex and class. Third, Hurston's literary career throws up questions about traditions and the academy since she was an active participant in the academic world, training with the anthropologist Boas, and studying at Howard University *and* a creative writer in the Harlem Renaissance and the South.

Together with Langston Hughes, Hurston founded the literary journal *Fire!*, which became a major vehicle of Black creative writing in the 1920s. Yet Hurston's term 'niggerati' for the Black 'literati' intelligentsia of that period reveals her sense of the ambiguous status of Black literature. So that while the writers Langston Hughes, W. E. B. Du Bois and Alain Locke were creating in effect a 'masculine' Negro canon, Hurston returned to her Southern roots to search out a very different culture of Black rituals, songs and proverbs (Humm, 1991).

Their Eyes Were Watching God challenges realism and deals directly with the empowerment of women. Janie, the heroine, demonstrates how the gaining of a Black female identity and independence comes from relinquishing masculine frameworks and from learning to combine private and public languages. *Their Eyes Were Watching God* begins in the home of Janie's grandmother and opens with the grandmother's story, which is the story of all Southern slaves. What Janie learns in the novel is to move beyond the limited gender roles her grandmother chooses for Janie (arranged marriage) as well as to refuse Black male constructions of appropriate feminine behaviour. Janie's childhood name of 'Alphabet' is replaced in turn by the names of her three successive husbands – Killicks, Starks and Woods. Naming is an important strategy. Janie's marriage to the farmer Killicks, as his name implies, almost 'kills' her youthful spontaneity. Starks, in Eatonville 'starkely', limits Janie's role to that of a wifely symbol of his bourgeois storekeeping success. When 'Tea Cake' Woods enters her life, Janie escapes with him into an irresponsible Afro-American itinerant existence. We gradually become aware of the way that the gender conventions of Black masculinity work together with white bourgeois society. Hurston describes Janie's story through metaphors of domesticity and clothing. Like Black feminist critics, Hurston draws on familial objects to challenge masculinity. Throwing away her apron, Janie elopes from Killicks with Starks, finding only that marriage to Starks brings with it a head-rag, symbolizing both women's physical and social constraints. In widowhood, after 'murdering' Tea-Cake, Janie triumphantly celebrates independence with the overalls she wears to return to Eatonville.

One of the great messages in *Their Eyes Were Watching God* centres on Janie's need to subvert patriarchal time with 'women's time', with a more complex historical and collective model of memory and subjectivity. As if agreeing with a Black feminist interest in dialogue, the novel is told from both third person and first person and tenses shift with point of view. The dispersed narrative voice calls attention to issues of audience and gendered 'rememory'. As Janie predicts in the opening of the novel 'Now, women forget all those things they don't want to remember, and remember everything they don't want to forget. The dream is the truth. Then they act and do things accordingly' (from *Their Eyes Were Watching God*, Virago, London, 1986, p. 9).

This is a view of memory and identity *outside* chronology. What distinguishes Black women's experience here is a sense of multiple voices – of dialogue with the other self which gradually develops in the space of the novel to dialogue with a wide range of others (judge and jurors at Janie's trial as well as Pheoby her friend). Hurston describes the moments in the lives of women characters as *performances* taking place on verandas outside the daily world of work and domesticity. It is as if the 'work' of dialogue, of story telling, replaces the work of rural production.

One good example of Hurston's attention to dialogue and performance is the episode of Janie's trial for Tea Cake's murder. Describing the moment of death, Janie mediates between the white world of the jurors and her own 'rememories'. Janie uses her acquired skills as a story-teller to act as a translator. Janie's 'bilingualism' and gift for language would be a key focus for Black feminist criticism. It ought to be remembered that throughout Hurston's lifetime most Blacks did not have access to higher education and that segregation severely restricted Black economic and educational progress, making 'translation' an important feature of Black writing.

They all leaned over to listen while she talked. First thing she had
to remember was she was not at home. She was in the courthouse
fighting something and it wasn't death. It was worse than that. It was
lying thoughts. She had to go way back to let them know how she
and Tea Cake had been with one another so they could see she could
never shoot Tea Cake out of malice.

She tried to make them see how terrible it was that things were
fixed so that Tea Cake couldn't come back to himself until he had got
rid of that mad dog that was in him and he couldn't get rid of the dog
and live. He had to die to get rid of the dog. But she hadn't wanted
to kill him. A man is up against a hard game when he must die to
beat it. She made them see how she couldn't ever want to be rid of
him. She didn't plead to anybody. She just sat there and told and
when she was through she hushed. She had been through for some
time before the judge and the lawyer and the rest seemed to know it.
But she sat on in that trial chair until the lawyer told her she could
come down.

(From *Their Eyes Were Watching God*, Virago, London, 1986, p. 278)

Hurston at first appears to tell Janie's story only in third person.
But quickly this realist viewpoint is interrupted. The scene shows
Janie refusing a conventional authoritative stance. She refuses to
use normal courtroom speech, preferring proverbs – 'A man is
up against a hard game when he must die to beat it' – as well as
holding to Black syntactical and grammatical forms 'Tea Cake
couldn't come back to himself until he had got rid of that mad
dog'. Janie's reported narrative carries a Black frame of reference
and way of thinking. Not only does she adopt Southern Black
speech habits but expresses a more complex sense of time 'she
had to go way back' as well as memory, 'First thing she had to
remember was she was not at home'. In this scene Janie's
memory is the path to knowledge. In a segregated world,
memory and the alternative personal identity which this
validates act as a kind of resistance. Janie gains a psychic (after
she 'remembers'), cultural ('mad dog') and linguistic presence
through her act of re-entering her memory and unfolding her
past in a different time and space: 'She had been through for
some time before the judge and the lawyer and the rest seemed
to know it.' Janie chooses to leave the safety of the domestic
'home' but reveals at once her ability to speak to a mixed audience

– 'They all leaned over to listen'. Janie's testimonial autobiography becomes publicly credible. The episode is a mixture of speech registers: on the one hand a densely metaphorical idiom of mad dogs, on the other hand the grammatically correct standard English 'it was worse than that'. Janie has to leave behind the internalized limitations of traditional narrative 'lying thoughts'; but she never subjugates Black expression to an Other public self.

The passage highlights Black feminist issues of race and gender difference. Janie creates a testament *composed* of racial differences and gives difference an expanded public presence. Janie speaks of her own gender difference from Tea Cake, who cannot survive his mad dog. The episode specifically demonstrates the importance of performance by showing how the meanings of various discourses can be employed. By overlaying one language on to another, Janie's linguistic facility allows her to control reality. Janie's strategy of code shifting subverts traditional courtroom English and appropriates the public space. Janie's code switching enables her to convince her listeners of the 'truth' of her memory and culture. Such language use embodies difference. As Alice Walker suggests, Hurston translates the power of oral culture, its textures and vocabulary, into a new cultural space (Walker, 1984).

The passage focuses issues of public and private speaking which confront Black women daily in a white-dominated society. The representation of two quite distinct ways of speaking and therefore of racial and cultural identities, *and* Janie's ability to code switch between these, demonstrate the function of translation in a racially divisive world. Janie manages to dismantle the jurors' assumptions about Black female identity and walks free, largely because her account reveals a very complex dynamic of dominant and subordinate thinking.

What distinguishes Black feminist criticism and creative writing is this attention to multiple languages and to the relation between power and language. The ability to speak in a plurality of voices gives Black women power and identity. Barbara Christian calls this 'creative dialogue', citing the work of the Black lesbian writer Audre Lorde as a marked example of the strength of self/other dialogues (Christian, 1986). Black women's narratives constantly engage in dialogue in order to deconstruct binary oppositions such as white subject/Black Other. Transcultural dialogues are a feature of Black feminist writing. This feature is much more than a simple linguistic game, for it marks the nature of Black feminist thought.

The narrative of *Their Eyes Were Watching God* cannot *begin* until Janie has a woman listen to her story.

> 'Looka heah, Pheoby, is Sam waitin' on you for his supper?'
>
> 'It's all ready and waitin'. If he ain't got sense enough to eat it, dat's his hard luck.'
>
> 'Well then, we can set right where we is and talk. Ah got the house all opened up to let dis breeze get a little catchin'.
>
> 'Pheoby, we been kissin'-friends for twenty years, so Ah depend on you for a good thought. And Ah'm talking to you from dat standpoint.'
>
> Time makes everything old so the kissing, young darkness became a monstropolous old thing while Janie talked.
>
> (From *Their Eyes Were Watching God*, Virago, London, 1986, p. 19)

What is at once characteristic about this piece, and what would interest Black feminist criticism, is its dialogic nature. Janie's story does not describe a static past series of events but will vary depending on Pheoby's response 'Ah depend on you for a good thought'. It is the cultural context of the telling, the performance and situation which will shape its reality. *Their Eyes Were Watching God* grows and is defined by dialogue, by code switching, by racial and gender difference. Like Black feminist criticism the novel celebrates Black culture.

SECTION 18: ELLEN KUZWAYO, *CALL ME WOMAN*

Black feminist criticism is not one single area because this would overlook cultural differences between nationalisms, between Black minority and Black majority criticisms and between languages. Yet, as an international cultural phenomenon, one common denominator in Black feminism is an opposition to Eurocentric, 'universal' critical models. Black feminists look outwards from a text at history and politics. While Black feminist criticism, like any other criticism, offers close readings of texts, these often involve critics in describing how criticism opens up new cultural possibilities. By addressing literatures with very different histories and cultures, Black feminist criticism problematizes any essentialist construction of 'Black women'. In this sense 'Black' and 'feminism' are coincident terms. In addition, Black feminist critics are interested in texts which themselves are 'outside' the canon. Black feminist critics read politically, neither foregrounding political ideas nor critical tools but making the case for linking literature and political change.

This is of crucial significance in South Africa, where women who struggled to liberate themselves from apartheid, like Ellen Kuzwayo, have very different political interests from white Western feminists. Whereas Western feminists first identified the family as a patriarchal institution, women in South Africa point to the *destruction* of Black families by apartheid. South African feminists argue that Black women suffer national, class/tribal *and* gender oppressions whose representations necessitate more complex cultural critiques. There are further contradictions for any critical recognition of African writing since economic deprivation, self-censorship as well as the censorship of oral and indigenous folk cultures, deprive Black writers of the security of their own history. What Elizabeth Spelman calls ampersand, or additive, criticism ignores these interrelations of oppression (Spelman, 1988). Black feminist critics insist that gender representations cannot be separated from other features of culture. Similarly there is no single 'sisterhood' of Black feminists, although many share particular critical strategies and political principles.

The question 'What *is* literature?' is at the heart of this enterprise. Black literature interfaces with traditional oral stories, as well as with political writing and criticism. As a result, Black feminist criticism is fundamentally opposed to examining *only* traditional genres. Ellen Kuzwayo, among other writers, incorporates and adapts a variety of genres (sociology, letters, poems, life history) into her work, making us question existing critical criteria and evaluative judgements. Nor is the issue a simple one of replacing traditional literary texts (the canon) with Kuzwayo's life history or any other text. Rather, Black feminist criticism aims to offer new reading practices based on new assumptions about writing. Audre Lorde's 'The master's tools will never dismantle the master's house' takes up this theme. Exploring issues of critical languages and institutions, Lorde argues that only *non*-patriarchal, *non*-racist criticism can empower women, not traditional tools (Lorde, 1984). In her essay 'Uses of the erotic: the erotic as power' Lorde redefines the function of erotic literature, suggesting it should be a source of change and creativity (Lorde, 1984). What Lorde produces is an alternative psycho/literary critique which eradicates the Black victim model of white sociologists.

Black feminist criticism incorporates several areas. First there is reclamation criticism, which widens traditional literary history to include Black women writers. A good example here is Mary Helen Washington's *Invented Lives*, which interweaves excerpts from Black women's writings with critical analyses (Washington, 1987). Washington brings to attention writers hitherto unavailable in print and she gives a clear account of Black writing strategies and the misassumptions of traditional literary criticism.

A secondary task is to eradicate stereotypes of Black femininity through attention to cultural history, for example Alice Walker's collection of essays *In Search of our Mothers' Gardens*. Walker sought out Black women's autobiographies revealing these to be rich and crucial texts and enlarged the field of Black literature (Walker, 1984). A third concern is to address the question of audience and relations between Black writers and readers Black and white. For example, Barbara Smith's *Home Girls*, an edited collection of essays, defines a Black feminist standpoint as one which is built on autonomy but not on separatism (Smith, 1983).

Finally, the relationship between Black women's writing and postmodernism and other theories is now under debate: see Barbara Christian's critique of the white academy in 'The race for theory'. Christian attacks white academic criticism for ignoring modes such as 'call and response' which have a long history in Black culture (Christian, 1989). She argues that Black feminist cultural/materialist readings are grounded in the concerns of the Black community and in a continuing dialogue with sexual politics. In her essays Christian takes up these issues by discover-ing positive images of mothering in Black slave narratives, utilizing terms such as 'rememory' to describe the force of reconstruction and widening 'literature' to include letters and diaries (Christian, 1980). In this way Black feminist criticism finds a strength in diversity. African feminist criticism is particularly diverse. It ranges from work on archetypes, on historic diasporal links between women of African descent and celebrates a heritage dating from prehistory. In *Ngambika* Carole Boyce Davies and Anne Adams Graves argue that Black women's literary representations are shaped as much by patriarchy, landscape and very different cultures and kinships as by the literary institution (Davies and Graves, 1986).

The focus of their research is on African and Caribbean women's writing, including oral literature, as well as on feminist aesthetics and children's literature. *Ngambika* illustrates the range of contemporary African feminist concerns including Ibo traditions and studies of Gikuyu writing. The collection's inclusion of oral literature helps to contest the conventional genres of traditional criticism and illustrates the strength and diversity of dialogue. What precisely, though, is being challenged by Black feminist critics? The first target is the idea that literary texts have single, coherent identities. Much African writing, for instance, describes collective story telling and communities with common traditions. Barbara Christian calls this creative dialogue, which is writing and speaking from more complex historical and cultural positions (Christian, 1980). For many Black feminist critics that 'creative dialogue' depends on an Afracentric world view (see Section 20). Alice Walker uses the term 'womanist' not 'feminist' to celebrate Afracentrism (Walker, 1984). The important moral and symbolic representations of community in writing are also the result of Afracentric thinking. Communal figures in Kuzwayo's work signify not her own individual history and politics but stand for a shared historical memory of co-operation and mutuality. Black feminist criticism looks for symbols and objects in narratives which are the repertoire of the community not those from psychobiography. Symbols are frequently chosen which reconcile individual characters with communities; so Kuzwayo often describes everyday objects such as blankets or pots which become important cultural emblems. The repetitive use of these symbols combines to give a sense of a strong collective history.

The most radical challenge, however, comes to the idea that texts should have a detached or objective narrator/interpreter. Interpreters, like Kuzwayo, are not objective but experience the impossibility of reconciling different discourses (urban/rural;

men/women). The role of Kuzwayo as interpreter is complex. She has to praise the value of progressive education and English while functioning *through* the text to preserve community history. All these concerns suggest that Black feminist criticism should offer a multiplicity of responses, both cultural and literary to what is a historical constant: the need for Black women to move beyond colonial systems, whether these are economic or critical.

Another consequence of this far-reaching Black feminist inquiry into the very nature of historical and individual representations is a frequent challenge to the idea that texts have authors with singular and unique perspectives. The narrating subject is no longer assumed to be writing her own life as a coherent, *personal* entity but as a formulation of a collective *Zeitgeist* – a double consciousness of personal and collective meanings. As Black feminism suggests, linked to this contesting of a unified individuality is a more general awareness that individual expression must be grounded in history. The recovery of personal memories can therefore be a mechanism for subverting a racist white history. Yet far from simply recovering the past as an intact 'object', critics understand that literary representations are continually positioned by, and in dialogue with, communal narratives of differing kinds.

A major focus of Black feminist criticism is therefore on *place*. In attempting to create local and regional cultures in the face of colonial displacement a widely shared concern is with images and themes of place, of landscape, or of domestic interiors. In this sort of context, writing becomes a kind of political work. Black feminist texts organize writing *and reading* resistances to colonial dominations and misrepresentations. Literature and popular culture could be discursive instruments of future power. The particular use of English by multilingual writers like Kuzwayo creates its own special problems. Many writers talk of their struggles with the Eurocentric concepts structuring English language. The most obvious complexity which feminist criticism has to address is the huge number of languages spoke by African writers from Anglophone to Francophone. In addition, many African writers utilize several genres. This is visible in the degree to which creative writing blurs with the political/historical as in *Call Me Woman*, which is scored through with social science 'reports' set into a personal history of unbridled and violent political events. Black feminist criticism therefore has to be constantly self-conscious about the status of language. All of these wide-ranging critiques help to contest the categories and conventions of traditional criticism, while developing an Afracentric feminist aesthetic. The task is urgent because Afracentric autobiographies in particular raise new questions about representations of self and life. Traditional Western standards of autobiography based on notions of a detached, retrospective life history are not appropriate to the burgeoning field of Afracentric writing. Subsequently, Black feminist critics are actively engaged in rethinking the tools and methods of literary criticism itself as well as reshaping the canon.

South Africa was not (until May 1994) a democratic independent state. All forms of communication, including literature, were state controlled. The imposition of two languages, English and Afrikaans, as well as censorship controls over journals and creative writing contribute to silence writers. One consequence is that oppositional writing, autobiography as well as novels or drama, is necessarily subversive. All such writing has to *politically* engage in subverting and appropriating available forms of expression whether these are everyday or institutional (like the literary academy). Ellen Kuzwayo, who trained as a teacher and social worker, is a community activist, former president of the Black Consumer Union and the Maggie Magaba Trust, who has made films (*Awake from Mourning* and *Tsiamelo, a Place of Goodness*) as well as writing her autobiography *Call Me Woman*. The book is a fine example of subversive writing as well as being a celebration of the heroic struggle of women in South Africa. Kuzwayo draws a huge historical panorama from prehistorical communities to the nineteenth and twentieth centuries as well as the history of African tribes and her family. While situating herself as an urban observer, Kuzwayo provides a penetrating examination of the cultural and economic conditions of apartheid. Kuzwayo's personal experience of domestic violence and police harassment have to be understood in a social context. Kuzwayo presents herself emerging from her world to tell her story as a public, collective account rather than a private document. Autobiography therefore has to play multiple roles rather than the conventional Western role of superior instruction. Paradoxically, as Kuzwayo grows more confident politically and more active in her community, the autobiography becomes more *personal*, more self-reflexive. Afracentric autobiography is a special form of writing within which the impulse to affirm one's own Black identity inevitably follows a historical or communal identity. In this sense autobiography resembles a testimonial. *Testimonios* grew as a new form of narrative in Latin America in the 1960s, and like that genre *Call Me Woman* communicates issues of poverty, imprisonment and survival which very much shape the narrative style. *Call Me Woman* makes women's oppression a discursive as well as a political issue by continually reflecting on Kuzwayo's status as a writer. Kuzwayo counters some of these oppressions by remembering episodes from childhood which are not synchronic with police brutality. Simultaneously she presents herself as a historical witness passing on the cultures and histories of Black South Africans. How, then, is Kuzwayo an autobiographical 'I'? How would Black feminist criticism describe Kuzwayo's autobiographical techniques?

On their heads they wore a frill of reeds, beautifully made, covering their faces and tied around their heads. Their faces, arms and legs were smeared with whiteish clay or soil called *phepa*. Around their loins they wore seemingly pleated skirts made of a type of grass. Their trunks were bare, displaying their beautiful, round, small breasts which were regarded as a symbol of virginity.

As a child from a Christian home, I was strictly forbidden to associate in any way with the girls who had accepted *Lebollo* as part of their lives. This restriction from my family did not dampen my burning desire and curiosity about what transpired at the school. I secretly and carefully planned a visit to see for myself the beautiful performance by *bale* so often described to us by *Lebollo* graduates or villagers who had watched their performance. I managed to watch them dance for about 15 to 20 minutes. It could have been more, because I stood there spell-bound by the harmony of the music, so common but striking in this country among blacks, their rhythm and graceful poise, their agile movement, all this accompanied by the joy and perpetual smile on each face. Perhaps in the final analysis the less sophisticated people with little or no education, who make no fuss about their religious affiliations, derive far more satisfaction and happiness out of their supposed primitive simple life. Their lives have far fewer 'don't' than the lives of professed Christians. They are, by and large, more open and they readily accept other people.

At the end of that beautiful performance, I quickly trotted home, an innocent, respectable little girl, keeping to myself this rare enjoyable experience, for fear of remonstration by my parents.

(From *Call Me Woman*, The Women's Press, London, 1985, p. 72)

The passage describes differences and offers a compelling metaphor of Kuzwayo's moving and difficult negotiation of those differences in her description of the *Lebollo*, or circumcision, ceremony. There is a permanent struggle with translation in the text of which this passage is a good example. Kuzwayo 'gazes' at the girls who are from a different tribe (Basotho), objectifying their difference 'so common but striking in this country among blacks'. She adopts the characteristic narrative tone of a colonial ethnographer 'their lives have far fewer "don'ts" than the lives of professed Christians'. Kuzwayo is 'an innocent, respectable little girl'. The 'other' girls are alien but not alarming. Their representation acts as a simile for absences in Black Christian upbringing. The Basotho are a curious, attractive spectacle moving before Kuzwayo's knowing gaze. They are essentially natural, 'less sophisticated' with 'perpetual smiles'. These images draw on several traditional narrative conventions of the primitive and the exotic, of a people whose 'little or no education' and physical ease throw into question Kuzwayo's need for personal striving and social advancement. The subordination of the girls' individuality to the unity of the dance is in strong contrast to Kuzwayo's, as a narrator fearful of 'remonstration by my parents'. In this register the passage seems a conventional conservative narrative, making a traditional distinction between a moral observing subject and an amoral savage.

This is the predicament of a writer who expresses herself in the 'dominant' language of Western publishing. The 'purpose' of the passage remains outside these rhetorical signifiers. There is also the presence of a gendered *attraction* to folkloric custom which subverts the apparent message of the passage. The intersection of these discourses (folkloric, Western ethnographer) creates ambivalence. There are a large number of qualifiers in the section of the passage which describe observation, but none in the section describing the girls' beauty: 'it could have been', 'perhaps', 'supposed primitive', 'by and large'. The girls' beauty and craft ability – 'reeds beautifully made' – create incoherences in any construction of a Western perspective. The admiration Kuzwayo experiences makes her 'spell-bound' wanting to keep 'to myself this rare enjoyable experience'.

It is the problematic status of the painted (*phepa*) and different female body 'beautiful, round, small breasts' which destabilizes Kuzwayo's dominant gaze. Kuzwayo's reconstruction of her memories reveals a love for an 'Other' which transforms her view of present oppressions and is an antidote to apartheid. Kuzwayo depicts a world of mystery but a world also of joy and beauty where individual identity stems from common rituals. Kuzwayo gives a central place to the Black female body and through this an understanding that Black women can be part of a non-oppressive world. In Black feminist criticism the body is a emblem of cultural resistance, as in Alice Walker's descriptions of the colour of Black vaginas in '*One* child of one's own'. Kuzwayo also identifies the female body with a religious or spiritual ceremony. Spiritual rituals provide a metaphoric emblem of an alternative moral world beyond the then current political order of South Africa and its Black stereotypes. The girls dance to, and for, their community, but Kuzwayo's account reveals a tension between self-portrayal and community experience. In this Kuzwayo confronts the problem of readership, a further and major area of concern in Black feminist criticism. Kuzwayo is not writing primarily for Black women but for white readers and this, too, affects her sense of how to present Black women, as well as her sense of the relation between gender and political representations.

The diversity of multiple voices here is a strength, not a fault, in Kuzwayo's text. Kuzwayo continually makes a self-reflexive commentary and engages with the multiple female selves of South Africa. Consequently *Call Me Woman* is not a private, personal account of struggle and a journey to success but a charting of more multiple and 'banned' Black identities. Kuzwayo has placed her own experience directly *inside* a Black religious experience which she does not personally undergo. Explicit aspects of African tribal practices attest to an alternative African reality. Kuzwayo's attention to culture is a good model of Black feminism's interest in reclamation writing and illustrates the function of Black writing in passing on stories about a symbolic past. The problem with Kuzwayo's honest portrayal is that this sometimes leads to stilted and somewhat cliché expressions: 'I quickly trotted home'. Yet the text constantly draws attention both to cultural differences between Black Africans lexically *and* places cultural distinctiveness at the heart of its content.

Another passage illustrates Kuzwayo's Black feminist techniques.

> I recall particularly one lady named Motena. She was a lovely person, warm and very orderly in her life as a mother and housewife. Her house was the only shebeen I ever ventured to enter. Except for a few benches for her customers and other guests, there was no other furniture. At the far end of the room was a pile of blankets, which clearly marked the corner used as the bedroom. The blankets were clean and fresh, because they were washed every week, a habit very common among the Basotho people. A piece of string fastened across the corner near the pile of blankets served as a wardrobe, where skirts, trousers and other clothing were hung. At the other end of the room were all the household utensils, which included a number of enamel plates and mugs, a few cups and saucers, a number of shiny spoons and a few different sizes of three-legged pots, some used for cooking meals, others for boiling the water used for brewing. There were also a number of empty shiny jam tins for serving beer to customers or guests. There were two or three well-built *stoeps* inside the house, like steps, measuring about one by one-and-a-half yards in size. These served as cupboards or dressers for the kitchen utensils. The air in this one-roomed shack was very fresh, from constantly smearing the smoothly-prepared floor with fresh cow dung. Within the constraints of that one-roomed house, in a yard congested with similar houses, spilling on to an untarred street which also carried all the dirty water from all the homes, I have every reason to credit Mama Motena (Mother Motena – a term of respect for addressing adults in the black community) with great qualities of cleanliness and tidiness. She showed great ability in maintaining the clearly defined boundaries of various room services in that one room. Many black women in congested urban accommodation share that quality.
> (From *Call Me Woman*, The Women's Press, London, 1985, pp. 27–8)

As Black feminists suggest, the personal is always bound up with the political; domestic and sensual descriptions often have metaphoric importance. Here Kuzwayo describes the objects 'the blanket' and 'three-legged pot' to which she constantly returns throughout the autobiography at moments of personal and social transition in her life. Just before leaving her dying mother Kuzwayo lovingly shares her blanket and, later, running from an abusive husband Kuzwayo has only a blanket for cover. Metaphors organize the narrator's objective experience in the passage allowing her to present Mother Motena as clean, tidy and respectable; but they also offer the reader a structured passage into Kuzwayo's more private and emotional experiences. The blanket metaphor matches Barbara Christian's call for positive images, for rememory and becomes a heterogeneous signifier of Black poverty as well as an emblem of personal/ communal pride (Christian, 1986). A writer's use of domestic imagery is a common focus for Black feminist criticism (exemplified in the name Kitchen Table Press). In some way this authorizes, as Audre Lorde suggests, an alternative standpoint, a way of seeing the world from the marginalized world of the mother, from inside an illegal 'shebeen' or from under the kitchen table (Lorde, 1984). Such a standpoint subverts colonial objectifications and controls over women's legal and illegal activities. The powerful textual presence of endorsing adjectives: 'warm', 'clean and fresh', 'very orderly' marks Kuzwayo's desire to bring her account of African women (Basotho and Christian) into dominant culture but not *silence* the experience of the marginalized. Kuzwayo's multiple discourses, her struggle *in* writing match very well Black feminism's attention to narratives which are cultural histories of Black women's struggles *and* resistance.

10 Lesbian criticism

SECTION 19: COLETTE, *CLAUDINE AT SCHOOL*

What is a lesbian text? Is it one describing lesbian relationships? Is it one written by a lesbian author? Is it one in which hidden kinds of pleasure are offered to an implied lesbian reader? Are texts lesbian if neither author nor content are *explicitly* lesbian? How much of a text has to be about lesbianism to be regarded as 'lesbian'? While in very general terms, lesbian texts start from 'women identified', 'lesbian' as a label, of course, is often used negatively. Many lesbian critics turn the negative itself positive by arguing that lesbian texts will usually be ignored and non-canonical but subvert heterosexual writing. The notion that the *difference* of sexuality must shape the representation of sexuality is itself intensely problematic. These are all points of discussion in lesbian criticism. Emerging from these debates is a more fundamental and underlying question: how far *can* 'lesbian' representations be regarded as essentially different from feminine representations or, indeed, from feminist? Issues of historical construction, self and social censorship, and language are knotted together.

A further issue remains. Is a 'lesbian' reading 'essentially' different or can this be constructed or chosen and what differences (Black/white) inform different lesbian readers? Here the *object* of reading can suggest the focus. A lesbian reading must allow space for recognitions and identifications, must create a sense of ownership for a lesbian reader, if not a sense of community. Lesbian criticism takes its cue from these issues, sometimes focusing on an undermining of realism or on utopianism to describe lesbian experiences hitherto marginal, sometimes on a celebratory delight in positive lesbian heroines with whom reader and author can create the space 'lesbian'.

Lesbian criticism is not one homogenous approach. There is no single method but many shared concerns. Drawing on the work of over two decades of feminist research, lesbian critics have made major and crucial contributions to feminist theory by investigating cultural constructions of sex and gender. All critics agree that fictional language is not a representation of reality but a system of signification which is socially constructed *and* contested. New representations of gender identity or, more usually, confusions about old ones, indicate fragile breaks in these significations. Yet as lesbian critics point out, although the deconstructionist approach currently dominates criticism and usefully challenges the view that sexuality is essentially un- changing, the *materiality* of lesbianism (a different sexual *practice*) must not be lost sight of (Palmer, 1993).

Lesbian criticism addresses several areas: female narrators and heroines and processes of subjectivity and social construction; textual and subtextual 'messages' heavily dependent on analogy, metaphor and simile; autobiography; and representations of eroticism which may frequently involve strategies of displace- ment. Because many of these features can be said to appear in heterosexual as well as lesbian texts, lesbian critics often turn to historical differences in writing. Colette's writing is a very good example of historical constraints. *Claudine at School* was published in 1900 at a time when *fin-de-siècle* homosocial writing had secured a foothold in literary history but lesbian writing lacked a literary and cultural place. Representations of sexuality were constrained by rules of masculine and feminine behaviour. One key problem for lesbian criticism is how to decode what a dominant culture silenced, how to evaluate writing like Colette's, that pre-dates second wave 'coming out' literature. Here lesbian criticism is much in debt to the sexual histories of Michel Foucault, the French philosopher. Foucault's *History of Sexuality* was a landmark study which offered many suggestive insights into the historical construction of sexuality in the West. In brief, Foucault suggests that the growing volume of medical, biological and pedagogical discourses at the turn of the century do not indicate any *openness* about sexuality. Rather, the proliferation of sexual categories *limited* sexuality to particular norms, like the third sex or invert term for lesbian in Radclyffe Hall's *The Well of Loneliness* (Foucault, 1980). Following Foucault, any exploration of sexual constructions depends very much on literary critical concerns: on the forms, concepts and vocabulary of texts.

Lesbian literary criticism also owes a good deal to the strong presence of lesbian theory in the last decades. In the early 1970s the concept 'women identified women' was an important lesbian slogan. According to lesbian theorists a lesbian was a woman who believed in the primacy of women. 'Lesbian' was a source of an alternative model of female identity, not simply a choice of sexual activity (Radicalesbians, 1973). Later theorists focus more on sexuality. Like the Radicalesbians, Luce Irigaray argues that 'lesbian' necessarily opposes the constructions imposed by heterosexuality and represents an alternative sexual discourse (Irigaray, 1977). Monique Wittig suggests that lesbians are not women because the sign 'woman' carries with it too many constructions and associations. According to Wittig 'lesbian' is outside sexual categories and therefore 'outside' literary constructions. In her own work, for example, Wittig subverts linguistic order by allowing pronouns and characters to mingle and fuse, as in 'j/e' (Wittig and Zeig, 1980). This questioning of identity is shared by Judith Butler, who suggests that a post-modern concept of 'lesbian' utilizing parody and performance, challenges the construction of *heterosexuality* (Butler, 1990).

Theoretically challenging though these ideas are, they are contradictory. The notion of continuum, put forward by Adrienne Rich in her hugely influential essay 'Compulsory heterosexuality and lesbian existence', offers more inclusive representations. Building on de Beauvoir's premise that women are originally homosexual, Rich argued that 'lesbian continuum' could include all women identified experience whether or not women desire *sexual* experience with women. Rich's parallel concept was 'lesbian existence' which represented that more specifically sexual component of lesbian practice (Rich, 1980b). Attacked subsequently for devaluing lesbian sexuality, Rich's essay greatly enlarged the categories of 'lesbian', which has important consequences for feminist literary criticism. Critics could highlight more long-term and diffuse representations of female friendship in literature and clarify arbitrary assignations of sexual preference. In theorizing representations of female bonding, Rich drew on the work of Nancy Chodorow to suggest that critics could look for representations of proximity and fluidity rather than active/male passive/female dichtomies such as those in *The Well of Loneliness* (see Section 9).

One focus might be on interchangeable gender characteristics. Colette dispenses with social constructions of masculinity. Her heroes frequently have feminine traits. Gender ambiguity extends into Colette's choice of vocabulary and representations of eroticism. Women's bodies are not objectified but described as active and full of sensuality and appetite. The vocabulary of female sexuality is often both masculine and feminine. Colette deliberately searches out unusual metaphors and invents nouns in order to subvert conventional and stereotypical representations.

A number of these issues are taken up in *Claudine at School*. Colette wrote the novel for her husband Willy (Henri Gauthiers-Villars) under some duress as a collection of memories of her own education. Colette and Willy were actively engaged in journalism and Willy was the author of several popular erotic novels. Originally published under his name, the commercial success of *Claudine at School* encouraged Colette to write several sequels. The Claudine series traces the story of a rural, innocent girl growing from childhood to womanhood whose eroticism ensured the series a wide and devoted readership. In this sense *Claudine at School* has a place outside the canon of great works of literature, although it could be argued that Colette created a narrative of some sophistication.

Claudine at School is a novel of the gynaeceum. Such novels describe the 'women identified' worlds of girls' schools and colleges and as such are frequently a focus for lesbian criticism (Marks and Stambolian, 1979). Descriptions of warm female friendships and schoolgirl eroticisms form the focus of study.

> I burst into the classroom, pushing open the door as if I had no idea that their Lordships might be inside. Then I stopped, pretending to be confused, in the open doorway. Mademoiselle Sergent arrested by course with a 'Control yourself, Claudine' that would have cracked a water-jug and I tiptoed away like a cat. But I'd had time to see that

> Mademoiselle Aimée Lanthenay was laughing as she chatted to Duplessis and was setting herself out to charm him. Just you wait, my hero wrapped in Byronic gloom! Tomorrow or the day after there'll be a song about you or some cheap puns or some nicknames. That'll teach you to seduce Mademoiselle Aimée.
>
> (From *Claudine at School*, Penguin, Harmondsworth, 1979, p. 24)

By the moment of this scene, Claudine is already an outstanding pupil, knowledgeable and able to control social relationships. In addition she lacks some attributes commonly thought of as feminine – she is unable to sew. The passage shows Claudine's jealous reaction to a possible liaison between Mademoiselle Aimée and the young male master Armand Duplessis which she aims to block. What Colette creates in the scene, a lesbian critic would argue, is a triad of female homosocial desire. Claudine resolves to join Aimée in some kind of relationship whose bond can occur only with the displacement of the male. The scene illustrates one major theme of lesbian criticism, which is that lesbian bonding involves the overt suppression of hetero-sexuality. For this new configuration to appear, critics would suggest, the male must be diminished, for example by being made the butt of jokes: 'there'll be a song about you or some cheap puns or some nicknames'. Claudine 'is' the male because she displays physical power ('burst' and 'push'). Claudine has incorporated the masculine as part of a new kind of female representation. Masculinity and femininity co-exist in Claudine in a rare fluidity which she constantly negotiates. Although the novel was written before Colette became acquainted with the lesbian *demi-monde* of Paris, in some ways the novel's signature 'Willy' perhaps allowed Colette the freedom of sexual ambiguity.

Let us take a later scene from the novel.

> I'd aimed it with all my might, adding a 'Mind your own business' for good measure. The class, completely out of hand, buzzed like a bee-hive; Mademoiselle Sergent descended from her desk for so serious an affair. It was so long since I had hit one of my companions that people were beginning to believe I had become rational. (In the old days, I had the annoying habit of settling my quarrels on my own, with kicks and blows, without thinking it necessary to tell tales like the others.)
>
> (From *Claudine at School*, Penguin, Harmondsworth, 1979, p. 88)

This passage continues the theme of Claudine's gender ambiguity. Claudine rejoices in characteristics conventionally signified as masculine – 'might', 'hit', 'kicks', 'blows'. But masculinity does not denote 'mannish'. Claudine is not simply or crudely acting as a surrogate male since we already know that she has hair 'whose colour varies according to the season between dull chestnut to gold' (p. 28). In *Claudine at School* gender is not *stabilized* by signifiers of masculinity or femininity but shares of both. Lesbian critics would also draw attention to Colette's refusal of gender hierarchy: there are no binaries of superior/inferior, male/female.

A final brief passage introduces the reader early in the novel to the erotic features of schoolgirl friendships.

> Our intimacy is progressing very fast. Her nature is like a demonstrative cat's; she is delicate, acutely sensitive to cold, and incredibly caressing in her ways. I like looking at her nice pink face, like a fair-haired little girl's, and at her golden eyes with their curled-up lashes. Lovely eyes that only ask to smile!
>
> (From *Claudine at School*, Penguin, Harmondsworth, 1979, p. 15)

The erotic impact of this passage is striking. The notion of a lesbian couple is not elusive but directly confronted. A number of features contribute to the effect. It is significant that Aimée is old and the teacher while Claudine is the schoolgirl. For this reason their relationship can replicate the mother–daughter nexus, described by Rich, as an important part of the 'lesbian continuum' and erotic friendship. However, Claudine reverses that hierarchy in her preoccupation with Aimée's sensuality. It is Aimée who is placed in the infant role in the semiotic (mother/infant bonding) with 'her nice pink face, like a fair-haired little girl's'. Equally significant in this regard is that Aimée is watched by a female narrator, who openly 'likes looking'. Claudine is the bearer of the gaze and Colette creates a dialectical relation between the desiring female subject and masculine sexual practice. Lesbian critics would celebrate Colette's subversion of the hierarchies of heterosexuality. Clearly this relationship will not be an 'imperfect' copy of a heterosexual relationship. Claudine's ability to work *through* a series of gender constructions and claim a successful education and self-identity is the key theme of the novel.

Lesbian critics would also pay attention to Colette's use of pronouns. The circular movement from first to third person and paraphrased dialogue allows the reader to identify with Claudine's diary-like address with its frequent use of the present tense. Finally, Colette's repeated use of a simile of a cat for both narrator and Aimée is another indicator of a lesbian text. Animals need not be gendered but cats are often perceived as 'female'. Throughout Colette's work animals play important roles. Animals are often more knowing than humans and have personal and differentiated characteristics. The passage subverts the normal hierarchy between cat and human worlds to hint that there may be other, similar absences of differences (masculinity/femininity). Colette's use of a simile 'like a demonstrative cat', rather than metaphor, is strategic. The narrator/Aimée/cat are not merged but share characteristics. There is an extensive use of simile throughout *Claudine at School* which is both visually striking and thematically suggestive. A lesbian critic would suggest that the use of simile parallels, or *enacts*, Colette's refusal of a hard division between hetero- and homosexuality.

The problematizing and parodying of sexual roles, described by Judith Butler, are also a feature of the novel. Claudine betrays a strong interest in masquerade, in a fantasy of changing appearance. 'I had time to be meticulous over every detail ... Now for the wreath. Ah, how well it suited me! A little Ophelia' (p. 240). Lesbian fiction characteristically gravitates towards artifice and romance. In this final tableaux Claudine delights in playing with literary signifiers of gender, such as 'Ophelia'. Claudine's physical glamour has a literal *tableaux vivant* quality as Claudine apes the patriarchal closure of the feminine – the weak, passive Ophelia.

Just as there is no single definition of 'lesbian' so there is no single method of lesbian criticism. Each critic is marked both by her moment and by the ways in which she came to call herself lesbian. Lesbian criticism, as I hope I have demonstrated, does have unique strengths to offer. Lesbian criticism shows that 'difference' is both a concept, something that can be analyzed and discussed, and also something staged in positive alternatives to heterosexual patterns. Lesbian criticism provides critical strategies which subvert traditional literary theory as well as subverting everyday sexual stereotypes.

SECTION 20: AUDRE LORDE, *ZAMI*

Black lesbians face particular problems claiming an identity when representations of race and sexuality are split and contradictory. Identity is further problematized: socially by the denial to Black lesbians of a public *Black* self and, critically, by poststructuralist ideas of fragmented selves. Even the term homosexuality was not available, at least in the English language, until the late nineteenth century. Black lesbian critics suggest that for these reasons writers often display a double consciousness, being familiar with the language and conventions of the oppressor while hiding independent self-definitions.

Lesbian criticism's main aim, therefore, is to clarify the ways in which critics *can* discover a lesbian aesthetic in a wide range of texts. One of the first, and most influential, lesbian feminist essays was Adrienne Rich's 'When we dead awaken: writing as re-vision'. The essay forcefully insists on addressing issues of visibility and invisibility; on seeing with fresh eyes; and on the need for a new literary history and new critical principles. These would include, among other things, the retrieving of lost women writers; an attention to mothering, and to a wider range of subjective, autobiographical and physical experiences (Rich, 1980a). An equally significant lesbian essay is Barbara Smith's pioneering *Toward a Black Feminist Criticism*, which widened the contours of Black lesbian criticism by including texts previously assumed heterosexual (Smith, 1977). Among other pioneering critics are Elly Bulkin, who celebrated the positive lesbian role models ignored by traditional literary history, and Lillian Faderman who identified a lesbian tradition (Bulkin, 1981; Faderman, 1981). Indeed, Faderman redesignated as lesbian, writers hitherto regarded as heterosexual.

Underlying these concerns with lesbian representations was an ideological project never far from the surface: an optimistic assessment of the possibility of a lesbian aesthetic. Taking this on board, lesbian critics searched literary history for features which could be called lesbian (Zimmerman, 1991). The 'coming out' story was one. Autobiography, like Audre Lorde's *Zami*, and *Bildungsromans* (or the growing into consciousness story) became a key focus of lesbian criticism. Lesbian critics argued that a feminist criticism with a serious commitment to understanding representations of sexual difference would take a very different form than hitherto, for example, attending to new kinds of syntax and new vocabulary. Lesbian critics suggest that *all* criticism is ideological, not simply that produced by lesbian critics. All criticism is a culturally constructed reflection of particular historical values. Second, lesbian critics attend much more readily to popular as well as to high art. Lesbian critics are also attracted to works which themselves illustrate fluid ego boundaries, such as the fluidity of mother–daughter representations. Much lesbian criticism involves this return to the mother and an interest in autobiographical and fictional representations of mothering.

It was the work of the Black lesbian critics and lesbian women of colour in their powerful analyses of the racism in literary, and much feminist criticism, which gave new impetus to that intellectually vital area of lesbian criticism. Audre Lorde invented a new critical term for this kind of metaphorical investigation – 'biomythography' – or composite representations of mothers, friends and lovers. The term is carefully chosen to mark the way in which all gay people's pasts are constructed mythologies. Lorde's formulations of lesbian difference have been hugely influential in lesbian criticism. The idea that lesbian relationships could replicate mother–daughter bonds suggests another kind of consciousness. For many Black critics that consciousness is part of Afracentric feminism. Afracentrism draws on African religions, on the values and languages of Black communities, on orality, and in particular on the cultural significance of mothering.

For Afra-American women inequalities of race and class are sexualized. Audre Lorde's 'Uses of the erotic: the erotic as power', like her term 'biomythography', similarly draws together the emotional with the political. Lorde makes very clear that there is no *one* experience and no *one* language of sexuality. Lorde argues that current definitions of sexuality rest upon problematic and culturally specific oppositions, such as intellect/passions; but Western representations do not capture the experiences of Black women.

These issues of mothering, male power and violence and the cultural history of Africa are the central themes of Lorde's writing. Audre Lorde was a Black lesbian feminist poet, autobiographer and critic who describes the year 1968, when her first book was published (*The First Cities*) and she made her first trip to the deep South, as pivotal because it inspired Lorde's intense concern with issues of repression and representation. Lorde frees the concept of 'difference' from a hierarchical superior/inferior binary. When Lorde calls herself Sister Outsider (the title of her major collection of essays) she is claiming a tension *between* identities and creating a connection between two apparently contradictory positions. Believing that sexual and ethnic identities have interlocking features, Lorde argues that a Black lesbian feminist standpoint must be holistic. Affirming that women are culturally different but that we all share a need to survive, Lorde makes an extensive mapping of matrilineal diasporas in her meshings of history, myth and autobiography.

Audre Lorde's *Zami* focuses these themes. The book is an autobiography of Lorde's childhood in 1940s' New York, and her subsequent sexual, political and work experiences in America and Mexico. 'Zami' is a term from the Caribbean meaning 'women-identified-women'. As the title suggests, Lorde aims to describe lesbian, race and class differences. Lorde divides her story into three phases. The first is her early childhood, and her family and school experiences. The second begins with her first strong female friendship and her gradual move away from her mother, first psychologically and then in reality. The third section is devoted to her friendships with women and her growing sexual experience and understanding of lesbian lifestyles. The book is full of social and political history with its rich evocation of period styles (clothes, music and expressions) as well as black culture (food, patois and myths). *Zami* covers the decade of the 1950s and overlaps Lorde's left-wing politics with the anti-Communism and homophobia of the McCarthy era. In addition *Zami* recognizes as fundamental the need for psychological and spiritual connections between self-identity, families and, in particular, mothers. Lorde especially favours scenes which not only provide a tapestry of Black and lesbian lifestyles but which can also convey a sense of the kind of metaphorical political values which the detail of objects, clothes or food can carry. One major source of difference in lesbian writing comes from the tense, but compelling, relationships many lesbian authors have with their mothers. Lorde is no exception.

I never caught cold, but 'got co-hum, co-hum' and then everything turned 'cro-bo-so', topsy-turvy, or at least, a bit askew.

I am a reflection of my mother's secret poetry as well as of her hidden angers.

Sitting between my mother's spread legs, her strong knees gripping my shoulders tightly like some well-attended drum, my head in her lap, while she brushed and combed and oiled and braided. I feel my mother's strong, rough hands all up in my unruly hair, while I'm squirming around on a low stool or on a folded towel on the floor, my rebellious shoulders hunched and jerking against the inexorable sharp-toothed comb. After each springy portion is combed and braided, she pats it tenderly and proceeds to the next.

I hear the interjection of *sotto voce* admonitions that punctuated whatever discussion she and father were having.

'Hold your back up, now! Deenie, keep still! Put your head so!' Scratch, scratch. 'When last you wash your hair? Look the dandruff!' Scratch, scratch, the comb's truth setting my own teeth on edge. Yet, these were some of the moments missed most sorely when our real wars began.

I remember the warm mother smell caught between her legs, and the intimacy of our physical touching nestled inside of the anxiety/pain like a nutmeg nestled inside its covering of mace.

The radio, the scratching comb, the smell of petroleum jelly, the grip of her knees and my stinging scalp all fall into – *the rhythms of a litany, the rituals of Black women combing their daughters' hair.*

(From *Zami*, Sheba, London, 1982, pp. 32–3)

Taking a close look at the passage, lesbian critics would point to how Lorde depicts lesbian identity as close to a mother's nurturance and sexuality. In addition, Lorde draws on a mythical past: the island of Carriacou and its 'topsy-turvy' language, rituals and nutmeg crop. Lorde gains her identity through identifying with her mother and *not* objectifying the mother. Verbs and adverbs are active and present: 'sitting', 'squirming', 'tenderly', 'combing'. Lorde's mother is allowed her own narrative space with quoted dialogue: 'Deenie, keep still! Put your head so!' This early passage in the book prepares the reader for Lorde's later thoughts about the lesbian body and lesbian writing. The body which centres the vocabulary of the passage is the body of the mother. The passage's scene of maternal nurturance mixes italicized poetry, direct patois, remembered life history and dramatized dialogue. Lorde directly links the maternal with writing '*I am a reflection of my mother's secret poetry*'. One of Lorde's central claims is that her lesbian 'drives' stem from, and return her to, the maternal body. Lesbian critics would focus on the ways in which Lorde symbolizes and brings into narrative play a continuous dependence on the maternal, which Lorde believes is part of lesbian identity.

Lorde's account of the semiotic, that world of *jouissance* experienced by mother and child, revolves around the sensuality of touch, sound and smell. Lorde describes the 'pre-symbolic' maternal power: 'gripping', 'tenderly', 'scratching'. Lorde's lyrical, but carefully balanced, celebration of these maternal moments is consistent with Nancy Chodorow's idea that the lesbian self is not a discrete or isolated subjectivity (Chodorow, 1978). The image of the 'nutmeg' is a metonymy of her mother's home (the nutmeg isle of Carriacou); of the sexuality and security of her mother from Audre's vantage point between her legs; as well as the similar colours and smells of mother and mace. The scene erotically connects the maternal, or here the matrilineal, with lesbian identity.

An equally pertinent and close following scene is the episode where Lorde crushes spices with her mother's elaborately carved mortar and pestle. Again Lorde feels an orgasmic awareness of the connection between her body (on the day of her first menstruation), the 'sexed' mothering pestle and the smell of souse and its resonant place in Black women's culture.

It is this metonymic recreation of the psychic, incestuous sensuality experienced by some mothers and daughters which is Lorde's major contribution to lesbian literature. It is also part of a Black lesbian aesthetic. In her essay with that title, bell hooks suggests that a key feature of a Black aesthetic is a 'heightened awareness', specifically the intensification of one's capacity to experience reality sensually (hooks, 1991, p. 112). Similarly, in *Zami*, Lorde avoids a conventional linear autobiography to return to her mother's aesthetic space. The constant circling involves Lorde in new ways of thinking and writing about the maternal. *Zami* has multiple voices and genres including poetry and songs, those most intensely lyrical and emotional forms. Alongside Lorde's evocation of the maternal are Lorde's ideas about lesbian difference which the maternal helps to define. It is in the nutmeg scene that Lorde is first aware of the sensual power of her body. The intensity of that moment is replicated later in Lorde's exploration of a range of lesbian differences in the Greenwich Village bars of the 1950s.

> For some of us there was no one particular place, and we grabbed whatever we could from wherever we found space, comfort, quiet, a smile, non-judgement.
>
> *Being women together was not enough. We were different. Being gay-girls together was not enough. We were different. Being Black together was not enough. We were different. Being Black dykes together was not enough. We were different.*
>
> Each of us had our own needs and pursuits, and many different alliances. Self-preservation warned some of us that we could not afford to settle for one easy definition, one narrow individuation of self. At the Bag, at Hunter College, uptown in Harlem, at the library, there was a piece of the real me bound in each place, and growing.
>
> It was a while before we came to realise that our place was the very house of difference rather the security of any one particular difference. (And often, we were cowards in our learning). It was years before we learned to use the strength that daily surviving can bring, years before we learned fear does not have to incapacitate, and that we could appreciate each other on terms not necessarily our own.
>
> (From *Zami*, Sheba, London, 1982, p. 226)

The concept of difference which this passage explores is complex. Lorde is not suggesting that difference is shaped by binaries of insider/outsider, Black/white, or self/other but rather that difference is always multidimensional, continually intersecting ethnic and sexual preference. Lorde creates a history of Greenwich Village lesbian life, while simultaneously questioning its every feature. The key questions which interest lesbian critics are carefully focused here. How *many* selves represent lesbian difference? What form does difference take in relation to class/ education, race and demography? Lorde suggests that 'the strength that daily surviving can bring' is of prime importance to 'the house of difference'. Lorde recreates the semiotic in the unexplored space of that house (standing both for a maternal space and Black lesbian sexuality): the 'quiet', 'a smile, non-judgement'. Lorde constructs a world of additives: 'black', 'gay', 'dykes' which begins with being women together. Lorde suggests that all those racist, homophobic terms of abuse if *collectively* combined can be turned into an affirmation. Similarly, in *Speculum of the Other Woman*, Irigaray suggests that it is the recognition by women identified women of their physical similarities, and the ways they reproduce themselves and their mothers, which create a lesbian identity (Irigaray, 1974). Lorde's description of a Black lesbian popular culture is rooted in her sense that this culture has to do with a mothering home/'house'. Rather than emphasize an autobiographical *uniqueness*, Lorde's insistent incorporation of many differences 'a piece of the real me bound in each place, and it was growing' celebrates women affiliation.

My final example of *Zami's* Black lesbian aesthetic ties these threads together.

> I grew Black as my need for life, for affirmation, for love, for sharing – copying from my mother what was in her, unfulfilled. I grew Black as *Seboulisa*, who I was to find in the cool mud halls of Abomey several lifetimes later – and, as alone. My mother's words teaching me all manner of wily and diversionary defenses learned from the white man's tongue, from out of the mouth of her father. She had had to use these defenses, and had survived by them, and had also died by them a little, at the same time. All the colors change and become each other, merge and separate, flow into rainbows and nooses.
>
> *I lie beside my sisters in the darkness, who pass me in the street unacknowledged and unadmitted.* How much of this is the pretence of self-rejection that became an immovable protective mask, how much the programmed hate that we were fed to keep ourselves a part, apart?
>
> (From *Zami*, Sheba, London, 1982, p. 58)

A lesbian reading would start from Lorde's identification of Black identity with the maternal 'copying from my mother', and an identity which creatively *completes* her mother's 'unfulfillment'. Most lesbian critics deny the concept of a lesbian 'essence' which Lorde also denies here by celebrating her mother's role playing including using 'the white man's tongue'. In other words a lesbian self is not fixed and static, although some will be beautiful 'rainbows' and some dangerous 'nooses'. The dichotomy of 'rainbow' and 'noose' dissolves in the continuous merging and separating of 'colors'. Lesbian critics would consider such marks of sexual fluidity tend to confirm a lesbian aesthetic. In addition,

Lorde celebrates African mythology: 'the cool mud halls of Abomey' with a lesbian lover. What Lorde argues very plainly, and yet with complexity, is that Black and lesbian are not parallel terms but intersecting and mutually affirmative. Lorde both asserts that the Black maternal *is* the source of lesbian identity, *and* that a *knowledge* of matrilineal history, 'defenses' and 'deaths', *changes* the representation of lesbian identity. Lorde describes a plurality of identities: 'Black as *Seboulisa*', sisters Black and white, her mother, which 'change and become each other'. The affirmation of African origin combines with the 'we were different' of 1950s' Harlem and Greenwich Village in a collective lesbian identity. As bell hooks suggests, the Black aesthetic is 'a particular location, a way of looking and becoming' (hooks, 1991, p. 104).

All lesbian critics share a concern to *change* the literary map, not merely to understand it. All value literature's support in transforming sexual politics and displacing heterosexist patterns of meaning making. This often requires lesbian critics to search out the mythical, the experimental and the sensual: all the qualities which make Audre Lorde's *Zami* a brilliant and challenging text.

11 Third World feminisms

SECTION 21: JOSEPH CONRAD, *HEART OF DARKNESS*

The history of European colonialism has the same time frame as the history of the European novel. In each century, as Edward Said and Gayatri Spivak have shown, cultural representations and imperialism shape each other (Said, 1983; Spivak, 1987). Jane Austen's novels describe the financial support taken from a Caribbean economy by the emerging British bourgeoisie. Charlotte Brontë's *Jane Eyre* describes the missionary impulses as well as Caribbean exploitations of that class later in the century. Further, the actual *forms* of the novel – its confidence in a positivist narrative voice and subjectivity – could be described as imperial. It could be argued that many nineteenth-century novels flesh out the social and cultural representations of imperialism because they represent a self-sufficient and enclosed European world view.

It is against this historical backcloth that we can read Joseph Conrad's *Heart of Darkness*. Conrad problematizes the nature of imperial values by problematizing the notion of a coherent, unchanging narrating hero: a hero whose ideology depends on the subordination of others. A Third World critique of *Heart of Darkness* and Conrad's ideas about the imperial project in the African Congo – the setting of the novel – would focus on Conrad's fictional representation of a historical, real world. *Heart of Darkness* has been called one of the most important and mythic novels written in English. First appearing serially in *Blackwood's Magazine* (1899) and reprinted in *Youth* (1902), *Heart of Darkness* transforms Conrad's experience of travelling to the Congo in 1890, although the novel was written a decade later. The novel's chief narrator, Marlow, tells readers (through the listening figure of the Accountant, the Chief of Companies) about his Congo command – his search for the 'lost' European Kurtz and, following Kurtz's death, his visit to Kurtz's 'Intended' fiancée on return to London. Conrad's story arguably could be read as imperial history because it is grounded firmly in the history of Conrad's *life* story and is an imperial 'romance' about the conquest of Africa. As critics point out, however, *Heart of Darkness* also *critiques* imperialism by presenting the colonial experience as demoralizing for all involved, colonialists and colonized. The novel also, a Third World critic would argue, reveals behind this surface of realistic and historical detail, the more elusive quality of the imperial experience: a universalizing, transhistorical project. Earlier critics, like Albert Guerard, paying attention to the artistic unity of *Heart of Darkness*, saw the novel as a dream of man's self-discovery (Guerard, 1958). Others, such as Bruce Johnson, placed Conrad in a philosophical tradition which included Immanuel Kant and Jean-Paul Sartre (Johnson, 1971). From this perspective Marlow becomes an alienated, existential character organizing the novel's only moral schema. Still other critics, such as Ian Watt and Frederick Karl, preferred to see the novel as an expression of mythical ideas in its development of literary as well as philosophical themes (Watt, 1979; Karl, 1979). But the novel is also a text about the racist European colonizers of Africa. Third World critics would want to argue that *Heart of Darkness* might be a philosophical/literary truthful representation of an alienated nineteenth-century figure but it is also, and simultaneously, a political representation of a *European imperial* figure. The novel is additionally a key example of those themes which interest Third World *feminist* critics. A major feature of Conrad's story of colonization is the interrelation of *patriarchal* with imperialist ideas. It is the women characters, above all, in *Heart of Darkness* who reveal that ideology, particularly in Marlow's different accounts of Black and white women. The two representations he describes – the sight of a 'savage' Black woman in the Congo contrasted with the whiteness of Kurtz's Intended – reveal the fundamental hostility to, and fear of, Others, particularly female Others, at the heart of the patriarchal-imperial project.

With the addition of feminism to Third World criticism the binary opposition between colonized peoples and white exploiters, and the literary representations of that opposition in contrasts of Black/White static/progressive time, are seen to depend crucially on the repression of women. Third World feminist criticism, a more recent development in contemporary criticism, is flourishing. What is involved in naming an area of feminist criticism Third World? Questions of definition are not easy. The term 'Third World' is frequently applied to geographical entities and to oppressed 'underdeveloped' peoples. But clearly women in the Third World are not necessarily more 'underdeveloped' or oppressed than Western women, white or Black. Third World also implies oppositions between 'First' 'Second' and 'Third Worlds' as well as the subsidiary status of 'Third'. Yet many feminists *prefer* the term 'Third World' because the term encompasses a *political* position and underlines the similarity between white oppressions in the USA and Europe and imperial oppression elsewhere. The critics Chandra Mohanty, Gayatri Spivak and Gloria Anzaldúa, among others, argue that Third World feminist criticism makes a rich and dense engagement with ideas from First and Third Worlds and offers a mobile unity of international sisterhood (Mohanty, 1991; Spivak, 1987; Anzaldúa, 1987).

Third World feminist criticism draws on a wide spread of disciplines and techniques, including psychoanalysis, deconstruction, semiotics as well as cultural history. But all critics start from the assumption that the sign 'woman' is a key feature of colonial writing. All critics share the belief that unequal relations between the imperialist West and the marginalized non-West are represented discursively in gendered terms. So that, for example, Black women are usually conflated with nature, animals or the exotic as in *Heart of Darkness*. Many feminist historians share these concerns: Gerda Lerner, in *The Creation of Patriarchy*, argues that patriarchy even *begins* and takes its shape from the enslavement of women of other races (Lerner, 1986). Third World feminist critics, whatever their differences, would argue that Conrad's literary representations of gender cannot be critiqued as individual creations distinct from their imperial underpinnings.

What key critical techniques come from these ideas? Third
World feminist criticism favours deconstruction. A constructed
Eurocentric narrative perspective often breaks revealingly when
it tries to distance women as Others. Deconstruction helps critics
to pull apart this noticeable feature of imperial narrative – the
breaks and absences in gender representations – in order to
question racist and misogynist stereotypes. For example, Conrad
portrays the Intended as an emblem of white purity against the
Black Other. Third World feminist critics deconstruct those
processes of signification, which establish race in specific ways.
One major focus is on textual repressions: the use of a vocabulary
of authority such as 'primitivism'. In many texts, including *Heart
of Darkness*, Black women are represented as monolothic
constructs.

In her critique of colonial stereotyping in 'Under Western eyes:
feminist scholarship and colonial discourse' Chandra Talpade
Mohanty argues that imperial texts construct two artificial
entities: the colonizer and the colonized. Mohanty examines
the textual implications of this practice which allows the
colonized only those representations derived from the colonizer.
Mohanty's examples of monolithic images are the veiled woman,
the powerful mother, the chaste virgin and the obedient wife –
all images represented in *Heart of Darkness* (Mohanty, 1985).
Imperialism often imposes a homogenous narrative order by
means of repetition and an excess of gender stereotyping.
Collapsed into imperial writing are two myths about Black
women. The first is that 'native' women are 'outside' the
progressive time/history of the colonizers and therefore represent 'primitive' values. The second myth is that 'native' women
encapsulate all that is most natural/exotic and therefore most
threatening and *different* about the Third World to the imperial
invader. Thus Third World feminist criticism pays much
attention to psychoanalysis. Psychoanalytic terms such as
'fetishism' (meaning the obsessive erotic satisfaction some men
gain from single female features such as hair or shoes), are often
deployed by Third World feminist critics. In novels the whole
female body may be fetishized in order to counter the threat of
sexual difference and women's independence.

The fetishism of the Other, Third World feminists argue, is at
its most transparent when the imperialist substitutes natural or

generic categories (of emotion or primitivism) for those that are *socially* constructed. Black = emotion while white = rational are the extremes of imperial gender representations. In the colonial male psyche a Black/white female opposition is expressed in terms of Black she-devil/white goddess. The association of the 'Otherness' of a Black woman with a feared lack of sexual control is an extensive feature in many Victorian novels (see Herman Melville's *Pierre* and Nathanial Hawthorne's *The Blithedale Romance*). Similarly, in *Heart of Darkness* Africa is a sign of destruction, chaos and evil, a primeval world to be penetrated by white explorers. Conrad also represents these signs as characteristics of Black women. *Heart of Darkness* takes up all of these themes creating a world of insistent paired opposites whose colonial values are represented in two directly opposed scenes: Marlow's encounter with an African woman, on his journey, and Marlow's reporting of Kurtz's 'last words' to Kurtz's Intended. Because the novel is constructed episodically scenes can be isolated.

> She walked with measured steps, draped in striped and fringed cloths, treading the earth proudly, with a slight jingle and flash of barbarous ornaments. She carried her head high; her hair was done in the shape of a helmet; she had brass leggings to the knee, brass wire gauntlets to the elbow, a crimson spot on her tawny cheek, innumerable necklaces of glass beads on her neck; bizarre things, charms, gifts of witch-men, that hung about her, glittered and trembled at every step. She must have had the value of several elephant tusks upon her. She was savage and superb, wild-eyed and magnificent; there was something ominous and stately in her deliberate progress. And in the hush that had fallen suddenly upon the whole sorrowful land, the immense wilderness, the colossal body of the fecund and mysterious life seemed to look at her, pensive, as though it had been looking at the image of its own tenebrous and passionate soul.
>
> (From *Heart of Darkness*, Macmillan, Basingstoke, 1989, p. 76)

A use of first person male narrative voice is the first distinctive feature of the passage. The voice adopts a perspective of objectivity and narrative distance. Marlow uses a vocabulary drawn from nineteenth-century travellers' stories where Africa is a strange, primitive, erotic place. Part of the values of any novel

are in the *ways* in which stories are told. Marlow stands back from
any *personal* feelings allowing emotions to be displaced onto the
woman he describes. The fear and desire of the observing white
male are the position of domination; the woman is an 'appari-
tion', 'ominous and stately'. Marlow objectifies her by representing not her *qualities* but her figure as a symbol of the 'mysterious
life' of the jungle. Marlow *evades direct* description. Everything
non-white is 'mysterious'. Black representations are transposed
into universal qualities. Throughout the passage the specific
social detail of the woman's appearance or setting is conflated
with an ahistoric eternal image. The woman is an object not a
subject. In his account, Marlow the colonizer is able to
mythologize Africa itself as female, as treacherous and desirable,
needing a firm and paternal European control. The woman is
seen from outside. Marlow does not guess at inner feelings or,
indeed, any possible facial representation of such feelings only
her 'cheek'. Third World feminist critics would see the objectification of a Black woman in the fetishization of 'hair in the shape of
a helmet', on a 'bizarre' and 'wild-eyed and magnificent' woman.
Patriarchal imperialism is featured in the ways in which the
woman's body is commodified. Marlow's employers are searching for ivory and she embodies an immense wealth of 'elephant
tusks'. Because the entry of the woman has no narrative status
in the novel she is given no independent African power. The
scene intersects Black gender oppression with colonial oppression. It turns the woman into a metaphor of Africa, leaving the
reader dependent on Marlow's explanations.

Indeed, throughout *Heart of Darkness*, Conrad carefully
manipulates the 'I' narrator, switching between Eurocentric
perspectives. Because Marlow both describes retrospectively *and*
in continuous present, the effect is to dislocate the reader and
encourage reader dependence on the authoritative narration.
The Black woman is not allowed a voice. Marlow's vocabulary is
stereotypical in reproducing in 'excess' the clichés of Black
African women as exotic and sexual. It is as if the incomprehens-
ibility of Africa as a *geographical* location can only be managed if
Marlow distances the country as a female stereotype. Somehow
the very *excess* of cliché, a Third World feminist would argue,
paradoxically indicates Marlow's vulnerability, which he is
forced to displace *on to* the Black Other. Marlow's narrative

foregrounds a collision between the rhetoric of the colonizer and the reality of colonization. By moving into timeless, abstract vocabulary he covers over such contradictions and legitimizes the absolute unchanging face of imperialism.

The scene of the visit to Kurtz's Intended, on the other hand, is shot through with images of whiteness. Because *Heart of Darkness* does not describe the physical battles between imperialists and others, Black and white oppositions have to be realized *visually* in frequently gendered vocabulary. Such scenes can be read from a Third World feminist perspective as a metonymy of the way in which white imperialists struggle to control the 'Other' within themselves.

> A grand piano stood massively in a corner; with dark gleams on the flat surfaces like a sombre and polished sarcophagus. A high door opened – closed. I rose.
>
> She came forward, all in black, with a pale head, floating towards me in the dusk. She was in mourning. It was more than a year since his death, more than a year since the news came; she seemed as though she would remember and mourn for ever. She took both my hands in hers and murmured, 'I had heard you were coming.' I noticed she was not very young – I mean not girlish. She had a mature capacity for fidelity, for belief, for suffering. The room seemed to have grown darker, as if all the sad light of the cloudy evening had taken refuge on her forehead. This fair hair, this pale visage, this pure brow, seemed surrounded by an ashy halo from which the dark eyes looked out at me. Their glance was guileless, profound, confident, and trustful. She carried her sorrowful head as though she were proud of that sorrow, as though she would say, I – I alone know how to mourn for him as he deserves. But while we were still shaking hands, such a look of awful desolation came upon her face that I perceived she was one of those creatures that are not the play-things of Time. For her he had died only yesterday.
>
> (From *Heart of Darkness*, Macmillan, Basingstoke, 1989, p. 90)

Unlike the first scene where Marlow was able to distance himself from the 'primitive' Black woman, here Marlow breaks the flow of narration to allow the Intended to speak 'I had heard you were coming'. Yet in both scenes the woman is statuesque either living in a continuous present or frozen in the belief that the past *is* the present as well as the future: 'she would remember and mourn forever'.

What is striking here is Marlow's continued use of timeless patterns. There is a mythic emphasis on the *lack* of history 'for her he had died only yesterday'. Marlow ostensibly visits Kurtz's Intended in order to shore up the illusion that Kurtz was a 'remarkable man'. The scene distances the white woman 'floating', with 'pale visage, this pure brow' into an icon which is the binary opposite of the earlier and similarly objectified Black woman. The first sentence here juxtaposes the black piano 'sarcophagus' and its ivory keys with the Intended 'all in black, with a pale head'. This similarly commodifies the white woman where the earlier scene constructed the Black woman as 'savage'. Here 'woman' is embedded in a Victorian iconography of an angel 'surrounded by an ashy halo'. The scene is emblematic of Third World feminist concerns: a gendered white iconography; 'fair hair', 'pure brow' which covers over colonial exploitation represented by the piano's ivory keys. The Intended's 'admiration' of Kurtz's supposed virtues must be preserved just as the imperial venture must be preserved and continue. Imperialism constructs a 'mirroring' woman who can represent everything which imperialism wishes to believe about itself: 'guileless, profound, confident, and trustful'. Neither white nor Black woman is permitted internal thoughts, a psyche and hence individuality or individual ethics. The double oppression of women in both African and English patriarchal worlds is very marked.

In addition to the colour-coded iconography, Third World feminists would draw attention to the way in which imperialism depends on a firm belief in evolutionary time. Imperial fictions usually describe Western societies as if such societies 'own' a progressive linear history. In opposition, the Third World is frequently described as ahistorical, existing in a timeless unprogressive present. The 'mysteriousness' of the Black woman is not only a *Black* 'Otherness' but also a temporal one. Africa, that 'immense wilderness', can only look statically inwards at an image of its 'own soul'. What Marlow describes, and what the novel endorses textually, is a fantasy of gender. Even if, as many critics argue, the novel is a *reluctant* affirmation of imperial capitalism, its deliberate and structured *gender* representations ensure that *Heart of Darkness* affirms imperial *patriarchy*. Rational and mythic are interchangeable with white and Black. Africa becomes a primitive *woman's* body. Any use of imperial patriarchal vocabulary supports Third World feminists' view that dominating systems of patriarchal representation will inevitably construct the Third World as a Black *female* Other.

SECTION 22: JEAN RHYS, *WIDE SARGASSO SEA*

Third World feminists attack two key features of mainstream literary theory: its use of literary conventions which are shaped by dominant Western social ideas; and its belief in the power of a Western canon of 'great' literary masterpieces. A major task of Third World feminists is to create a criticism which both exposes the valorization of patriarchal and imperial values by the West and replaces these with more complex constructions of gender, ethnicity and writing. Third World criticism examines representations of patriarchal authority, or the loss of authority, in colonial settings, as well as problematizing traditional literary conventions.

The kinds of literary processes which interest Third World feminists are those which subvert a humanist notion of aesthetic authority as well as those which subvert Western literary representations. Another area of concern is to examine the impact of history. Novels which attract Third World critics are those which incorporate these processes, like the multiple stories of *The Woman Warrior* or Jean Rhys's *Wide Sargasso Sea*. Critics argue that Third World cultures should neither be objectified into a set of minority literary products nor read as an idealized version of essentialism. Many Western critics write as if the Third World were a monolith, instead of a label the West has created for its own convenience, ignoring a wide range of distinct national and international writings.

Third World critics eclectically utilize theories from post-structuralism, psychoanalysis and feminist theory as well as those of differing cultures. What Third World feminists bring to feminism is a fresh insistence on the *provisional* quality of literary and cultural identities and that texts will reveal struggles over *ethnic*, as well as gender, positions.

If we turn to a text which was written 'inside' Britain's empire but 'outside' that empire's own values – Jean Rhys's *Wide Sargasso Sea* – a Third World feminist approach seems ideal. This would acknowledge that any account of a historical moment of imperialism (for Rhys the effects of the ending of slavery in the Caribbean) would be problematized from the point of view of a Creole woman author. What this means for literary criticism is that the focus will shift. Rather than describing only the 'Otherness' of Black and Creole characters, for example, or static, essential patriarchal characters, such an approach could also attend to narrative *processes* and *contradictory* structures. For example texts in which representability is itself a problem in the colonial context can be read as subversive in their implied criticism of traditional Western culture. Where representability (of Black to white and Creole woman to white man) is a text's main theme, what we often find is a doubly coded text. Literary criticism would then pay attention to the lack of a coherent narrator standpoint, to the lack of a linear plot as well as to the lack of mastery (by characters or author) over vocabulary choices and homogenous narration.

Jean Rhys's *Wide Sargasso Sea* takes up many of these issues. The whole novel is a novel of opposites: of Black/white representations and strategies of doubling and representation as well as a novel which celebrates a Caribbean home. The title itself reflects that sense of the impossibility of an easy 'passage' through history and representations. The Sargasso Sea is a still, warm part of the Atlantic Ocean in which light winds and seaweed combine to prevent ships from passing through with ease. In *Wide Sargasso Sea*, the sea metaphorically lies between the England of the imperial character Mr Rochester and the Caribbean home of the 'colonized' Creole woman Antoinette.

Wide Sargasso Sea is Jean Rhys's most complex novel of race and gender, although a consistent theme in all her writing is the issue of dispossession brought about by race and gender discriminations. *Voyage in the Dark*, *Good Morning*, *Midnight* and her letters and autobiography *Smile Please* describe Caribbean, French and English cultures in terms of issues of insiders and outsiders, home and exile. Rhys shares concerns with Third World feminism: an engagement with colonialism and an incipient anti-colonialism and a recognition of the international power of patriarchy (although Rhys would never couch her fictions in these terms).

All women characters in Rhys's fictions are mercilessly exposed to the financial and gendered constraints of an imperial world. Although Jean Rhys would fly from the term 'feminist' or even woman writer (particularly since her *nom de plume* is constructed from the names of her first husband Jean and her father Rees) she addresses a key concern of Third World feminists: the relation between gender identity and imperial material history. *Wide Sargasso Sea* is a fictional account of the early life of Mrs Rochester – the mad Bertha in *Jane Eyre*. Using elements from the 'mothering' text Rhys reshapes Bertha's history – now with her full name Antoinette Cosway – to criticize and repudiate the imperial history of Charlotte Brontë. Antoinette is imaginatively reconstructed as an emotional vulnerable young girl living in Jamaican isolation with her mother Annette because of her mixed race (Creole) and poverty. The marriages of Annette to Brontë's Mr Mason and Antoinette subsequently to Mr Rochester bring with them the constraints of English customs and patriarchal appropriations of their estate.

In opposition to these discriminations Rhys contrasts the warm and reciprocal relations between Antoinette and her Black nurse Christophine and Black childhood companion Tia. Both Christophine and Tia are strong, independent figures. Christophine has a facility in English, French and patois as well as valuable knowledge of Obeah and Arawak history. It is Christophine who succours and nourishes Antoinette from Rochester's brutal domestic tyranny. The novel raises a number of specific issues about imperial history and fictions that would deserve a Third World feminist study. First, imperial linear history is contested structurally by the three part organization of the novel. The first section is told by Antoinette whose voice is succeeded in Part 2 by Rochester's own account of Jamaica and his unsuccessful marriage. The last brief section is Antoinette's 'mad' account of incarceration in the attic room of Charlotte Brontë's Thornfield Hall. All of this problematizes the concept of narrative authority, particularly of a white masculine authority, sandwiched as Rochester is between the two powerful stories told by Antoinette. *Wide Sargasso Sea* does not ignore Brontë's history but deliberately problematizes its racism and concepts of gender.

Wide Sargasso Sea also poses questions about the actual imperial history on which Brontë (and in turn Rhys) draw, and on the idea of family or autobiographical 'reality'. The novel is set at a crisis point in Caribbean history of the 1840s after the Emancipation Act replaced slavery with 'apprenticeships', and the British government withdrew its protection of Jamaica's sugar market in 1846. The word Creole itself personifies imaginary history. It originated from the Spanish *criar* (to imagine) and *colon* (a colonist). In general terms *Creole* can refer to European settlers or to people of mixed race living in the colonies. *Wide Sargasso Sea* also draws on Rhys's family history in the sense that the landscape of Antoinette's estate Coulibri resembles Rhys's birthplace Dominica, not the less equatorial Jamaica where the novel is set. In addition, in October 1837 James Lockhart, Jean Rhys's great-grandfather, died leaving a widow (significantly called Jane) to manage the plantation. In the Black riots which followed a colonial census (as in the riots of *Wide Sargasso Sea*) the house was burnt down.

To Third World feminist critics such life histories and collision between women's histories and imperial histories, make a major challenge to traditional literary narratives. Critics draw attention to the importance of historical representations for writing groups historically denied access to literary production. Rhys also shows Christophine and other Black women to be repositories and transmitters of an earlier pre-imperial history. Rhys's exploration of race and gender does not fall into the trap of a futuristic identification with Black culture but allows Black women's memory to make sense of the imperial past and present. *Wide Sargasso Sea* deliberately confronts and subverts the intertextual echoes of *Jane Eyre* and offers a more complex and problematic version of colonial history. Two scenes in particular focus the difference between the creole Antoinette's intimate, intuitive understanding of a Third World landscape and white Rochester's strong fear of its dangerous sexual and racial freedoms.

> Our garden was large and beautiful as that garden in the Bible – the tree of life grew there. But it had gone wild. The paths were overgrown and a smell of dead flowers mixed with the fresh living smell. Underneath the tree ferns, tall as forest tree ferns, the light was green. Orchids flourished out of reach or for some reason not to be

touched. One was snaky looking, another like an octopus with long thin brown tentacles bare of leaves hanging from a twisted root. Twice a year the octopus orchid flowered – then not an inch of tentacle showed. It was a bell-shaped mass of white, mauve, deep purples, wonderful to see. The scent was very sweet and strong. I never went near it.

   All Coulibri Estate had gone wild like the garden, gone to bush. No more slavery – why should *anybody* work?

(From *Wide Sargasso Sea*, Hodder and Stoughton, London, 1989, p. 2)

At Coulibri Antoinette and the estate share an iconography of fertility. The family garden is a convincing image of the power of the semiotic (the pre-Oedipal world of mothers and infants). It is the maternal space of Antoinette's childhood. Third World feminists would draw attention to the emblematic religious significance of the Caribbean – 'the tree of life' – and to Antoinette's exact knowledge of plant forms – 'tree ferns' – as well as to their tropical intensity – 'gone wild'. Coulibri stands for the wild zone of Antoinette's childhood before her abusive marriage to Rochester. The passage is constructed from opposites: 'dead'/'fresh, living', 'snaky', 'twisted'/'bell-shaped'. Antoinette's narrative *incorporates* opposites. Her character mimics the Black Tia and her name mirrors in nomenclature that of her mother Annette. These are not pictures of Black and white women like the opposite and *distinct* portraits drawn by white imperialists. Antoinette does not use 'essentialist' or romantic images to describe Coulibri. She understands its dangers – 'I never went near it', 'orchids were not to be touched' – and respects the autonomy of the landscape. The figure of Antoinette is significant. Away from the appropriating colonizer Rochester she is self-reflexive, thoughtful and serious and, most significant, happy to be alone and independent.

The passage is written in the first person and therefore examines from the inside Antoinette's interior thoughts – her sensations of scents, 'very sweet and strong' – and her feelings of enchantment – 'wonderful to see'. The juxtaposition of binaries, 'dead'/'fresh', suggests that Antoinette might be able to encompass future contradictory and complex experiences. But there is a particular use of symbolism here, as in the opposition of 'snaky'/'bell-shaped' as well as 'mauve, deep purples'. The symbolism refers to Antoinette's first menstruation which marks her passage into womanhood and the 'threat' of marriage. Blood symbolizes different things, of course, to Rochester who is terrified of miscegenation, of mixed races as well as of any blurring of ethnic appearance in speech and dress.

To a Third World feminist the passage could represent Antoinette's verbal dexterity and her strong independent sensuality. The garden is clearly a woman's site, displaying the power of Creole female sexuality with its 'mauve' and 'deep purples'. Questions of ethnicity and gender become inextricable from questions of environment, of place and ultimately of power. What this means for Antoinette's subsequent abuse and 'hysterization' is that such abuse will be seen for what it is: an abuse of nature. Throughout Antoinette's section we see the power of 'feminine' vocabulary and female experience in opposition to the harsh asensual character of Rochester.

A passage from Part 2, Rochester's narrative, shows the patriarchal subject in conflict with his colonial environment.

Antoinette collapsed on the sofa and went on sobbing. Christophine looked at me and her small eyes were very sad. 'Why you do that eh? Why you don't take that worthless good-for-nothing girl somewhere else? But she love money like you love money – must be why you come together. Like goes to like.'

I couldn't bear any more and again I went out of the room and sat on the veranda.

My arm was bleeding and painful and I wrapped my handkerchief round it, but it seemed to me that everything round me was hostile. The telescope drew away and said don't touch me. The trees were threatening and the shadows of the trees moving slowly over the floor menaced me. That green menace. I had felt it ever since I saw this place. There was nothing I knew, nothing to comfort me.

I listened. Christophine was talking softly. My wife was crying. Then a door shut. They had gone into the bedroom. Someone was singing 'Ma belle ka di', or was it the song about one day and a thousand years. But whatever they were singing or saying was dangerous. I must protect myself. I went softly along the dark veranda. I could see Antoinette stretched on the bed quite still. Like a doll. Even when she threatened me with the bottle she had a marionette quality. 'Ti moun', I heard and 'Doudou ché', and the end of a head handkerchief made a finger on the wall. *'Do do l'enfant do.'* Listening, I began to feel sleepy and cold.

I stumbled back into the big candlelit room which still smelt strongly of rum. In spite of this I opened the chest and got out another bottle. That was what I was thinking when Christophine came in. I was thinking of a last strong drink in my room, fastening both doors, and sleeping.

(From *Wide Sargasso Sea*, Hodder and Stoughton, London, 1989, p. 81)

Rochester's imperial power depends on the displacement of Others, particularly female Others. Throughout his section Rochester records numerous personal moments of terror and dismay at any failure of *control* over his colonial environment. Rhys's use of the masculine narrative voice here allows Rochester's unconscious thoughts and feelings to emerge for the reader in a place 'where everything was hostile'. Rochester also fears women's sexuality (after Antoinette's retaliation 'my arm was bleeding and painful'). Both thoughts and fears distance Rochester from a reader, especially a female reader.

The overriding romance of colonial fiction is one where a male hero comes into rightful possession of a 'female' territory by marrying its white heroine and exerting paternal authority over willing indigenous natives. An insistent theme in this passage is Rochester's attempt to 'map out' his territory to prevent 'shadows of trees moving slowly' and 'that green menace'. Safety is found only by 'fastening both doors'. Third World feminists would draw attention to Rochester's patriarchal urge to make relationships into power games. For example, Antoinette becomes 'a doll' who Rochester can manipulate like a 'marionette'.

An additional area of concern to Third World feminists would be the novel's contrast between Antoinette and Christophine's memories and 'language' of songs *'Ma belle ka di'* (their alternative to patriarchal history) – and Rochester's monocular patriarchal gaze and the static quality of his feelings 'ever since I saw this place'. The iteration of the feminine in *Wide Sargasso Sea* and in Rhys's other books is in the voice. Rhys actively contests the male colonial gaze here with the old language which was handed down from mother to daughter. Rochester fears the strength of 'women's time' – 'whatever they were singing or saying was dangerous'. Hence, as Third World feminists would argue,

Rochester tries to contain female sexuality by denying Antoinette access to his speech and hence to recognition in the symbolic. The syntactical structure is significant. Rochester's narrative relies on very short sentences, on simple verbs 'I listened', 'I stumbled back' as Rochester both desperately attempts to control his feelings and alienate himself from his unconscious desires to feel 'sleepy and cold'. The objectification of a Creole woman as a doll is a key example of patriarchal imperialism. The authority of colonialism depends on its *repeated* recognition of difference and distance just as here Christophine's 'small eyes' have observed Rochester's attacks on Antoinette and forced him to displace his guilt by absenting himself from their presence and by stereotyping Christophine and Antoinette.

Jean Rhys deals seriously and imaginatively with issues at the heart of Third World feminism: questions about colonial female identity and subjectivity, patriarchal domination, the sexual/racial constructions of imperialism and the impact of all of these on literary conventions and forms. Rhys writes Third World women *into* history not simply by celebrating an 'essential' and Other *past* but by revealing the contradictions in patriarchal history and its vulnerability to 'women's time'. Jean Rhys fissures colonialism here with discrete breaks: first, she limits a patriarchal imperial territorial control in favour of the warm semiotic Coulibri; second, she contrasts creole and Black multiple histories and memories with a more limited patriarchal chronology. Third World feminist critics would celebrate Rhys's taming of patriarchal imperialism as well as her more complex matrix of motherland.

Glossary

Binary
Two terms which are opposites – rational/irrational, white/black, man/woman. The first term in any binary ('man') is usually seen as positive and superior to the other term ('woman') but to depend on the second term for its meaning.

Canon
A term for the list of literary *master*pieces in traditional literary studies. The canon is an informal institution of literature whose specific inclusions and exclusions, deletions and exceptions are nowhere codified.

Catachresis
An incorrect use or misuse of words; for example, the use of a proper term like 'true manhood' or 'true womanhood' to describe something which does not exist.

Codes
The disparate way of using a system or collection of signs, marking different social memberships. Codes may be conscious or unconscious and identities claimed or refused by codes selected: clothes may be codes, for instance.

Critical theory (literature)
In general a critical theory is a framework of general principles which critics use when describing literature and criticism. A feminist critical theory describes the relationship between literary forms and gender ideologies.

Critical theory (sociology)
Feminist critical theory attempts to discover and expose domin-ant ideologies, practices and beliefs which restrict women's freedom. Its research aim is to emancipate rather than to predict and control or simply to understand.

Cultural theory
Theories of the symbolic realm of the arts. Feminist theory extends the definition to include all symbolic products of society. This frees women from being defined by the expression 'sub-culture'.

Diegesis
A statement of a case or an account of events, a story or narrative. The diegesis of a novel is its total *content*, including plot, characterization, symbols and so forth.

Discourse
A shared vocabulary of meaning. If you use the 'discourse' of literary criticism you would use words like metaphor. The discourse of a novel includes the language as well as the 'social messages' represented by particular vocabulary.

Discourse analysis
The study of patterns and rules controlling language and representations used in films, literature, pictures and texts.

Discursive practices
The practice of using a special discourse (like the technical vocabularies of literary criticism or sociology) which carries with it a particular ideology (that books are meant to be 'true to life').

Epistemology
Theories of the way in which we perceive and know our social world.

Genre
A grouping, classification or category of works of art or literature, such as the 'thriller' or the 'romance'.

Images of women criticism

A term which describes the method used by feminist literary critics in the late 1960s and early 1970s. Kate Millett in *Sexual Politics* examines images of women in the work of D. H. Lawrence and other writers to conclude that these images are sexist and represent patriarchal ideology.

Intertextuality

A term used by Julia Kristeva to describe the ways in which texts are often composed of different discourses; a novel, for instance, might include popular songs or verbatim quotations from TV. Kristeva argues that texts also include the 'text' of the writer's unconscious.

Logocentrism

The primacy of the spoken word. A belief in a definitive truth, reality or 'word' of the transcendental signifier (such as a God) which provides a foundation for all language, thought and experience.

Metanarratives (also known as master-narratives or grand narratives)

An approach to explaining social reality by a universal philosophy or social theory; Marxism is an example.

Metaphor

A figure of speech implying but not explicitly stating a comparison between two objects or actions. Metaphors occur in both speech, text and representation and not only reflect reality but help to compose it. We use metaphors of war to describe arguments such as 'attacking a position' or 'shoot down in flames'.

Metonymy

The substitution of one object name for another which is representative of the object rather than a literal alternative, as in 'crown' for 'king'. This most commonly occurs when the two objects are habitually connected.

Narrative

A spoken or written account of connected events; a story, myth, legend, fable or tale.

Polyphony
A term derived from music meaning a combination of parts, each having its own melody played simultaneously in harmony.

Sign, signified, signifier
A sign is a signifier which signifies or carries with it a concept or meaning. For example a red traffic light (signifier) signifies stop (signified). Deconstructionists argue that the signified (meaning) is not immediately obvious from a sign because the relation between sign and signified is arbitrary. Signs appear in different contexts and thus meanings are not entirely the same; red means different things outside the sign system of traffic lights. For Saussure the distinction was between the term, the signifier, and the concept signified by the term, the signified; so 'woman', 'lady' and 'girl' are signs or signifiers with different meanings (the signified) depending upon the context in which they are used.

Stereotype
An erroneous, conventional, generalization about individuals, groups or objects: 'girls like dolls' and 'boys like cars'.

Subject
A topic or theme which is described, discussed or represented. Something submitted to examination or analysis. Subject can also mean the speaker or actor in a text. Texts construct subject positions, for example describing women as feminine, and encourage readers to identify with these subject positions. Not surprisingly, subject positions are a key focus of feminist criticism.

Symbolic
In French feminist theory 'symbolic' means the language of patriarchy. Using techniques drawn from linguistics and psycho-analysis writers such as Hélène Cixous and Luce Irigaray argue that the symbolic represents not only a form of language but a way of thinking and ordering the world to the benefit of men. Opposed to the symbolic is the feminine semiotic or the representation of mother–child relations.

Syntax
The order and grammatical arrangement of words in a sentence and the rules or analysis of this.

Bibliography

Althusser, L. (1971) *Lenin and Philosophy and Other Essays*, trans. B. Brewster, New Left Books: London.

Anzaldúa, G. (1987) *Borderlands/La Frontera: The New Mestiza*, Spinsters/Aunt Lute: San Francisco.

Bakhtin, M. M. (1981) *The Dialogic Imagination*, University of Texas: Austin.

Barrett, M. (1982) 'Feminism and the definition of cultural politics', in *Feminism, Culture and Politics*, eds. R. Brunt and C. Rowan, Lawrence and Wishart: London.

Barthes, R. (1966) 'Introduction à l'analyse structurale des récits', *Communications*, 16.

Barthes, R. (1970) *S/Z*, Seuil: Paris; trans. R. Miller (1975) Cape: London.

Barthes, R. (1986) 'The death of the author', in *The Rustle of Language*, trans. R. Howard, Hill and Wang: New York.

Baym, N. (1978) *Women's Fiction: A Guide to Novels by and about Women in America 1820–1970*, Cornell University Press: Ithaca.

Belsey, C. (1980) *Critical Practice*, Methuen: London.

Brooks, C. (1947) *The Well Wrought Urn*, Harcourt, Brace and Co: New York.

Bulkin, E. (1981) *Lesbian Fiction*, Persephone Press: Watertown, MA.

Butler, J. (1990) *Gender Trouble: Feminism and the Subversion of Identity*, Routledge: London.

Chodorow, N. (1978) *The Reproduction of Mothering*, University of California: Berkeley.

Christ, C. (1980) *Diving Deep and Surfacing*, Beacon Press: Boston.

Christian, B. (1980) *Black Women Novelists: The Development of a Tradition 1892–1976*, Greenwood Press: Westport, CT.

Christian, B. (1986) *Black Feminist Criticism*, Pergamon: New York.

Christian, B. (1989) 'The race for theory', in *Gender and Theory*, ed. L. Kauffman, Blackwell: Oxford.

Cixous, H. (1974) *Prénoms de Personne*, Seuil: Paris.

Cixous, H. (1976a) 'The laugh of the Medusa', *Signs*, 1:4.

Cixous, H. (1976b) *The Exile of James Joyce*, trans. S. Purcell, John Calder: London.

Cixous, H. (1979) *Vivre l'orange/To Live the Orange*, bilingual text, trans. A. Liddle and S. Cornell, des femmes: Paris.

Cixous, H. and Clément, C. (1986) *The Newly Born Woman*, trans. B. Wing, Manchester University Press: Manchester.

Daly, M. (1978) *Gyn/Ecology: The Metaethics of Radical Feminism*, Beacon Press: Boston.

Davies, C. B. and Graves, A. A. (eds) (1986) *Ngambika: Studies of Women in African Literature*, Africa World Press: Trenton, NJ.

Davis, T., Durham, M., Hall, C., Langan, M. and Sutton, D. (1982) 'The public face of feminism: early twentieth-century writers on women's suffrage', in *Making Histories: Studies in History, Writing and Politics*, eds. R. Johnson *et al.*, Hutchinson: London.

de Beauvoir, S. (1949) *Le Deuxième Sexe*, Gallimard: Paris; trans. H. M. Parshley (1953) Jonathan Cape: London.

Derrida, J. (1976) *Of Grammatology*, trans. G. C. Spivak, Johns Hopkins University Press: Baltimore.

Disraeli, B. (1961) *Sybil, or the Two Nations*, Dolphin: Garden City, New York.

Du Plessis, R. B. (1980) 'For the Etruscans', in *The Future of Difference*, eds H. Eisenstein and A. Jardine, G.K. Hall: Boston.

Eagleton, T. (1976) *Marxism and Literary Criticism*, Methuen: London.

Ellmann, M. (1968) *Thinking About Women*, Harcourt Brace Jovanovich: New York.

Faderman, L. (1981) *Surpassing the Love of Men: Romantic Friendship and Love Between Women from the Renaissance to the Present*, Columbia University Press: New York.

Fetterley, J. (1978) *The Resisting Reader: A Feminist Approach to American Fiction*, Indiana University Press: Bloomington.

Fiedler, L. (1965) *Waiting for the End*, Jonathan Cape: London.

Firestone, S. (1970) *The Dialectic of Sex*, W. M. Morrow: New York.

Foucault, M. (1972) *The Archaeology of Knowledge*, trans. A. M. Sheridan Smith, Tavistock: London.

Foucault, M. (1980) *The History of Sexuality*, Vintage: New York.

French, M. (1978) *The Women's Room*, Sphere: London.

Freud, S. (1980) *Art and Literature*, Penguin: Harmondsworth.

Fuss, D. (ed.) (1991) *Inside/Out: Lesbian Theories, Gay Theories*, Routledge: London.

Gilbert, S. and Gubar, S. M. (1979) *The Madwoman in the Attic: The Woman Writer and the Nineteenth Century Literary Imagination*, Yale University Press: New Haven.

Gilbert, S. and Gubar, S. M. (1988) *No Man's Land*, Yale University Press: New Haven.

Gramsci, A. (1971) *Prison Notebooks*, Lawrence and Wishart: London.

Greer, G. (1971) *The Female Eunuch*, Paladin: London.

Griffin, S. (1978) *Woman and Nature: The Roaring Inside Her*, Harper and Row: New York.

Guerard, A. J. (1958) *Conrad the Novelist*, Harvard University Press: Cambridge.

Hirsch, M. (1989) *The Mother/Daughter Plot: Narrative, Psychoanalysis, Feminism*, Indiana University Press: Bloomington.

hooks, b. (1991) *Yearning: Race, Gender and Cultural Politics*, Turnaround: London.

Humm, M. (1986) *Feminist Criticism: Women as Contemporary Critics*, Harvester: Brighton.

Humm, M. (1991) *Border Traffic: Strategies of Contemporary Women Writers*, Manchester University Press: Manchester.

Hurston, Z. N. (1978) *Mules and Men*, Indiana University Press: Bloomington.

Irigaray, L. (1974) *Speculum de l'autre femme*, Editions de Minuit: Paris; trans. G. C. Gill (1985) Cornell University Press: Ithaca.

Irigaray, L. (1977) *Ce Sexe qui n'en est pas un*, Minuit: Paris; trans. C. Porter and C. Burke (1985) Cornell University Press: Ithaca.

Jacobus, M. (1986) *Reading Woman*, Methuen: London.

Jameson, F. (1984) 'Postmodernism or the cultural logic of late capitalism', *New Left Review*, 146, pp. 53–92.

Jardine, A. A. (1985) *Gynesis: Configurations of Woman and Modernity*, Cornell University Press: Ithaca.

Johnson, B. (1971) *Conrad's Models of Mind*, University of Minnesota Press: Minneapolis.

Jung, C. (1976) *Symbols of Transformation*, Princeton University Press: Princeton, NJ.

Karl, F. (1979) *Joseph Conrad: The Three Lives*, Farrar, Straus and Giroux: New York.

Krauss, R. (1981) 'The originality of the avant-garde: a postmodern repetition', *October*, 18 (Fall).

Kristeva, J. (1980) *Desire in Language: A Semiotic Approach to Literature and Art*, Blackwell: Oxford.

Kristeva, J. (1981) 'Women's time', *Signs*, 7:11.

Lacan, J. (1972) 'Seminar on "The Purloined Letter"', *Yale French Studies*, 48, pp. 39–72 (originally published in *Écrits* (1966)) Seuil: Paris.

Lacan, J. (1977) *Écrits*, Tavistock: London.

Laing, R. D. (1960) *The Divided Self*, Tavistock: London.

Lerner, G. (1986) *The Creation of Patriarchy*, Oxford University Press: New York.

Lorde, A. (1984) *Sister Outsider*, The Crossing Press: Trumansberg, New York.

Lukács, G. (1971) *Theory of the Novel*, Merlin: London.

Lyotard, J-F. (1984) *The Postmodern Condition: A Report on Knowledge*, trans. G. Bennington and B. Massumi, University of Minnesota Press: Minneapolis.

Marks, E. and Stambolian, G. (eds) (1971) *Homosexuality and French Literature: Cultural Contexts/Critical Texts*, Cornell University Press: Ithaca.

Marxist-Feminist Literature Collective (1978) 'Women's writing: *Jane Eyre, Shirley, Villette, Aurora Leigh*', *Ideology and Consciousness*, 3 pp. 27–49.

Millett, K. (1970) *Sexual Politics*, Doubleday: New York.

Mitchell, J. (1974) *Psychoanalysis and Feminism*, Penguin: Harmondsworth.

Mitchell, J. (1984) *Women: The Longest Revolution*, Virago: London.

Mitchell, J. and Rose, J. (1982) *Feminine Sexuality: Jacques Lacan and the École Freudienne*, Macmillan: London.

Moers, E. (1976) *Literary Women*, Doubleday: New York.

Mohanty, C. T. (1985) 'Under Western eyes: feminist scholarship and colonial discourse', *Boundary*, 2:2, pp. 333–59.

Mohanty, C. T. (ed.) (1991) *Third World Women and the Politics of Feminism*, Indiana University Press: Bloomington.

Morris, M. (1988) *The Pirate's Fiancée: Feminism, Reading, Postmodernism*, Verso: London.

Morrison, T. (1992) *Jazz*, Chatto and Windus: London.

Olsen, T. (1978) *Silences*, Delacorte Press/Seymour Lawrence: New York.

Palmer, P. (1993) *Contemporary Lesbian Writing: Dreams, Desire, Difference*, Open University: Milton Keynes.

Pankhurst, C. (1913) *The Great Scourge and How to End It*, E. Pankhurst: London.

Piercy, M. (1972) *Small Changes*, Doubleday: New York.

Rabinowitz, P., (1987) 'Eccentric memories: a conversation with Maxine Hong Kingston', *Michigan Quarterly Review*, 16:1, pp. 177–88.

Radicalesbians (1973) 'The woman identified woman', in *Radical Feminism*, eds A. Koedt, E. Levine and A. Rapone, Quadrangle: New York.

Radway, J. (1987) *Reading the Romance: Women, Patriarchy and Popular Literature*, Verso: London.

Rhys, J. (1969) *Good Morning Midnight*, Penguin: Harmondsworth.

Rich, A. (1976) *Of Woman Born: Motherhood as Experience and Institution*, W. W. Norton: New York.

Rich, A. (1980a) 'When we dead awaken', in *On Lies, Secrets, and Silence*, Virago: London.

Rich, A. (1980b) 'Compulsory heterosexuality and lesbian existence', *Signs*, 5:4, pp. 631–60.

Riley, D. (1984) *Am I That Name? Feminism and the Category of 'Women' in History*, Macmillan: London.

Russ, J. (1972) 'What can a heroine do? or why women can't write', in *Images of Women in Fiction*, ed. S. K. Cornillon, Bowling Green University Popular Press: Bowling Green, OH.

Said, E. (1983) *The World, the Text and the Critic*, Harvard University Press: Cambridge, MA.

Selden, R. and Widdowson, P. (1993) *A Reader's Guide to Contemporary Literary Theory*, 3rd edn, Harvester Wheatsheaf: Hemel Hempstead.

Showalter, E. (1977) *A Literature of Their Own: British Women Novelists from Brontë to Lessing*, Princeton University Press: Princeton, NJ.

Showalter, E. (1985) 'Toward a feminist poetics', in *The New Feminist Criticism: Essays on Women, Literature and Theory*, ed. E. Showalter, Pantheon: New York.

Smith, B. (1977) *Toward a Black Feminist Criticism*, Out and Out Books: Brooklyn, New York.

Smith, B. (ed.) (1983) *Home Girls: A Black Feminist Anthology*, Kitchen Table Press: New York.

Spelman, E.. (1988) *Inessential Woman: Problems of Exclusion in Feminist Thought*, Women's Press: London.

Spillers, H. J. (1984) 'Interstices: a small drama of words', in *Pleasure and Danger*, ed. C. S. Vance, Routledge and Kegan Paul: London.

Spivak, G. (1987) *In Other Worlds*, Methuen: London.

Tate, C. (ed.) (1983) *Black Women Writers at Work*, Oldcastle Books: New York.

Tompkins, J. P. (1985) 'Sentimental power: *Uncle Tom's Cabin* and the politics of literary history', in *The New Feminist Criticism: Essays on Women, Literature and Theory*, ed. E. Showalter, Pantheon: New York.

Walker, A. (1983) *The Color Purple*, Harcourt Brace Jovanovich: New York.

Walker, A. (1984) *In Search of Our Mothers' Gardens*, The Women's Press: London.

Walker, A. (1989) *The Temple of My Familiar*, The Women's Press: London.

Washington, M. H. (1987) *Invented Lives: Narratives of Black Women 1860–1960*, Anchor/Doubleday: New York.

Watt, I. (1979) *Conrad in the Nineteenth Century*, University of California Press: Berkeley.

Waugh, P. (1992) *Practising Postmodernism, Reading Modernism*, Edward Arnold: London.

Williams, R. (1963) *Culture and Society 1780–1950*, Penguin: Harmondsworth.

Wittig, M. (1971) *Les Guérillères*, trans. D. LeVay, Picador: New York.

Wittig, M. and Zeig, S. (1980) *Lesbian Peoples: Materials for a Dictionary*, Virago, London.

Woolf, V. (1928) *Orlando*, Hogarth Press: London.

Woolf, V. (1929) *A Room of One's Own*, Hogarth Press: London.

Woolf, V. (1942) *The Death of the Moth and Other Essays*, Hogarth Press: London.

Woolf, V. (1944) *The Second Common Reader*, Penguin, Harmondsworth.

Woolf, V. (1979) *Women and Writing*, ed. M. Barrett, The Women's Press: London.

Zimmerman, B. (1991) *The Safe Sea of Women: Lesbian Fiction 1969–1989*, Beacon Press: Boston.

Index

Note: Major references are indicated by emboldened page numbers